REASSESSING FATHERHOOD

REASSESSING FATHERHOOD

New Observations on Fathers and the Modern Family

Edited by
Charlie Lewis and Margaret O'Brien

$)SAGE Publications
London · Newbury Park · Beverly Hills · New Delhi

SAGE Publications Ltd
28 Banner Street
London EC1Y 8QE

SAGE Publications Inc
275 South Beverly Drive
Beverly Hills, California 90212
and
2111 W. Hillcrest Drive
Newbury Park, California 91320

SAGE Publications India Pvt Ltd
C-236 Defence Colony
New Delhi 110 024

British Library Cataloguing in Publication Data

Reassessing fatherhood: new observations
  on fathers and the modern family.
  1. Fathers
  I. Lewis, Charlie   II. O'Brien, Margaret,
  1954–
  306.8'742   HQ756

Library of Congress Catalog Card Number 87-060199

ISBN 0-8039-8019-1
ISBN 0-8039-8020-5 Pbk

Phototypeset by Fakenham Photosetting Ltd, Fakenham, Norfolk
Printed in Great Britain by J.W. Arrowsmith Ltd, Bristol

Dedications

For two important Irish father-figures: my grand-fathers Michael Conway (from Ballycroy) and Thomas O'Brien (from Cootehill). (**M.O'B.**)

For those who, in their own ways, have helped me reflect upon parenthood: Rosemary Smith, Tom W. Lewis, Camilla Lewis, Ken and Kath Smith, Tom (TNT) and B. Lewis and Alex (Babushka) Moore. (**C.L.**)

78/94

Acknowledgements

I am grateful to my colleagues in the Department of Sociology at the North East London Polytechnic (especially the Psycho-Social Studies team) for providing a stimulating environment in which to be a psychologist and to study fathers. My clinical experience in family therapy at the Marlborough Family Service opened new horizons for considering the role of the father. I would like to thank the therapists there, especially Ann Miller. We were unhappy that Dr Lorna McKee was unable to write about her work on fathers in a health educational context. I would particularly like to acknowledge the importance of her continuing intellectual support and friendship.

Margaret O'Brien

We would like to thank Jennifer Jones for her magnificent work in preparing the manuscript and the Sage team in London, particularly Farrell Burnett, for their enthusiasm and encouragement.

Charlie Lewis and Margaret O'Brien

Contents

1
Constraints on fathers:
research, theory and clinical practice

Charlie Lewis and Margaret O'Brien

There is now a large body of literature on fathers which has grown immeasurably over the past ten years. Recent emphasis has shifted from the influence of the man upon his child's development (Lamb, 1976, 1981a) to, first, the personal experience of fatherhood itself (Beail and McGuire, 1982; Hanson and Bozett, 1985; Jackson, 1984; Lamb, 1986a; Lewis, C., 1986a; Lewis and Salt, 1986; McKee and O'Brien, 1982) and, second, attempts to change this experience, both at the individual (Lamb, 1982; Russell, 1983) and societal (Lamb and Sagi, 1983) levels. The recent interest in male domesticity has been accentuated by the ideology of the 'new father' — the man who is both highly nurturant towards his children and increasingly involved in their care and the housework. However, as Lamb (1986b: 3) points out: 'rhetorical exchanges concerning the new father abounded; unfortunately, rhetoric continues to outpace serious analysis'.

In contrast to much of the literature, this book reflects critically on the 'new father'. Despite the wave of optimism driving contemporary accounts, the evidence for the existence of such a man is much less convincing. The authors draw upon research and discussion which has highlighted the problematic nature of fathering roles. Such a perspective has entered public and academic debate less often than the 'new father' orientation. As editors, we contend that an explicit statement about the constraints imposed upon men's involvement in the family will enhance our theoretical understanding of fatherhood and throw new light on families for those working in the helping professions.

The three parts of this book examine fatherhood from complementary perspectives. The first reviews the paternal role in what are termed 'traditional' families — two-parent nuclear households. It will be seen that the father's role is enacted within clear institutional constraints: historical (Richards, Chapter 2), societal (Moss and Brannen, Chapter 3; Horna and Lupri, Chapter 4) and in the inter-personal relationships between family members over the life-course (Backett, Chapter 5; Cunningham-Burley, Chapter 6). The second part of the book looks more closely at the evidence to support the 'new father' image by examining families which attempt to change the paternal role. Each chapter reveals the problems involved in effecting major shifts in parental responsibility, again at various levels of analysis. The final part, which is aimed primarily at workers in the 'helping professions', describes how constraints on male parents evident in 'traditional families' manifest themselves especially in times of family dissolution or personal crisis.

In this chapter we will attempt to sketch why a theoretical shift in our understanding of paternal involvement seems to be needed. Studying men's involvement in the family is notoriously difficult not only because they are less available to researchers than mothers but also, we suggest, because theoreticians are so influenced by the 'new father' image. The first section criticizes the notion of change embedded in most research on contemporary fathering roles, drawing upon a large but hitherto less cohesive body of literature which paints a different picture. The second part argues that recent accounts of fatherhood should be replaced by an understanding of paternal involvement in the context of the continuing domination of women by men in the public sphere, and in certain respects within the family itself. It will be argued that the social institution of fatherhood contains inherent contradictions since on a societal level men dominate, while individually they may show and develop close reciprocal relationships with women and children. The third part of this chapter sketches the ways in which men might be constrained in the execution of their paternal duties. Expanding on this analysis, the final section examines the position of fathers as clients in clinical settings. It will be suggested that the helping professions, like researchers, will better understand the fathers they work with by considering the contradictions of paternal involvement.

Theoretical constraints: the ideology of change

Many authors have assumed that men are becoming more involved in family life (e.g. Dorn and Ryan, 1979; Entwisle and Doering, 1981; Fein, 1978; Lewis, R.A., 1986). Yet such contentions are hard to justify. To begin with, there are two reasons why comparisons of paternal involvement over time might give rise to problems of interpretation. First, it may be that respondents today are under greater pressure to appear to be more involved than those a few years ago. This suggestion is certainly hinted at in a recent analysis of cartoons in the *New Yorker* magazine and *Saturday Evening Post*, which found a marked decrease in the number of derogatory depictions of the father's involvement with his children during the 1970s (Mackey, 1985). Second, we have to understand the nature of paternal involvement within the context of other social and technological changes (e.g. Duvall, 1967). The postwar decades have witnessed great shifts in work and family patterns. Thus it is especially hard to measure alterations in paternal involvement without considering the increases in maternal employment and changes in family size and structure (e.g. Hoffman, 1977). Moreover, there are many methodological difficulties in measuring couples' division of labour in child-care and housework (Cronenwett, 1982; McKee, 1982).

 In addition to these conceptual problems, no single study has set out to measure paternal involvement over many years. Researchers have had to rely upon data derived from different sources or comparisons over very brief time-spans. The results of these comparative analyses are often contradictory. Some suggest significant shifts in the father's role. For example, Davis (1982) and Juster (cited in Lamb, 1986b) reported significant increases in paternal involvement, but in both analyses men still did far less domestic work than their wives at the later date (one-third according to Juster and one-sixth in the Davis paper). Other studies on men's participation in the home show no change between the 1960s and 1970s (Coverman and Sheley, 1986; Sanik, 1981; Stafford, 1980). For example, Coverman and Sheley found that, in 1965 and 1975, men's daily contributions to domestic work in Michigan were 81.39 minutes and 82.4 minutes, respectively. This stability in findings has to be understood in terms of a daily decrease in paid work of one hour and an increase in leisure activities of 40 minutes over the ten-year period.

 It seems most likely that change in fathering roles has been restricted to particular areas of family life. For example, Lewis, C. (1986a: 175) found in the period 1960–1980 an increase in paternal involvement around the time of childbirth, but little difference in the performance of chores like nappy changing or bathing the baby.

 Given that discussion about the 'new father' far outweighs evidence to demonstrate his existence, it seems necessary to consider briefly the very notion of change within contemporary accounts. As Lewis, C. (1986a) has argued, implicit within the notion of the 'new father' are the assumptions that fathers have only recently been discovered by researchers and that in previous generations fathers were not involved in child-rearing. However, a brief examination of the literature shows, first, that there has been a stream of papers on fathers over the past fifty years which repeatedly claim that little has been written on the topic (Lewis, C., 1986a: 3). Second, family researchers throughout this century have tended to depict two contrasting marriage patterns. Some have almost disregarded the father's nurturant role. The obvious examples are the psychoanalysts Bowlby (1954) and Winnicott (1965) and the sociologist Parsons (Parsons and Bales, 1955). At the same time, others (e.g. Mowrer,

1930) have regarded contemporary husbands as being much more involved in family life than fathers from previous historical periods. In each generation some authors feel that men are breaking new ground, even though it is recognized that respondents might be doing this for different reasons. A similar dialogue has been happening more recently among family historians.

Badinter (1981: 322), in her analysis of French family life, has argued that the contemporary father is rejecting his authoritarian past and becoming 'a father–mother'. This position has been criticized by Laslett (1981: 7) who comments that we should acknowledge that it is not yet known how innovatory this is. Involved fatherhood may have always existed, but only have become a fashionable research topic in recent years.

In other words fathers often find themselves like a ball in a tennis court bouncing between conflicting ideologies; at one time 'vestigial' (Gorer, 1948), while at another 'a most important factor in family stability' (Mogey, 1957: 234) or even 'a mother' (Badinter, 1981). As Dybwad (1952: 3–4) comments:

> As one reviews recent books and articles in the field of family life which make specific reference to the father's role, one finds that while some authors see today's father as less active and further removed from the family, others quite to the contrary observe that he has found his way back to the family and shares actively and creatively many activities with wife and children. Apparently it depends on the author's vantage point whether and in what areas he discerns progress.

Constraints on research: the paradox of patriarchy

Within the world of fatherhood research, other constraints and tensions have been apparent. In most studies in the 1970s and early 1980s there was an underlying rejection of the so-called mother-focused paradigm embedded in social scientific enquiry into familial relationships. It was noted that many conventional research practices tended to be centred on the mother. For instance, data about fathers were more than likely collected from mothers, who in turn were more often seen by investigators — fathers, like the investigators, were out at work. (Richards et al., 1977). Only slowly have we come to realize that this research procedure was important in itself. Social scientists have tended to study either men in employment or women in the family. Yet men and many women are located in both spheres and their experience of each sphere can be highly interdependent (Allen and Barker, 1976; O'Brien, 1982; Pleck, 1979).

One purpose of the father-centred research orientation was to give paternal accounts of family life a hearing and a place centre-stage (McKee and O'Brien, 1982: ix). In doing so, studies in this tradition have been taken to task by some feminist writers (e.g. Pollock and Sutton, 1985) for being politically unsound and for omitting any consideration of the privileges and status attached to fatherhood. Such criticisms have reminded fatherhood researchers (although some would say that they have never forgotten) that the experience of fathering should be set in the context of the social institution of fatherhood and the more general divisions of power between the sexes.

It seems that an analysis of fathering which derives in part from feminist discussion has more credibility than that which merely assumes significant increases in the involvement of men in the home and, moreover, that the consequences of such increases are always positive. Women writers have long pointed out the caste-like divisions between the sexes (e.g. Gillespie, 1972), particularly at work. Most women are restricted to a limited number of occupations, they are paid less for jobs which often offer part-time work on temporary 'contracts' and have few, if any, training and career possibilities (Martin and Roberts, 1984; Ratner, 1980). As Ratner points out, such patterns continue despite equal opportunities directives and legislation. At the same time it is assumed that women will enter into full-time child-care by what Russo (1976) calls the 'motherhood mandate'. Often the attraction of motherhood and the home is much stronger than the pull of the market-place for women. The presentation of child-rearing as a relatively conflict-free state adds to this dynamic; a position which has been noted for some time:

> The pains, the dangers, the risks of child-bearing are tabooed as subjects of conversation. The drudgery, the monotonous labor, and other disagreeable features of child-rearing are minimised by the 'social guardians'. On the other hand, the joys and compensations of motherhood are magnified and presented to consciousness on every hand. Thus the tendency is to create an illusion whereby motherhood will appear to consist of compensations only and thus come to be desired by those for whom the illusion is intended. (Hollingworth, 1916: 27)

Like women, men as fathers have to be considered in terms of the broader relations between the sexes. The fatherhood mandate, which encourages a consolidation and development of men's position in the public sphere of work, seems to bring more gains than losses. Absence from the home allows some freedom from domesticity, especially the dreary and repetitive aspects of housework and child-care. The energy devoted to a work role at one and the same time enhances the self professionally and financially while also providing the family with social status and financial support. In most societies material provision is the embodiment of male parenting and although the act often incorporates an altruistic dimension it also accrues social and familial power. Moreover the resilience of father as 'breadwinner' especially in times of economic recession, has to be recognized and has been shown in studies of male unemployment (McKec, 1983).

The provider role with its distant location may be an important mechanism in the maintenance of father rule or 'patriarchy'. As Pollock and Sutton (1985: 597) suggest, a voluntary level of childcare participation can accentuate gender divisions and their generational transmission within the family.

The ways in which fathers relate to children stems from their social position in the family. Their privileged status, authority, rewards and access to resources as men, relative to women, allows for a particular form of involvement. They play rather than carry out the more mundane tasks. They select what they do and the commitment they feel they are willing and able to make; mothers are left with the rest.

There is evidence from recent research which indicates that men are often somewhat detached from family life and envy the close relationships between mothers and children (e.g. Lamb, 1981b; Lewis et al., 1982; Lewis, C., 1986a). The paradox of patriarchy, therefore, is that, while a father may be 'head' of his family, simultaneously he is constrained from being a central character within it. We will examine the effects of this paradox in the next section.

Constraints on fathers: institutional and individual
When the collected mass of data on paternal involvement is examined, two contrasting, yet compatible, conclusions can be drawn. On a social level, men perform a far less important nurturant role than women in all societies (Katz and Konner, 1981) despite a few exceptional families like those discussed in Parts 2 and 3 of this book. However, close examination of paternal involvement suggests that the variations between individual fathers can themselves be considerable. Such a finding emerges within relatively homogeneous communities irrespective of whether mothers (Newson and Newson, 1963; Pedersen and Robson, 1969), fathers (Lewis, C., 1986a) or children (Herbst, 1952) are the source of data collection. It is also evident in cross-cultural comparisons (Katz and Konner, 1981). The very heterogeneity of fathering roles, itself related to the male's marginality in the family, invalidates general statements about 'the father'.

In this section we shall consider three areas of research literature which highlight constraints on the father's role: research focusing on the developmental implications of 'traditional' familial roles; writings on the man's relationship with the mother of his children; and finally investigations into the man's status and identity as a father. Research in each of these areas underlines the complexity of mediating processes which structure the institution and experience of fatherhood. The very polarity of adult sex roles has been emphasized in theoretical accounts of 'traditional' (i.e. differentiated) parental roles. For example, Alice Rossi (1984) has pointed out how biological sexual dimorphism channels parents into distinctive gender roles. The obvious example is that of child-bearing. Since this temporarily 'confines' the mother and temporarily distances her from employment it is more likely, but of course not essential, that she will assume a major role in child-care in the early months. Such biological influences give socially constructed gender ascriptions apparent credibility. These tend to be manifested in relationships between parent and child as well as between spouses. For instance, psychological studies of very young children show that parents discriminate between boys and girls early in life, even in the delivery room (see Lewis, C., 1986b for a review), and that fathers are more likely to differentiate between their children on lines of gender (Power, 1981). Bell and Newby (1976: 160) argue that such parenting styles develop 'in a manner which is consistent with the existing ideological hegemony' of men dominating women and is 'a, if not *the*, vital social mechanism of this ideological control'.

Just how such patterns of family relationships pass from one generation to another is hard to establish. However, theorists using an object relations framework have offered a plausible account of how mothering and fathering styles might be transmitted (Chodorow, 1978; Dinnerstein, 1978; Seidler, 1985; Richards, 1982). The account places great import on the psychological consequences of male absence from, and female domination of, child care. A seminal paper by Irene Josselyn (1956) highlighted the effects of the near monopoly of maternal care in the early years. The following extract describes such influences upon a son:

The American male's childhood is spent in a world dominated by women. His primary experiences with tenderness, protectiveness and learning are through his relationship with women. . . . As a result the boy child attributes those characteristics, especially those involving tender love, that are so important to him in childhood to the female; but he also finds them within himself. To fulfil his biological heritage of being a man he must repress that which he sees in himself, that he has experienced chiefly in his relationship to women. . . . (p. 268)
When childhood is controlled by women, and especially the mother figure, achievement of maturity is considered attained when the male can escape from the mother to the outside world populated by men . . . A man, wishing on the one hand to find a complementary figure in the woman, feels belittled in his relationship to her because those characteristics he values in her must be denied since they represent, as a result of his

past, femininity. In order to strengthen his denial of that part of himself, he depreciates those components (pp. 270–271).

However, a process like this is not ubiquitous, since many children do not grow up under the exclusive care of their mothers (Rapoport et al., 1977), and research on alternative families shows that men and women can overtly reject — at least on a behavioural and conscious level — the patterns established by their parents (Eiduson et al., 1982). For instance, O'Brien (1984: 427) found that lone fathers were less likely than married fathers to rear their children in the traditional gender roles. While the latter often adopted a tougher orientation to sons than daughters, lone fathers expressed less inhibition about being strict with daughters and affectionate to sons.

A second constraining influence upon a father's involvement with his children derives directly from his usual role as secondary care-giver. Research on the transition to parenthood shows that as soon as the first child is born (and maybe at the point of marriage according to Brannen and Moss in Chapter 8) marital roles become clearly diffe-rentiated, like the division of labour outside the home (Entwisle and Doering, 1981; Kotelchuck, 1982; Shereshefsky and Yarrow, 1973). Mother becomes the 'instructress in primary care tasks' and 'the correspondent of the baby's affairs' to her partner (McKee, 1979: 20). Survey evidence suggests that after the first child's arrival the father's participation in domestic work continues to decline (Hoff-man and Manis, 1978). As Myrdal and Klein (1956) pointed out, even working mothers assume a primary role, while husbands are seen to 'help out' in the home. This difference has been found in many subsequent studies. For example, Oakley (1974) suggested that the key factor in child-care is the issue of responsibility. It is mothers who are judged both by the upkeep of the home and the appearance of their children, even in families where their partners help out. In her subsequent study of new mothers, one-third of their husbands saw their babies for less than half an hour per day. Fathers squeeze child-care into the limited time they have available. This has rami-fications beyond the father–child relationship:

> In many cases it HAS become more acceptable for a husband to 'help' his wife; provided he doesn't help TOO much, it is regarded as probable that his masculinity will survive. The concept of 'help' here is obviously politic-al: because they 'help', fathers do not take the main responsibility for child care, or because theirs is not the responsibility, they must only help (Oakley, 1979: 211, her emphasis).

Therefore, despite any lip service which couples may make to the 'equality' in their relationship, behavioural indicators point to a very different reality. This representation–action mismatch can create quite complex conjugal interactions. Ralph La Rossa (1977), for example, found that women used their 'sick role' in pregnancy to gain power in their marital relationships, getting their husbands to perform chores they would otherwise not do. Likewise Lewis, C. (1986a) reported that parents were often surprised and upset about similar assertions of power. Husbands expressed dismay, for example, about being excluded from decisions concerning the child's daily routine. At the same time over half (53 percent) of mothers were critical of their husbands' reluctance to discipline their one-year-olds. At this age, men are still forging a relationship with their children and most are hesitant to take part in any battle of wills between mother and child. In Chapters 5 and 6, Backett and Cunningham-Burley focus specifically upon the ways in which couples cope with the imbalance of power and knowledge between them at different stages of child-rearing.

A third constraint on fathers lies in the very statuses and identities which they construct. In most cases men have a less clear 'job description' of their parental roles within the home than their partners. When confronted by a researcher many suggest that the 'expert' in the family is the wife (Lewis, C., 1986a). Just as many men rely upon their wives for knowledge of, and access to, their children, so too have accounts of male identities emerged in relation to issues concerned with the experiences of women and mothering (Hacker, 1957; Pleck and Brannon, 1978; Richards, 1982).

A growing number of polemical accounts of masculinity have depicted a range of personality failings and weaknesses. These describe men being, for example, unable to express their emotions (Farrell, 1974), competitive (Lewis, R.A., 1978), brutal in the way they use their muscular strength (Solomon and Levy, 1982) and incapable of showing intimacy apart from during sexual contact (Fasteau, 1974). It seems that the language and communicational styles of the public arena are judged as inappropriate for home-based relationships. However, men's distance can also be seen as a strength. Fathers are often depicted as unflappable 'sturdy oaks', the emotional pillars of their families (e.g. Benson, 1968).

The literature on masculinity tends to assume that the failings of men are inbuilt or derive from their socialization (Solomon and Levy, 1982). Yet this analysis does not consider the context of men's actions. As researchers on fatherhood, not masculinity, we have both been struck by the very involvement of men in their paternal relationships. As a comment from one father of two young children suggested, fatherhood may challenge the unidimensionality of the image of detached masculinity, even to the man himself:

I suppose I've been surprised at my emotions, but ... yeah, to me, without the kids, you now, I don't know what I'd do ... And things like this ... and if anything ever happened to them I'd crack up, actually ... you know, that sort of emotion and ... you're probably just as dependent on them as they are on you. (An engineer's clerk, quoted in Lewis, C., 1986a: 165)

Therapeutic constraints: fathers in clinical settings

So far we have considered the institution and experience of fatherhood mainly in terms of empirical and theoretical debates from within the social sciences. We have described the contradictions and ambiguities inherent in being a father. In this section we shall explore these tensions further by examining fathers in therapeutic settings. The clinical implications of research findings on fatherhood for working with male clients have entered discussion only recently (Blackie and Clark, Chapter 12; Parkinson, Chapter 15; Lamb, 1986a). In contrast, there is a long tradition of writings about the female 'client' and the impact of motherhood on women's mental health (see Howell and Bayes, 1981; Williams, 1984 for reviews).

A starting point for many clinicians working with 'families' which include fathers is the realization that a majority of such men, for whatever reason, tend to be absent from consultations. The research evidence to date indicates that when there are relationship problems in presenting families (either conjugal or parental) it is mothers rather than fathers who make the initial approach to an agency for help. The father has been described as 'disengaged' in literature on individual psychotherapy (Kirshner, et al., 1982; Solomon, 1982), marital counselling (Brannen and Collard, 1982) and family therapy (Atkins and Lansky, 1976; Heuback et al., 1986), although we do not know whether the man himself would concur with such a description. Similarly, men and fathers are relatively absent in other health-related public settings — for instance, child health clinics (Kerr and McKee, 1981), family planning centres (Gordon and DeMarco, 1984) and antenatal classes (Lewis, C., 1986a). It seems that the ideology of the involved father, central to many clinicians' philosophies and training, is not reflected in the interactions between professionals and clients in the clinic. Recently, clinicians have been trying to understand *why* men are underrepresented in help-seeking settings and *how* fathers can be more effectively *engaged* in therapy. These developments will be described in the context of the tension between paternal involvement and paternal control outlined above. Bringing fathers into therapy may facilitate perceived gains for men, despite their initial reluctance to participate. However, we have yet to articulate the implications of such changes, for instance in enhancing father–child relationships, and/or the lives of mothers.

Why fathers do not attend clinical settings
Most of the ideas about the relative absence of fathers from the help-seeking domain usually conflate the categories 'man' and 'father' in the analysis. So, for instance, it is assumed that since men evince lower personal self-disclosure than women, making them less open to helping professionals (Solomon and Levy, 1982), this characteristic is equally true of men who happen to be fathers. The evidence for this sort of generalization has still to be produced — a point which should be kept in mind. However, such reasoning is heuristically useful at this stage. Many factors have been put forward to explain why men experiencing personal or emotional difficulties are less likely than comparable women to seek professional assistance. These range from those that highlight individual attributes to those that focus on institutional practices.

One suggestive finding is that men are less attentive to their internal bodily states than women, for instance being less likely to perceive symptoms of personal distress and anxiety (Pennebaker, 1982). It may well be that this difference in 'internal attentiveness' (Skevington, 1986) carries over into interactions with others so that, in a familial context, men are slower than women in perceiving the indicators of relationship difficulties. Certainly research data indicate that men are more likely than women to report marital happiness, are less often the first spouse to express marital complaints and are less likely to be the petitioner in divorce cases (Bernard, 1976; Thornes and Collard, 1979; Hetherington, 1986). In fact, Brannen and Collard (1982) noted that despite contrary information many husbands attributed a *mutual* marital problem to causes emanating solely from their wives. They were unable or unwilling to recognize their own contribution to the difficulty. Where men do recognize familial or marital problems, expressive norms associated with conventional masculinity at least in western cultures, can inhibit articulation, especially in the public domain (Solomon and Levy, 1982).

Writers ascribing to this view argue that the existence of familial difficulties might be suggestive of a degree of personal weakness and so, in line with traditional gender rules, is more appropriately communicated to outsiders by female family members. Men's reluctance to attend hospital, even in the face of possible heart attacks, and the instrumental role of wives in engineering admission gives some support to this argument (Finlayson and McEwen, 1977).

As far as specifically child-related problems are concerned, there is some evidence that both mothers and fathers accept the normal prescription of the mother as the child-care expert and the specialist in dealing with health professionals (Kerr and McKee, 1981; Graham, 1984). The mother both receives (Gluck et al., 1980) and transmits the emotional atmosphere of the family and moreover is reinforced in this position by the feedback she receives from others outside the home. In the majority of families there is, of course, a material basis to this transaction since women take on the main responsibility for child-care, and also some would argue for adult-care:

> As the principal carer, the mother acts not only as the home nurse, home doctor and home tutor, she is also the person in contact with the professionals who perform these roles in the public domain. Typically it is mother who seeks out health professionals; she is the one, too, who is sought out by them. (Graham, 1984: 164)

Kerr and McKee (1981) show that fathers tend to attend child health clinics when requested by their wives or when there is a 'serious' developmental issue to consider such as immunization. Social service involvement, for instance in cases of child abuse, may also result in fathers being compelled to attend a therapeutic setting (O'Brien, 1987).

Further factors which influence the involvement of fathers in clinical milieux are the nature of the therapeutic institutions and the therapists they contain. A clinic might seem, to the eyes of both potential clients of each sex and the therapists themselves, a woman's place located in woman's time. Just as research on the family takes place in men's *working* hours and often excludes fathers, so too does therapy with the family. Also therapists and other health workers might share the societal belief of some of their male clients that expressing concerns about fatherhood or husbandhood is indicative of weakness and femininity. Even if therapists do not consciously hold this belief, Atkins and Lansky (1986: 183) suggest that male clients might through the course of treatment project these feelings onto therapists and so create in turn quite a debilitating institutional countertransference for fathers.

> Shared social values surrounding masculinity can generate conflicts around a man's more 'feminized' past, rendering a father anxious and/or hostile toward a treatment situation he sees as passive, or as inflicting passivity or powerlessness, or as dominated by women or by 'affected, panty-waisted men'. The mental health system then becomes the inheritor, through projection, of shared inner conflicts surrounding masculinity and femininity, activity and passivity, and power and weakness.

Other researchers into gender issues in psychotherapy have noticed the 'discomfort' some therapists feel when treating men and indeed the 'deficiencies in fledgling male therapists' appreciation of emotional issues' (Kirshner et al., 1982: 271).

Although the gender of a clinician or therapist has always been considered a potent dimension in the therapeutic relationship, systematic research into this area is only a recent development and has been especially pronounced in the USA. We know very little about gender and therapeutic relationships elsewhere. Data from the USA indicate that male psychotherapists are more involved in marital, family and group therapy than their female counterparts. By contrast, female psychotherapists spend a larger part of their therapy time doing individual work when compared to their male colleagues (see Dryden, 1984).

As far as fathers are concerned there is growing evidence that a male therapist in the early stages of family therapy can facilitate whole family engagement (Heubeck et al., 1986). In this situation a father might feel that he is not entering into women's territory, that he is 'in with a chance' and that he might even have an ally who can understand him.

Whatever the characteristics associated with fathers' lack of involvement with the helping professions, there is certainly a current concern to engage the peripheral father. This motivation might originate from the philosophical assumptions underlying a particular intervention, as is the case in the systemic approach of family therapy. Alternatively, wider political orientations, such as a belief in shared parental responsibility for child-care, may be in operation. It could be said that the persuading and cajoling of fathers to enter into the inner sanctum of the consulting-room resonates with some of the strategies used by women to encourage more male involvement in the emotional life of the home.

Fathers in the consulting-room:
interactions with helping professionals
Just as there are often conflicts of interest between mothers and fathers in the home these may also occur during consultations with helping professionals. Men and women in such settings may want the same outcome, for example help with children's sleep problems or relief from chronic marital arguments, but their investment in the consultation and expectation of treatment may vary considerably. Brannen and Collard (1982) found that men were less satisfied than women with an unstructured, 'ventilative' style of marital counselling, expressing a preference for more structured advice-giving or goal-setting. One reason for this might be a transfer of work-talk into the therapeutic encounter, a strategy that might be preferable to men especially when they are under threat (Weiss, 1985). Some of the

active techniques used in structural family therapy, such as the enactments of dysfunctional transactions between parents and children, have also been favoured by fathers (Russell et al., 1984). The expressive skills considered necessary when talking about emotional and personal difficulties may need to be fostered in men during therapeutic encounters and here, as in other matters, the gender of the therapist might be important. As Goldner (1985: 45) suggests:

> A male therapist telling a father to shape up can be a rude awakening, a female therapist with the same message can be just another nag.

However, the manner in which particular male family therapists align with fathers has come under criticism, especially from feminist therapists. For instance Hare-Mustin (1981: 558) argues that some therapeutic manoeuvres reinstate stereotypical gender roles and may in fact create an even more 'one-down' position for women:

> Minuchin (1974) sees himself as modeling the male executive function, forming alliances, most typically with the father and through competition, rule setting, and direction, demanding that the father resume control of the family and exert leadership as Minuchin leads and controls the session ... These illustrations reveal how the unquestioned acceptance and reinforcement of stereotypic sex roles takes place in much of family therapy, despite the possibilities inherent for change in the systems point of view.

Similarly, there has been concern that the philosophical assumptions of systems thinking, for example the insistence that all actors play a part in the maintenance of recurring sequences of dysfunctional behaviour, can have negative consequences for women in families where men are violent (McIntyre, 1985). Such approaches, McIntyre (1985: 253) posits, overlook the social dominance of men in the public sphere and fallaciously assume equal power in the home. In the consulting-room, as the interaction between the couple becomes highlighted, the woman's status is redefined from victim to 'co-conspirator'.

Conclusion: involving fathers in families and therapy
We have argued in earlier sections that a full appreciation of fatherhood necessitates analysing the phenomenon at an *individual–experiential* level as well as at an *institutional* level. While 'the rule of the father' or patriarchal domination may be apparent from both perspectives it is also clear that in many households fathers, mothers and children find deep affection and happiness with each other. Moreover, it is usually women who activate change or recruit help from outsiders about 'relationship problems'. Researchers suggest that, in enlisting this help, women are not rejecting close rela-

tionships but instead are trying to make them more successful (Gluck et al., 1980). Involving fathers in therapeutic encounters and so engaging them more in the emotional arena may be part of this general process. Indeed, research indicates that paternal involvement, for instance in family therapy, can create closer father–child relationships and so enhance men's self-esteem as fathers (Heubeck et al., 1986). Also when abusing fathers take responsibility during therapy for the part they have played in physical or sexual child abuse a more favourable *family* prognosis is indicated (Tyler, 1986).

However, involving fathers in clinical settings, as mentioned above, may have negative consequences. In the current sex-gender system the emotional arena is, in the main, a specialist area for women. It is there that women can show competence and be powerful. Male movement into this domain may therefore result in a depowering rather than an empowering of women. Given the continued patriarchal character of the work-place, which in many ways operates to discourage maternal entry, any transformation of men into competent parents and emotionally sensitive partners begs the question: What areas are left in which women can excel and derive meaning? Paradoxically, while many women want their male partners to be more caring in the home, they have also a rationale to resist movements in this direction.

Note

With many thanks to Lorna McKee, Michael Rustin and Rex Stainton Rogers for their poignant criticisms of the penultimate draft of this chapter.

References

Allen, S. and Barker, D.L. (1976) 'Introduction: The Interdependence of Work and Marriage', in D.L. Barker and S. Allen (eds) *Dependence and Exploitation in Work and Marriage*. London: Longman.

Atkins, R. and Lansky, M. (1986) 'The Father in Family Therapy: Psychoanalytic Perspectives', in M.E. Lamb (ed.) *The Father's Role: Applied Perspectives*. New York: Wiley.

Badinter, E. (1981) *The Myth of Motherhood: An Historical View of the Maternal Instinct*. London: Souvenir Press.

Beail, N. and McGuire, J. (1982) 'Fathers, the Family and Society: The Tide of Change', in N. Beail and J. McGuire (eds) *Fathers: Psychological Aspects*. London: Junction Books.

Bell, C. and Newby, H. (1976) 'Husbands and Wives: The Dynamics of the Deferential Dialectic', in D.L. Barker and S. Allen (eds) *Dependence and Exploitation in Work and Marriage*. London: Longman.

Benson, L. (1968) *Fatherhood: A Sociological Perspective*. New York: Random House.

Bernard, J. (1976) *The Future of Marriage*. Middlesex: Pelican Books.

Bowlby, J. (1954) *Child Care and the Growth of Love*. Harmondsworth: Penguin.

Brannen, J. and Collard, J. (1982) *Marriages in Trouble.* London: Tavistock.

Chodorow, N. (1978) *The Reproduction of Mothering.* Berkeley: University of California Press.

Coverman, S. and Sheley, J.F. (1986) 'Change in Men's Housework and Child-Care Time 1965–1975', *Journal of Marriage and the Family* 48(5): 413–22.

Cronenwett, L. (1982) 'Father Participation in Child Care: A Critical Review', *Research in Nursing and Health* 5: 63–72.

Davis, M.R. (1982) *Families in a Working World: The Impact of Organisations on Domestic Life.* New York: Praeger.

DeFrain, J. (1975) 'The Nature and Meaning of Parenthood', PhD dissertation 1976, 36, 8: 5578. University of Wisconsin: Madison.

Dinnerstein, D. (1978) *The Rocking of the Cradle and the Ruling of the World.* London: Souvenir Press.

Dorn, R.S. and Ryan, J.L. (1979) 'Shared Parenthood', in R.F. Levant and E.T. Nickerson (eds) *Mothering and Fathering: Dispelling Myths, Creating Alternatives.* Weston: Mass, Boston Professional International.

Dryden, W. (1984) *Individual Therapy in Britain.* London: Harper and Row.

Duvall, E.M. (1967) *Family Development.* New York: J.B. Lippincott.

Dybwad, G. (1952) 'Fathers Today: Neglected or Neglectful?', *Child Study* 29(1): 3–5.

Eiduson, B.T., Kornfein, M., Zimmerman, I.L., and Weisner, T.S. (1982) 'Comparative Socialisation Practices in Traditional and Alternative Families', in M. Lamb (ed.) *Nontraditional Families.* Hillsdale, NJ: Erlbaum.

Entwisle, D. and Doering, S. (1981) *The First Birth: A Family Turning Point.* Baltimore: Johns Hopkins University Press.

Farrell, W. (1974) *The Liberated Man.* New York: Random House.

Fasteau, M. (1974) *The Male Machine.* New York: McGraw Hill.

Fein, R.A. (1978) 'Research on Fathering: Social Policy and an Emergent Perspective', *Journal of Social Issues* 34(1): 122–35.

Finlayson, A. and McEwen, J. (1977) *Coronary Heart Disease and Patterns of Living.* London: Croom Helm.

Gillespie, D. (1972) 'Who Has The Power? The Marital Struggle', in H.P. Dretzel (ed.) *Family, Marriage and the Struggle of the Sexes.* London: Collier Macmillan.

Gluck, N., Donefer, E. and Milea, K. (1980) 'Women in Families', in E. Carter and M. McGoldrick (eds) *The Family Life Cycle.* London and New York: Gardner Press.

Goldner, V. (1985) 'Feminism and Family Therapy', *Family Process* 24(March): 31–47.

Gordon, P. and DeMarco, L. (1984) 'Reproductive Health Services for Men: Is There a Need?', *Family Planning Perspectives* 16(1): 44–9.

Gorer, G. (1948) *The Americans: A Study of National Character.* New York: W.W. Norton.

Graham, H. (1984) *Women, Health and the Family.* London: Wheatsheaf Books Ltd.

Hacker, H.M. (1957) 'The New Burdens of Masculinity', *Marriage and Family Living* 19(3): 227–33.

Hanson, S.M.H. and Bozett, F.W. (1985) *Dimensions of Fatherhood.* Beverly Hills: Sage.

Hare-Mustin, R.T. (1981) 'A Feminist Approach to Family Therapy', in E. Howell and M. Bayes (eds) *Women and Mental Health.* New York: Basic Books.

Herbst, P.G. (1952) 'The Measurement of Family Relationships', *Human Relations* 5: 5–36.

Hetherington, E.M. (1986) 'Family Relations Six Years After Divorce', in K. Pasley and M. Ihinger-Tollman (eds) *Remarriage and Stepparenting Today: Research and Theory*. New York: Guilford.

Heubeck, B., Watson, J. and Russell, G. (1986) 'Father Involvement and Responsibility in Family Therapy', in M.E. Lamb (ed.) *The Father's Role: Applied Perspectives*. New York: Wiley.

Hoffman, L.W. (1977) 'Changes in Family Roles, Socialisation and Sex Differences', *American Psychologist* 32: 644–57.

Hoffman, L.W. and Manis, J.D. (1978) 'Marriage Influences of Children on Marital Interactive and Parental Satisfactions and Dissatisfactions', in R. Lemer and G. Spanier (eds) *Child Influences on Marital and Family Interaction: A Life Span Perspective*. New York: Academic.

Hollingworth, L.S. (1916) 'Social Vices for Inspelling Women to Bear and Rear Children', *American Journal of Sociology* 22(1): 19–29.

Howell, E. and Bayes, M. (1981) *Women and Mental Health*. New York: Basic Books.

Jackson, B. (1984) *Fatherhood*. London: Allen and Unwin.

Josselyn, I.M. (1956) 'Cultural Forces: Motherliness and Fatherliness', *American Journal of Orthopsychiatry* 28: 264–71.

Katz, M. and Konner, M.J. (1981) 'The Role of the Father: An Anthropological Perspective', in M.E. Lamb (ed.) *The Role of the Father in Child Development*. New York: Wiley.

Kerr, M. and McKee, L. (1981) 'The Father's Role in Child Health Care', *Health Visitor* 54(2): 47–51.

Kirshner, L.A., Hauser, S.T. and Genack, A. (1982) 'Research on Gender and Psychotherapy', in M.T. Notman and C.C. Nadelson (eds) *The Woman Patient*. New York: Plenum Press.

Kotelchuck, M. (1982) 'The Nature of the Child's Tie to His Father'. PhD: Harvard.

Lamb, M.E. (1976) *The Role of the Father in Child Development*. New York: Wiley.

Lamb, M.E. (ed.), (1981a) *The Role of the Father in Child Development*, 2nd edn. New York: Wiley.

Lamb, M.E. (1981b) 'Fathers and Child Development: An Integrative Overview', in M.E. Lamb (ed.) *The Role of the Father in Child Development*, 2nd edn. New York: Wiley.

Lamb, M.E. (ed.), (1982) *Non-Traditional Families*. Hillsdale, NJ: Erlbaum.

Lamb, M.E. (1986a) *The Father's Role: Applied Perspectives*. New York: Wiley.

Lamb, M.E. (1986b) 'The Changing Role of Fathers', in M.E. Lamb (ed.) *The Father's Role: Applied Perspectives*. New York: Wiley.

Lamb, M.E. and Sagi, A. (eds) (1983) *Fatherhood and Family Policy*. Hillsdale, NJ: Erlbaum.

La Rossa, R. (1977) *Conflict and Power in Marriage: Expecting the First Child*. Beverly Hills: Sage.

Laslett, P. (1981) 'Mothering', *London Review of Books* 16–19 August: 6–7.

Lewis, C. (1986a) *Becoming a Father*. Milton Keynes: Open University Press.

Lewis, C. (1986b) 'Early Sex Role Socialisation', in D. Hargreaves and A. Colley (eds) *The Psychology of Sex Roles*. London: Harper and Row.

Lewis, C., Newson, J. and Newson, E. (1982) Father Participation Through Childhood and its Relation to Career Aspirations and Delinquency, in N. Beail and J. McGuire (eds) *Fathers: Psychological Perspectives*. London: Junction.

Lewis, R.A. (1978) 'Emotional Intimacy Among Men', *Journal of Social Issues* 34(1), 108–21.

Lewis, R.A. (1986) 'Introduction: What Men Get Out of Marriage and Parenthood', in R.A. Lewis and R.E. Salt (eds) *Men in Families*. Beverly Hills: Sage.

Lewis, R.A. and Salt, R.E. (eds) (1986) *Men in Families*. Beverly Hills: Sage.

Mackey, W. (1985) *Fathering Behaviours: The Dynamics of the Man–Child Bond.* New York: Plenum.

Martin, J. and Roberts, C. (1984) *Women and Employment: A Lifetime Perspective.* London: HMSO.

McIntyre, D. (1985) 'Domestic Violence: A Case of the Disappearing Victim?', *The Australian Journal of Family Therapy* 5(4): 249–58.

McKee, L. (1979) 'Fathers' Participation in Infant Care'. Paper presented at British Sociological Association Fatherhood Conference. Warwick University, April.

McKee, L. (1982) 'Fathers' Participation in Infant Care: A Critique', in L. McKee and M. O'Brien (eds) *The Father Figure*. London: Tavistock.

McKee, L. (1983) 'Wives and the Recession'. Paper presented at the Conference on Unemployment and its Effects on the Family, Birmingham Postgraduate Medical Centre.

McKee, L. and O'Brien, M. (eds) (1982) *The Father Figure*. London: Tavistock.

Mogey, J.M. (1957) 'A Century of Declining Paternal Authority', *Marriage and Family Living* 19(3): 234–9.

Mowrer, E.R. (1930) *The Family: Its Organisation and Disorganisation.* Chicago: University of Chicago Press.

Myrdal, A. and Klein, V. (1956) *Women's Two Roles: Home and Work.* London: Routledge and Kegan Paul.

New, C. and David, M. (1985) *For the Children's Sake: Making Childcare More than Women's Business.* Harmondsworth: Pelican.

Newson, J. and Newson, E. (1963) *Infant Care in an Urban Community.* London: Allen and Unwin.

Oakley, A. (1974) *The Sociology of Housework.* Oxford: Martin Robertson.

Oakley, A. (1979) *Becoming a Mother.* Oxford: Martin Robertson.

O'Brien, M. (1982) 'The Working Father', in N. Beail and J. McGuire (eds) *Fathers: Psychological Perspectives.* London: Junction.

O'Brien, M. (1984) 'Fathers Without Wives: A Comparative Psychological Study of Married and Separated Fathers and Their Families', PhD dissertation. LSE: University of London.

O'Brien, M. (1987) 'Men and Fathers in Therapy'. Paper presented at the British Psychological Society Annual Conference, April.

Parsons, T. and Bales, R.F. (1955) *Family, Socialisation and Interaction Process.* New York: Free Press.

Pederson, F. and Robson, K. (1969) 'Father Participation in Infancy', *American Journal of Orthopsychiatry* 39: 466–72.

Pennebaker, J.W. (1982) *The Psychology of Physical Symptoms.* London: Longman.

Pleck, J.H. (1979) 'Men's Family Work: Three Perspectives and Some New Data', *The Family Coordinator* 28: 481–8.

Pleck, J.H. and Brannon, R. (1978) 'Male Roles and the Male Experience: Introduction', in J.H. Pleck and R. Brannon (eds), *Male Roles and Male Experience*, a special edition of the *Journal of Social Issues* 34(1).

Pollock, S. and Sutton, J. (1985) 'Fathers' Rights, Women's Losses', *Women's Studies International Forum* 8(6): 593–9.

Power, T. (1981) 'Sex Typing in Infancy: The Role of the Father', *Infant Mental Health Journal* 2: 226–40.

Rapoport, R., Rapoport, R.N. and Strelitz, Z. (1977) *Fathers, Mothers and Others.* London: Routledge and Kegan Paul.

Ratner, R.S. (1980) 'The Policy and the Problem: Overview of Seven Countries', in R.S. Ratner (ed.) *Equal Employment Policy for Women.* Philadelphia: Temple University Press.

Richards, M.P.M. (1982) 'How Should We Approach The Study of Fathers?', in L. McKee and M. O'Brien (eds) *The Father Figure*: 57–71. London: Tavistock.

Richards, M., Dunn, J. and Antonis, B. (1977) 'Caretaking in the First Year of Life: The Role of Father's and Mother's Social Isolation', *Child Care, Health and Development* 3: 23–36.

Rossi, A. (1984) 'Gender and Parenthood', *American Sociological Review* 49: 1–19.

Rubin, Z., Hill, C.T., Peplan, L.A. and Dunkell-Schetto, C. (1980) 'Self Disclosure in Dating Couples: Sex Roles and the Ethic of Openness', *Journal of Marriage and the Family* 42(2): 305–17.

Russell, G. (1983) *The Changing Role of Fathers.* Milton Keynes: Open University Press.

Russell, C.S., Atilano, R.B., Anderson, S.A., Jurich, A.P. and Bergen, L.P. (1984) 'Intervention Strategies: Predicting Family Therapy Outcome', *Journal of Marital and Family Therapy* 10: 241–51.

Russo, N.F. (1976) 'The Motherhood Mandate', *Journal of Social Issues* 32(3): 143–53.

Sanik, M.M. (1981) 'Division of Household Work: A Decade Comparison — 1967–1977', *Home Economics Journal* 10(2): 175–80.

Seidler, V. (1985) 'Fear and Intimacy', in A. Metcalfe and M. Humphries (eds) *The Sexuality of Men.* London: Pluto.

Shereshefsky, D., and Yarrow, L. (1973) *Psychological Aspects of a First Pregnancy and Early Post Natal Adaptation.* New York: Raven Press.

Skevington, S. (1986) 'Sex Roles and Mental Health', in D. Hargreaves and Anne Colley (eds) *The Psychology of Sex Roles.* London: Harper and Row.

Solomon, K. (1982) 'Individual Psychotherapy and Changing Masculine Roles: Dimensions of Gender-Role Psychotherapy', in K. Solomon and N. Levy (eds) *Men in Transition: Theory and Therapy.* New York: Plenum.

Solomon, K. and Levy, N.B. (eds) (1982) *Men in Transition: Theory and Therapy.* New York: Plenum.

Stafford, F.P. (1980) 'Women's Use of Time Converging With Men's', *Monthly Labour Review*, 103 (December, 57–9).

Thornes, B. and Collard, J. (1979) *Who Divorces?* London: Routledge and Kegan Paul.

Tyler, A. (1986) 'The Abusing Father', in M.E. Lamb (ed.), *The Father's Role: Applied Perspectives.* New York: Wiley.

Weiss, R. (1985) 'Men and the Family', *Family Process* 24(March): 49–58.

Williams, J. (1984) 'Women and Mental Illness', in J. Nicolson and H. Beloff (eds) *Psychology Survey.* Leicester: B.P.S.

Winnicott, D.W. (1965) *The Family and Individual Development.* London: Tavistock.

I

CONSTRAINTS ON FATHERS

The chapters in this section have been selected to illustrate variations in fathering experiences as well as the limitations imposed on paternal involvement. They cover a variety of issues, but each attempts to unravel the problematic nature of fatherhood.

In Chapter 2 Richards examines the ideologies of parenthood within a specific historical period and locale — middle-class England at the turn of the century. This exercise allows the reader time for reflection about common themes in parenting over the years and historical change. Particularly relevant to contemporary social scientists is his speculation that the emergence of companionate marriage may well have led to a diminution of the father's involvement in the family, and not greater paternal participation as implied by the ideology.

The sexual divisions of parental responsibility described by Richards are shown very clearly when they are set in the context of contemporary employment patterns outside the home. Moss and Brannen's (Chapter 3) examination of paid work illuminates the persistence of gender-based career structures in western cultures. Men are more heavily engaged in their jobs, particularly during the years of active parenting. While many mothers work they are far less likely to embark upon careers and most regard the home as their domain. Despite governmental moves to equalize opportunities for women at work and men in the home (Moss and Brannen list all the current paternity leave schemes available to men in Europe to illustrate this point), the divisions continue, reinforced by tradition and the law.

Horna and Lupri (Chapter 4) examine parental roles in one north American city. Their data show the generalizability of Moss and Brannen's mainly European review. Horna and Lupri focus upon the domestic division of labour throughout the course of life and also explore the sphere of leisure, using innovative time-budget methods. Just as the husband assumes a greater work load outside the home (both in employment and 'yard work'), so too does his wife take on the bulk of both housework and child-care. Interestingly, the fathers in this study were more likely to perceive child-care as 'leisure', an indication perhaps of their voluntary engagement in this domain.

The final contributions to Part I examine descriptions of men as family members. Leading on from the chapters which indicate that parental roles are differentiated both at work and in the home, Backett (Chapter 5) shows at a 'micro' level how parents continue to profess a belief in the equality of contemporary parental roles. The discrepancy between attitudes and behaviour is maintained because, far from being fixed, parental roles are continually negotiated by couples. Parents with young children, the focus of this chapter, develop what Backett (1982) has previously called 'coping mechanisms' to avoid confronting the obvious mismatch between theory and practice.

While Backett and Horna and Lupri discuss the years of active parenting, Cunningham-Burley (Chapter 6) examines men at the stage of life when they are both fathers and grandfathers. Just as interviews of grandparents tended to be monopolized by grandmothers, so too do couples construct a lesser role for the grandfather — both at the symbolic level and we suspect in terms of their practical involvement. The accounts of grandfathering in this chapter echo the earlier descriptions which have emphasized a somewhat distanced father–child relationship. However, there are indications that a release from the breadwinning mandate sometimes gives space for grandfathers to have more contact with their grandchildren.

Reference

Backett, K.C. (1982) *Mothers and Fathers: A Study of the Development and Negotiation of Parental Behaviour*. London and Basingstoke: Macmillan.

2
Fatherhood, marriage and sexuality: some speculations on the English middle-class family

Martin Richards

Introduction

In part at least, the increased interest in fathers among developmental psychologists in the last decade or so arose from a dissatisfaction with a view of development which concentrated on mothers to the exclusion of all others in the child's life and which failed to place any of the psychological actors in their social world. To use Ingleby's (1972) analogy, mother and child were seen as if they were the sole inhabitants of a desert island. To some degree fatherhood research has helped to create more satisfactory theoretical frameworks, but all too often it has confined itself to questions about the relative contributions to child-care of the two parents without exploring the wider social context. At worst it has remained an academic extension of domestic quarrels about who should look after the baby.

One way to escape from these over narrow confines is to examine parent–child relationships and child-care within the broader context of marriage and domestic life. There have been a number of attempts to move the discussion in this direction. For instance, McKee (1986) has examined the influence of male unemployment on domestic life and child-care patterns and there is a quite extensive literature which examines connections between marital relationships and the arrival of children (e.g. Lewis, 1986). Here I would like to take this approach further and explore connections between father–child relationships and marriage and sexuality. Are there common characteristics of the relationship of husband and wife and father and child? If so, how can we explain the common features? I shall attempt to approach these questions by using some historical material. Historical work is not only important because it allows us to understand the formation of contemporary attitudes and institutions, but it also can help us to escape from our familiarity with our own social world and so question what we might otherwise take for granted. It can give us a new perspective from which to see our lives — a function not dissimilar to cross-cultural comparisons.

In order to provide anything beyond the most superficial pictures within the confines of a brief chapter, I will limit the discussion in a number of ways. I will only deal with English middle-class families, the social group about which we have the most detailed information. And I will concentrate on two points in time, the middle of the nineteenth century and the period just after the First World War. In choosing these two periods I am more concerned with the contrasts they provide than wishing to suggest that either may be particularly significant from the point of view of father–child relations.

Of course, there are considerable difficulties in trying to reconstruct the nature of domestic relationships in the past; after all, the task is hard enough in the present. However, thanks to a rapidly growing body of social history, much of it contributed by feminists, we have surprisingly detailed knowledge of the middle-class world of the nineteenth and early twentieth century. It is these secondary sources that I shall be drawing on for the most part. However, it is necessary to emphasize that the suggestions I will be making are tentative and often speculative. My aim is to sketch out a series of connections which require a good deal of further investigation to test their validity and generality.

There is a particular danger that we must avoid in an historical discussion of this kind, and it is the creation of simplistic stereotypes. All too many discussions use terms like 'Victorian women', paying little attention to variation within and across social class or through the span of a long reign. While we can immediately see the simplification involved in such generalizations about the present, they have less often been challenged when made about the past.

Marriage and parenthood in the mid-nineteenth century

By an Act of 1857 divorce became a civil matter for the first time. However, the Act did not embody any new view of divorce, or indeed marriage. It incorporated the principles that had been used in the granting of divorce by private Acts of Parliament in the first half of the century. Divorce was restricted to the affluent (numbers remained below 700 until the 1880s and did not exceed 1000 until after the turn of the century) and was almost always granted to men who would then retain custody of their children. It was founded on the patriarchal double standard under which middle-class women effectively were the property of men to be handed from father to husband at marriage. While it was generally assumed that men would have sexual relationships before and outside marriage, severe sanctions awaited any women who attempted to follow the same course. It was a world of strong contrasts and contradictions within and between the separate spheres of work and home which developed with the growth of industrialization and the professions to service this and their attendant imperialism. Home was a domestic world to which a man could return from the harsh world of commerce to be renewed and purified by the company of a woman. But the home, like the wider world, was divided by lines of gender and class. Not only did husband and wife have separate bedrooms, but, as far as the size of the establishment would allow, there were other rooms used principally by one or the other, the study, smoking- and billiard-rooms for men and particular day rooms, boudoir and dressing-rooms for women (see Girouard, 1979). During this period the nursery developed as a separate sphere for children. In the larger houses there would be a day and night nursery and a school-room. The class division within the house was represented by the green baize door dividing off the rooms used by servants — usually in the basement and the attic.[1]

From a modern standpoint perhaps the most striking feature of middle-class marriage of the period was separatedness of the spouses, not only represented by use of space in the home, and the relatively small amount of time the couple would spend together, but also their differing standards of education and experience which in many cases must have given them precious little to talk about. As Lewis (1984) remarks, it is the uncommunicative separate lives which are perhaps the most striking characteristic of middle-class Victorian autobiographies and popular literature.

The feature that later generations have used to characterize Victorian marriage is the 'passionlessness' of women (Cott, 1978). Many later writers on the subject have used the now famous quotation from Acton to make their point.

> I should say that the majority of women (happily for them) are not very much troubled with sexual feelings of any kind. What men are habitually, women are only exceptionally.

William Acton was a genito-urinary surgeon who had written a textbook of his subject and a volume on prostitution before his *The Functions and Disorders of the Reproductive Organs in Childhood, Youth, Adult Age and Advanced Life, Considered in Their Psychological, Social and Moral Relations* was published in 1857 (see Marcus, 1966). It is from this latter work that the famous quotation comes. While Acton's view as a prescriptive writer did reflect a widely held ideal, it cannot, of course, be taken as a statement of fact to be read in the way we might read a modern psychological survey.[2]

Were we to take it in this way, it would imply that female sexuality is capable of radical reconstruction over a relatively brief period of time, but there is growing evidence from other sources, including other professional writing of the time, and a very early survey of female sexuality carried out by an American woman doctor, that such unlikely conclusions are unnecessary (Degler, 1974).

In his writing Acton displays a series of beliefs about sexuality and marriage which were probably quite typical of someone in his position in the mid-nineteenth century. His ideas about male sexuality embody the assumption, common at the time, that the emission of sperm was debilitating leading in modest cases to a general loss of energy, especially of an entrepreneurial kind and, if frequent, to a whole series of chronic diseases. A common Victorian term for orgasm was 'spending' another part of what since has been called the spermatic economy (Barker-Benfield, 1972). So while Acton argues that for men any kind of sexual activity beyond occasional marital intercourse is dangerous and damaging to health, he also assumes they possess a strong drive, making masturbation common in childhood and youth, and pre- and extra-marital intercourse ('incontinence') general in adulthood. In discussing the latter, he displays the attitudes by which female sexuality is not only linked to disease but also social class. To continue the passage from Acton quoted above:

> It is too true, I admit, as the divorce courts show, that there are some few women who have sexual desires so strong that they surpass those of men . . . I admit, of course, the existence of sexual excitement terminating even in nymphomania, a form of insanity which those accustomed to visit lunatic asylums, must be fully conversant with, but, with these sad exceptions, there can be no doubt that sexual feeling in the female is in the majority of cases in abeyance . . . and even if aroused (which in many instances it never can be) is very moderate compared with that of the male. Many men, and particularly young men, form their idea of women's feelings from what they notice early in life among loose, or, at least, low and vulgar women. . . . Such women however give a very false idea of the condition of female sexual feeling in general . . . loose women (who, if they have no sexual feeling, counterfeit it so well that the novice does not suspect that it is genuine), all seem to corroborate such an impression . . . it is from these erroneous notions that so many young men think that the marital duties they will have to undertake are beyond their exhausted strength, and for that reason dread and avoid marriage . . . the married woman has no wish to be treated on the footing of a mistress.

This is the great divide of Victorian sexuality: dangerous, exciting, illicit sex with working class women and occasional visits to the bedroom of the pure and unresponsive wife for the dutiful procreation of children. While that ideology is clear enough from writing of the period, reliable accounts of sexual behaviour are almost nonexistent. However, there is every reason to think that sex for money or by exploitation of their social position was freely available to middle and especially upper middle class men and many, if not most, took advantage of it. Prostitutes were numerous, largely working class women aged between about 16 and 25 who found the apparent economic and social advantages of the 'gay' life more attractive than sweated labour or domestic service (Gorham, 1978 and Walkowitz,

1980). Acton regarded prostitution as inevitable and acknowledged its connection with poverty and the demand for money and position as a requirement for marriage (middle class men married around 30 at this time).

Like marriage, parent–child relationships are probably best characterized by their distance in both a physical and psychological sense. We may conclude that after what was probably a fairly brief period of breast feeding, children were cared for almost exclusively by servants. Precise information about how much time children spent with their parents is very hard to come by, but probably while most would spend some of the day with their mothers, time with fathers was generally very limited. Perhaps a brief encounter in the morning before he left the house but often they would be in bed long before he returned. Boys would be sent off to the somewhat brutal regime of the public school (Pearsall, 1971) while girls were largely educated at home.

There are at least two kinds of connection between parent–child relations and those of husband and wife which we might examine. The first are shared common characteristics that might exist, in part at least, because of common sets of attitudes as well as social conditions. A second link would be an ontogenetic one whereby the pattern of relationships in infancy and childhood created needs or desires in the children which led to certain patterns of adult interrelation.

As for the first, it is easy to see common characteristics in the two sets of social relations. Both were characterized by distance, undemonstrativeness, and separateness, at least in their public faces. Not only was the whole social system maintained by the exploitation of a working class at home and the imperial world abroad, but so also was the public decorum of marriage relationships underlain by sensuality across class, between nursemaid and child and gentleman and mistress. It was a socially and psychologically divided world in which middle-class women were perhaps more likely to find resolution in close emotional relationships with other women than in their marriages (Jeffreys, 1985).

Several authors have discussed the socialization of Victorian men (though less has been said about women). Cominos (1963) suggested that

> the whole socialization process to which the gentleman was subjected in order to establish his civilized self-control ... produced not merely a self-control of sorts, but often yielded a psychic condition of 'over-repression' among gentlemen and a rigidity of character-structure. Hence the social character of the gentlemen contradicted, as did the social system itself, the principle and possibilities of genuinely free association,

i.e. associations free of domination and submission both within and without the family.

Suggesting that the double standard was associated with an immature sexuality, he follows Thomas (1959) in proposing that this arose from a failure to bring together the two currents of love and sensuality in a relationship with one person.

> Freud ascribed the disassociation to the frustration of intense incestuous fixations, to the unsuccessful resolution of the Oedipus complex so that sexual attitudes were not freed from the parental models. The disassociated elements became polarized and were reflected in the respectable ideological opposition between sexual love, suspect and degrading, and ethereal love, honourable and exalting.

Clearly, psychological notions of this kind are likely to be very over-simplistic and run the risk of fixing explanation at a purely psychological level; however, it seems likely that, for many Victorian men, the intermittent and formalized relationships with their parents must have carried their marks into adulthood.

The 1920s
After the First World War advice to parents about children was dominated by the behaviourist views of Watson and Truby King (Hardyment, 1983). They appealed to science, presenting the mother at the centre of the stage, responsible for the development of her child's character and, most importantly, for anything that might go wrong. Routine and regularity were the basis of good child-care and it was necessary for the mother to keep a careful check on her own feelings and never to 'give in' to the baby. The style is well caught by the following quotations

> Obedience in infancy is the foundation of all later powers of self-control yet it is the one thing the young mother nowadays is most inclined to neglect. Instead of gently, wisely and firmly regulating her baby's habits and conduct, she tends to allow him to have his own way and to rule her and the whole household ... the establishment of perfect regularity of habits, initiated by 'Feeding and Sleeping by the Clock' is the ultimate foundation of all-round obedience. Granted good organic foundations, truth and honour can be built into the edifice as it grows. (Truby King, 1925)

Mrs J. Langton Hewer (1922) the midwife author of another popular baby book was aware of the difficulties.

> Mother must learn to vanquish many natural little temptations. She does not always want to part with her baby when he has finished a meal. She loves to feel his drowsy head nestling against her breast. But she must let sense triumph over sentiment, for her baby's sake. Immediately he has

finished a meal he should be laid in his cot ... a baby will require no 'patting' or rocking, which is so exciting and therefore dangerous to the nervous system: no dandling, no singing to sleep. ... Closely linked up to the good habits of feeding and sleeping come that of breathing THROUGH THE NOSE.

And looking ahead:

In the quiet of the evening hour, when curtains are cosily drawn, the tranquil lure of hearth and home filling them with a sense of benediction, parents direct their thought to the future for the beloved little one....
They will desire that by careful economy and management their son shall be brought up in the English tradition of 'playing the game' some already visualise his career from a good preparatory school through a famous Public School to a University, while others have ambitions less expensive to attain, yet better than the chances of haphazard life.
 Or if it be a daughter they will wish she to be equipped for the Battle of Life in one of the splendid modern colleges, and armed with a training for a profession. They will desire to be prepared should she marry for the provision of her trousseau and her dowry.[3]

Father played very little part in the scheme of things though some advised that mothers should be careful not to exclude him altogether. With the growing influence of Freud, the complexities of the father's position were increasingly pointed out. These points are well illustrated in an essay by Mrs C. Gasquoine Hartley (1924), a well known writer about women and family matters.

The mother is the first love-object and of supreme importance ... but the other parent, the superfluous father comes both as interrupter and friend in this mother–child circle. He plays with the children, opens up new delightful ways of interest. ... But also he is a disturber ... at a very early age jealousy of the father begins to stir and unsettle the nursery peace.
 Have we not read of the solitary polygamous father of the past, the Old Man of the Tribe, who drove his sons out of the home as they grew up, because in his greed he wanted all the women to be his wives? ... Pity and the gentler feelings of civilization enable the father to accept the son as a member of the family and as a companion instead of a rival. But echoes remain of the old instincts of jealous rivalry. No science is so difficult or so important as psychology. It is because parents do not understand their own minds or the minds of their children that they make such mistakes ... so do not let us be too alarmed if sons oppose fathers or if the fathers are wanting in sympathy with their sons.

Others simply accepted that the father was not of great significance beyond an economic provider. Russell (1929) presents this view in his famous attack on marriage.

No doubt the ideal father is better than none but many fathers are so far from ideal that their non-existence might be a positive advantage to children.

Instead Russell recommends a collaboration of mothers and the educational system for the bringing up of children.

It is not difficult to understand why the child-care manuals of the 1920s should have made such frequent appeals to psychology as their legitimating source. And within psychology, behaviourism lent itself to provide the method for training children while psychoanalysis could add to the agenda of issues that might concern parents. However, it is much less clear why fatherhood should be seen as an unimportant institution or why there was such a heavy emphasis on the necessity for mothers to control their own affectionate contact with children. These are matters to which I will return when I have discussed marital relationships in the period. But for the time being, it is worth pointing out that several authors of the day saw women's sexuality as a particular threat to children. To quote Russell again:

> A boy hates his father whom he regards as a sexual rival. He feels in regard to his mother, emotions which are viewed with the utmost abhorrence by traditional morality. . . . In later life, the effects of these turbulent passions are of the most diverse and terrible kind, varying from homosexuality at the best to mania at worse.

These Freudian dangers can be avoided, according to Russell, if the children's heterosexual emotions find an outlet in play and the mother's sexual feelings are engaged elsewhere. He concludes that there are:

> certain conditions which must be fulfilled if the psychological effect of family life upon children is to be good. The parents, especially the mother, must if possible not be unhappy in their sexual life.

But not only mothers are a risk, 'servant-girls and nurses, and in later years, schoolteachers, are quite as dangerous (as mothers), indeed, even more so, since they are, as a rule, sexually starved'.

The conventional picture of the postwar years is of the 'roaring twenties'; of women whose horizons had been extended by war work enjoying a new found sexual freedom inside and outside marriage. The work of the sexologists like Havelock Ellis and Krafft-Ebing (see Weeks, 1981) was used to support the idea that women, like men, had sexual needs and that sexual relations within marriage demand mutuality. Knowledge of and access to contraception became more widespread among the middle class (see Gittins, 1982).

But while it is undoubtedly true that some old patterns and attitudes had changed, it is also possible to argue that the First World War, like the Second, was followed by a period in which there was a reassertion of traditional values about marriage and the family. In both postwar periods the emphasis was on woman's place in the home (see Riley, 1984, for the 1940s). In the 1920s one of the most direct ways in which this occurred was by the imposition of a bar in many of the professions which forced women to give up their jobs on marriage (Lewis, 1984). While there is evidence of an increasing rate of pre-marital intercourse among women (Lewis-Fanning, 1949) the sexual liberation which is often described as characteristic of the period was extremely superficial. As Sheila Rowbotham (1973) put it,

> sexual defiance was a style, a fashionable cultural stance.... It was a release for a privileged minority, not a new way of living for the majority.

Whilst during the war there had been widespread pleas for under-standing and sympathy for 'war babies' and their unmarried mothers, after the war sexuality was firmly relocated within marriage. Women like Dora Russell and Irene Clephane who were calling for sexual freedom were part of a very small minority. As Marie Stopes herself later commented, women still regarded themselves as the passive partner and still were on the whole disappointed and dissatisfied by their sex lives (Lewis, 1984) and even in 1930 Helena Wright wrote that 'a woman's body can be regarded as a musical instrument await-ing the hand of a [male] artist'. Opposition to birth control was widespread as seen, for example, in the prosecution for the publica-tion of one of Margaret Sanger's books in 1922. The more liberal attitudes of the day may be illustrated by a report published by the Quakers in 1925 on 'The Problem of Birth Control' (Society of Friends, 1925). The report expresses concern at the declining birth-rate but recognizes that this, in part, is the result of 'moral advance of wider freedom won by women and increased respect for women', a rising standard of living and increased expectations of education. They give guarded support to the use of contraceptives but see dangers in that this may lead to overrating the importance of sex and to underrating the necessity of self-control within marriage. Sex, they say, is only the outward expression of the inward 'true spiritual love of man and wife'.

> We must note as of great social importance the tendency of use of contraceptives to make vice easier and less risky. Not only do these methods of conception control increase the temptation to 'vice' in the technical sense of the term, but they also encourage the cult of free love and the inclination, discernible in modern society, to follow the impulse of wayward passion, rather than to subject oneself to a disciplined affection. The use of contraception does definitely strengthen the downward Pagan tendencies in sex moralities at the present time. For that reason ... they may fall into the class of things which are lawful but not expedient. ...
> [But] the use of contraceptives does not make vice more vicious, nor does it make free love less objectionable.... The fundamental moral issue turns on the rightness or wrongness of extra-marital sexual relations. If these are sinful, their sinfulness is neither increased nor diminished by the use of contraceptives.

The report concludes with a medical section which emphasizes the dangers: 'Most of the leading specialists . . . state that sterility follows the frequent use of contraceptives by women' and quotes high rates of failure '71–88 percent' and points to the eugenic dangers; 'an alteration in the birth ratio between what we may term the socially desirable and the socially undesirable'.

In the 1920s the birthrate continued to fall and households became smaller (Gittins, 1982). Servants were harder to come by and many professional couples had to make do with a 'home help' who would come in each day. For those who did have servants, relationships with them were changed as physical and social distance was reduced. With the help of machines like the vacuum cleaner which were becoming commonplace, much of the domestic work was done by the wives themselves. Catering for these women were a growing number of magazines like *Home and Garden* and *Ideal Home* which

> all carried the same message — a woman's place is in the home and any normal woman should find cooking, shopping, sewing and mothering of all-absorbing interest. (Beauman, 1984)

Within the home the lives of husband and wife were less separate and evenings might often be spent at opposite sides of the same fire before retiring to their twin beds in the same bedroom. Many of the developing leisure activities — the cinema, motoring, the dance hall and tea dance — provided shared pursuits for husband and wife as well as meeting places for the unmarried. This shared life and an increasing joint experience of education and work (before marriage for women) extended the basis for a companionate marriage. This is not to say, of course, as we know from many accounts, that marriage and domestic life were not often extremely isolating for many women and Jane Lewis (1984) speculates that depression, or 'suburban neurosis' as it was called at the time, might have been as common then as neurasthenia and hysteria had been in the nineteenth century.

In such a world it may have been the growth in the idea of companionship in marriage and the increase in joint activity of husband and wife that, ironically, led to a reduction in fathers' involvement with children. Before the war when more child-care was provided by servants, the parents' role was not as caretakers but as amusers, educators, companions and figures of authority for children. As caretaking increasingly fell to the mother, and marriage became more companionate, it may have been that domestic division of labour was sharpened and so men's role in child-care was reduced. It was one thing for a husband and wife to share more of their leisure time, another for a man to become involved in domestic work.

Despite changing attitudes to male and female sexuality and

relationships in the 1920s, the double standard, of course, persisted and men were expected to be more likely to indulge in pre- and extra-marital sex. But it seems possible that while more women had relationships before marriage there may have been some decline for men, especially in the lower middle class. What also seems likely is that for men who did have sex outside marriage, it was much more likely to be with someone in their own class than would have been the case a generation earlier. This is the era when the concerns of the moralists shifted from the professional to the amateur. So that while the experience of sexuality may not have been very equal, the social backgrounds of the participants had become more so. Unfortunately, while a number of lines of evidence (for instance, the decline in the numbers of prostitutes) point in this direction, it cannot be stated as more than a speculative hypothesis. Sadly, historians of marriage and sexuality have, as yet, paid much less attention to the 1920s than they have to earlier periods. But if the hypothesis were true, it would mean that to some degree the split between sexual pleasure for men inside and outside marriage was reduced, at least in comparison with the two worlds of the mid-nineteenth century. It is perhaps somewhere in this shift that we can understand the (male) concern and anxiety about emotional closeness of mother and child. So that while men were able to see their love and sexual relationship as more of a whole, they projected their fears about female sexuality onto women as mothers and also onto relationships between women. In this connection, it might not be irrelevant to point out that lesbianism became a public issue in the 1920s with, among other incidents, an attempt to bring it into the scope of criminal law in 1921 and the prosecution of Radclyffe Hall's lesbian novel, *The Well of Loneliness* in 1928 (see Weeks, 1981).

I think it is reasonable to suggest that in the 1920s, for the first time, we may see middle class marriages that resemble those of today, and, indeed, marital affairs which share important characteristics with contemporary ones. But while in the 1920s a notion that a primary function of marriage was the raising of children was strongly retained, today the emphasis has shifted to the mutual psychological satisfactions of the spouses — but that is another story.

Conclusion
In this chapter I have used two historical periods as exemplars to suggest a number of connections between parenthood, marriage and sexuality. I am all too painfully aware how thin the evidence is for much of what I have suggested. However, I hope I may have indicated that there is an important area awaiting study. As our historical understanding of fatherhood increases, so will our ability to under-

stand the present. Historical work indicates connections that we may search out in the present. Today it is widely believed that fathers are increasingly involved in child-care, yet the evidence suggests that such changes that have occurred are very limited (Lewis, 1986). Similarly, at a time when research indicates the continuing disparity of power and status between spouses within marriage, there is widespread discussion of the symmetrical family (Young and Willmott, 1973). I hope my historical speculations may encourage someone to explore the connections between these two.

Notes

1. Class relationships were also represented by the placing of the house in the landscape. Knightshayes Court in Devon was built by William Burges for the Heathcoat–Amory family in 1869. It stands on a hill some two miles from the mill which was the centre of the family's lace-making business. The house faces the mill and the garden was landscaped with a central vista with the mill at its focus.
2. Using the example of child-care manuals, Mechling (1979) discusses some of the more obvious difficulties in trying to infer behaviour from the advice givers.
3. This volume is published by an insurance company which thoughtfully provided a list of recommended schools complete with their termly fees and details of suitable assurance policies that can be used to pay for these.

References

Barker-Benfield, B. (1972) 'The Spermatic Economy: A Nineteenth Century View of Sexuality', *Feminist Studies* 6: 45–74.
Beauman, N. (1984) *A Very Great Profession*. London: Virago.
Cominos, P. (1963) 'Late-Victorian Sexual Respectability and the Social System', *International Review of Social History* 8: 18–48, 216–50.
Cott, N.F. (1978) 'Passionlessness. An Interpretation of Victorian Sexual Ideology 1790–1850', *Signs Journal of Women in Culture and Society* 4: 219–35.
Degler, C.N. (1974) 'What ought to be and what was: Women's Sexuality in the Nineteenth Century', *American Historical Review* 79: 1467–90.
Girouard, M. (1979) *The Victorian Country House*. New Haven: Yale University Press.
Gittins, D. (1982) *Fair Sex. Family Size and Structure 1900–39*. London: Hutchinson.
Gorham, D. (1978) 'The "Maiden Tribute of Modern Babylon" Re-examined. Child Prostitution and the Idea of Childhood in Late-Victorian England', *Victorian Studies* 21: 353–79.
Hardyment, C. (1983) *Dream Babies. Child Care from Locke to Spock*. London: Jonathan Cape.
Hartley, C.G. (1924) *Women, Children, Love and Marriage*. London: Heath Cranton.
Hewer, J.L. (1922) *Baby From Bud to Blossom*. London: Eagle Star and British Dominions Insurance.
Ingleby, D. (1974) 'The Psychology of Child Psychology', in M.P.M. Richards (ed.) *The Integration of a Child into a Social World*. London: Cambridge University Press.
Jeffreys, S. (1985) *The Spinster and Her Enemies. Feminism and Sexuality 1880–1930*. London: Pandora.

Lewis, J. (1984) *Women in England 1870–1950: Sexual Division and Serial Change.* Sussex: Wheatsheaf Books.

Lewis, C. (1986) *Becoming a Father.* Milton Keynes: Open University Press.

Lewis-Fanning (1949) 'Family Limitation and its Influence on Human Fertility in the Last 50 Years'. Royal Commission on Population Papers, Vol. 1. London: HMSO.

Marcus. S. (1966) *The Other Victorians. A Study of Sexuality and Pornography in Mid-Nineteenth Century England.* London: Weidenfeld and Nicholson.

McKee, L. (1986) 'Having a Family in the Face of Unemployment', in J. Burgoyne and M.P.M. Richards (eds) *Public and Private Lives.* (In press.)

Mechling, J. (1979). 'Advice to Historians on Advice to Mothers'. *Journal of Social History* 9: 44–63.

Pearsall, R. (1971) *The Worm in the Bud.* Harmondsworth: Penguin Books.

Riley, D. (1984) *War in the Nursery.* London: Virago.

Rowbotham, S. (1973) *Hidden from History.* London: Pluto Press.

Russell, B. (1929) *Marriage and Morals.* London: Allen and Unwin.

Society of Friends (1925) *Marriage and Parenthood. The Problem of Birth Control.* London.

Stopes, M. (1918) *Married Love.* New York: Critic and Guide.

Thomas, K. (1959) 'The Double Standard', *Journal of the History of Ideas,* April, 207.

Truby King, E. (1925) *Feeding and Care of Baby.* London: Macmillan (original edition 1913).

Walkowitz, J.R. (1980) *Prostitution and Victorian Society.* Cambridge: Cambridge University Press.

Weeks, J. (1981) *Sex, Politics and Society. The Regulation of Sexuality since 1800.* London: Longman.

Wright, H. (1930) *The Sex Factor in Marriage.* London: Williams and Norgate.

Young, M. and Willmott, P. (1973) *The Symmetrical Family.* London: Routledge and Kegan Paul.

3
Fathers and employment

Peter Moss and Julia Brannen

Introduction

In this chapter, we describe some of the main characteristics of employment among men with dependent children and the dominant ideologies that promote and sustain these characteristics. We also consider why the present situation is problematic and how social policy might encourage change. First of all, though, it needs to be acknowledged that the employment of fathers is not at present a public issue to any great degree, in Britain or in most industrial countries. It is not recognized in legislation, nor by and large in the employment practices of individual employers: even for the most basic of entitlements — paternity leave — 'formal agreement is still the exception, not the norm' (Income Data Services, 1985). Politically too, there has been negligible interest in the subject. The only British government publication since 1945 about parenthood and employment confined itself entirely to 'services for young children with working *mothers*' (CPRS, 1978). By contrast, the employment of women with children has been long seen as a public issue. It has been and remains a contentious subject. 'Should mothers go out to work?' still seems to many people the central question to pose in relation to parents and employment.

Reflecting and reinforcing these dominant assumptions, research has paid far less attention to fathers' than to mothers' employment. In child development research, for instance, there is a substantial body of literature on 'maternal employment' and its implications for children (cf. the reviews by Lamb, 1982; Hoffman, 1979, 1984). But the student of child development will search the literature in vain for anything on 'paternal employment'. The same bias is evident in sociology. For instance, between 1980 and 1985, the *Journal of Marriage and the Family* had nine articles specifically on the employment of mothers, and six more on the employment of wives — but none on the employment of fathers. Industrial sociology, in the *Affluent Worker* study (Goldthorpe et al., 1968), began to make links between men's work-place attitudes and behaviour and their life cycle positions and orientations beyond their employment experiences; however, as Dex (1985) argues, the implicit importance of women and children upon men's work orientations was not taken up.

Earlier work on the relationship between men's employment and family roles tended to focus on extreme examples, for instance where occupations involved long periods of absence from home. More recently, there has been some increase in interest in male 'family-work' management and conflicts in more common circumstances (e.g. Berger and Wright, 1978; Pleck, 1980; Robertson Elliot, 1979; Russell, 1982; O'Brien, 1982). Although some of this research has involved the study of how time is used by household members, and in particular the allocation of time by husbands and wives between paid work and family work (cf. Pleck, 1985), little information exists on actual patterns of employment, beyond average times spent in paid work per day.

Some main characteristics of the employment of fathers in Britain

Continuity of employment
An increasing number of fathers do not live with all or any of their dependent children, while a small proportion — accounting for 1 percent of all households with children — are lone parents. Very little information exists on the employment of these groups; most of the information in this section refers to men living with their children in two-parent households. Even for this group, it is difficult to put together a complete picture of their employment. When it comes to statistical and other information, mothers' employment has, again, received more attention. Most recently, the Government's Women and Employment Survey (WES) (Martin and Roberts, 1984) has provided the sort of comprehensive and detailed account of women's and mothers' employment that is not available for men and for fathers.

WES data show how having children disrupts women's employment. Using this data, Joshi (1985) concludes that 'responsibility for children "costs" a representative mother around 6 to 7 years of labour force membership', made up of periods out of work and other periods of part-time employment. Economic losses are even greater: responsibility for children costs women 'about twice as many years worth of average annual earnings' (i.e. 12–13 years). The difference is due to women earning lower pay subsequent to child-bearing. This occurs for several reasons. Loss of work experience leads to missed increments and promotion, training and other opportunities, which affect later rates of pay; while the difficulties of combining paid work with domestic commitments cause women to return to low-paying jobs for which they are overqualified (occupational downgrading), or to get jobs which make full use of their skills, but reward them poorly (in 'crummy' jobs).

Men pay no such price for parenthood. They experience no discontinuities in their employment *because of parenthood* — with the exception of men bringing up children by themselves, a point to which we return. Even the birth of their children causes minimal interruption to paid work. In a study of first-time parents, for instance, most fathers took some time off for the birth and when their wives came home from hospital; however, only 8 percent had more than 2 weeks off work throughout this period and most (50 percent) had only a week or less (Moss et al., 1983). Similar findings come from a study which included time off in pregnancy, as well as for the birth itself and the postnatal period; 6 percent of men took no time off in this whole period, while most — 69 percent — took 2 weeks or less (Bell et al., 1983). By contrast, the small proportion of women who resume full-time employment within 8 months of giving birth take an average of 14 weeks' leave after the birth (Daniel, 1980). To make this comparison is not to suggest that women take too long a period of leave, or indeed that their circumstances are comparable to men's at this time: rather, the question is *should* men take more time off at this important point in their lives?

Many men do have breaks in employment during the period when they have dependent children. These breaks, though, are usually due to involuntary unemployment — the father who chooses to stay at home to care for his children is still rare. The 1983 General Household Survey shows 87 percent of men with dependent children were actually in paid work (OPCS, 1985). A proportion of those not in work — 4 percent — were economically inactive (e.g. retired or otherwise unable to work), but most — 9 percent — were actually unemployed. This proportion has trebled in the last 10 years, and the unemployment rate for fathers is now higher than for other men (7 percent). These figures represent the position at one point of time. The proportion of men unemployed for a spell during, say, a year's period is substantially higher; there are no published figures for fathers, but 16 percent of men aged 25–39 had had at least one period of unemployment in the 12 months preceding the 1983 GHS.

Unemployment is concentrated among certain groups of men with children. It is highest for men with children under five (12 v. 6 percent for men with a youngest child of secondary school age); for men with three or more children (13 percent for men with three children, 24 percent with four or more, compared to 8 percent for men with one or two children) (OPCS, 1985: Table 7.18); and for men in manual occupations (10 percent for men in skilled manual jobs and 19 percent in semi-skilled or unskilled manual jobs, compared to 2 percent for men in professional or managerial jobs) (OPCS, 1984: Table 6.23). Ages and numbers of children are related most strongly to unemployment among men in lower status jobs. Fathers in professional and managerial jobs, have low levels of unemployment, and numbers of children make little difference to this. For fathers in unskilled and semi-skilled manual occupations, men with three or more children are twice as likely to be out of work (16 v. 31 percent) (OPCS, 1984: Table 6.24).

Lone fathers are more likely than other fathers to be unemployed (George and Wilding, 1972; Ferri, 1973; Hunt, 1973; O'Brien, 1982). O'Brien's study confirmed Hunt's earlier conclusion that the major reason for these higher rates of unemployment among lone fathers was their inability to sustain full-time employment alongside sole responsibility for the care of their children.

Hours of work

Recent improvements in the annual report of the GHS provide details of *un*employment amongst men living with their dependent children, but there is no comparable source giving details of employment. We must rely instead largely on a few small, local studies. These leave many gaps and cannot be safely generalized to the whole country.

Two-thirds of employed mothers have part-time jobs. There are no comparable figures for fathers, but the proportion employed part-time is likely to be lower than the 4 percent figure for all employed men. Among the majority of fathers in full-time jobs, the evidence points consistently to long hours spent at work. Two studies, both conducted at the Thomas Coram Research Unit, provide detailed data — though for a relatively limited range of fathers. Both dealt with married men living in the London area; having a first child; and underrepresent men in semi-skilled and unskilled manual jobs. The Transition to Parenthood (TP) study covered the period of pregnancy and the first year after birth, for a sample of seventy-five men. The Day Care (DC) study has covered the first three years after birth — though only the first 18 months data are reported here — with an initial sample of 250 households, in three-quarters of which the mother resumed full-time employment after maternity leave. Fathers were interviewed in the TP study but not in the DC study.

Both studies found that fathers spent around 50–55 hours a week on average in paid work, if travel, overtime and second jobs were included. Similar figures come from two other studies. In a London-based study of men with children aged 5–11, married fathers averaged 10 hours paid work a day, though lone fathers worked less hours (O'Brien, 1982); and in an Australian study, fathers were at work for 51 hours a week on average (Russell, 1983). These average figures conceal large variations. In the DC study, when children were 18 months old, 27 percent of employed fathers spent less than 50 hours a week in paid work and 42 percent 50–59 hours; of the remainder, 21 percent worked 60–69 hours and 11 percent 70 hours or more. Where both husband and wife have full-time jobs, men work substantially longer hours than women, and this is the case both before and after having children. In the TP study, men averaged 10 hours a week longer at work before their first child was born; in the DC study, the difference was 8 hours 18 months after the birth for men whose wives were also in full-time employment.

There is no information on the effect of numbers and ages of children on the hours worked by fathers. The effect of occupation is also unclear. Some studies report no differences in total hours worked between men in manual and non-manual jobs (Bell et al., 1983; O'Brien, 1982). In the TP study, however, men in manual jobs worked longer hours a year after the birth of their first child; the same was true in the DC study, at 18 months after the birth — but only for men whose wives were in full-time employment. This in turn is at odds with the findings from Young and Willmott's larger-scale study (1973), where men (both with and without children) in professional and managerial occupations had the longest working week — because of more overtime and longer journeys — averaging a 57-hour week, compared to 52 among manual workers. Professional and managerial workers do, however, have longer holidays, which reduce the length of their working year. In the TP study, men in professional or managerial jobs were more than twice as likely as manual workers to have a holiday entitlement of 5 weeks or more.

Men's hours in paid work appear to be longest when they have dependent children — the reverse of the situation for women. In the TP study, hours of work (excluding travel) increased from 48 to 51 per week among men in manual occupations between early pregnancy and a year after the birth, though there was no change among men in non-manual occupations. Hours of work may be higher later in parenthood. A reanalysis of 1975 Family Expenditure Survey data showed 45 percent of men with a youngest child aged 2–4 working over 45 hours a week, compared to 38 percent for men with a youngest child under 2, and 30 percent for married men under 30 with no children.

Longer hours during parenthood are the result of increased overtime. *Paid* overtime is most common among younger married men, and especially those with children (NBPI, 1970). In Young and Willmott's study (1973), covering London and the home counties, married men under 30 and who had children worked four times as much paid overtime as men of similar age but with no children (8.5 v. 2.1 hours per week). *Unpaid* overtime was highest for men aged

30–49 and with children (2.4 hours v. 1.1 for younger fathers, and 1.0 for older and younger married men without children). Combining both types of overtime, younger fathers averaged 9.6 hours a week and older fathers 8, compared to 3 hours for married childless men under 30 and 4.6 hours among married men over 50.

Fathers' employment is characterized by hours that are not only long, but often irregular. Men with children, especially those in manual and less skilled jobs, are more likely than other men to work shifts (NBPI, 1970). Even among men who do not work shifts, many do not conform to a regular nine-to-five, 5-day working week. In the DC study, for instance, 61 percent of the fathers had worked some overtime in half or more of the weeks in the period 15–18 months after their first child's birth. Fifty-five percent had worked at least one evening, and 46 percent for part of the week-end, in half or more of the weeks in this period. Mothers in the sample who were in full-time employment, were less likely to have such irregular hours — 34 percent had worked some overtime in at least half the weeks in the 3-month period, 37 percent some evenings and 19 percent some part of the week-end.

Ideologies and structures
The main characteristics of employment among fathers that we have described — long and often irregular hours and no break in employment due to children — are the product of dominant ideologies and the structure of labour markets. These define the 'good' father and the 'good' worker in ways that sustain present patterns of male employment and which give priority to male employment as compared with unpaid work in the home. Ideologies legitimate structures, which in turn reinforce ideologies.

Central to the ideology of male parenting is the belief that the father *should* be the main breadwinner, and that breadwinning is the most important role for the father. In the TP study, for instance, three-quarters of both husbands and wives defined male parenting to include being the main provider. Such views are complemented by a belief that the 'good' mother's main responsibility is to care for her children. In WES, 85 percent of wives and 87 percent of husbands took the view that a married woman with children under school age should either stay at home or only go to work if she *really* needed the money. The TP study sample of first-time parents was similarly hostile to the idea of mothers going out to work from choice; three-quarters of the men and two-thirds of the women were opposed to women working until children had reached a certain age, usually 5, and only then, in most cases, if certain conditions were met, in particular that they tailored their work hours to the school day.

A year after their child's birth, fathers in the TP study were asked what would have been the ideal employment arrangement for themselves and their partners during their first year of parenthood. For themselves, they opted mainly for part-time or full-time employment (40 and 47 percent respectively). They opted overwhelmingly, though, for their wives to be at home full-time (91 percent).

Belief in a gendered division of work remains, therefore, particularly strong in Britain, and contributes to employment rates among women with young children that are low, both relative to most other industrial countries (Moss, 1986), and in absolute terms. The great majority of women — over 80 percent — with children under 5 are at home or else are employed for very short part-time hours (i.e. less than 16 hours a week). Even employed women with children over 5 mostly work in part-time jobs (Martin and Roberts, 1984: Table 2.16). Consequently, the financial contribution of mothers who are employed, though crucial to many households with younger children, is overall relatively low. Only 5 percent of women *with children* in dual earner households earn as much or more than their partners (Rimmer, 1986).

Men respond to this situation by seeking to earn as much as possible through taking up opportunities to work shiftwork, overtime and second jobs, so further reinforcing the gendered division of labour. Financial pressures are probably greatest in families with two or more children, one at least of whom is under 5 — hence, probably, the peak in men's work hours when they have a child aged 2–4. Women are least likely to be employed at this stage and, if employed, are most likely to be working very short hours. Savings accumulated before parenthood have run down, and the costs of more and older children are constantly increasing.

These economic pressures are likely to be felt most by men in semi-skilled and unskilled manual jobs. Their earnings are lower, they have on average more children, and fewer have a wife in employment — 18 percent with a youngest child under 5, compared to 32 percent of men in professional and managerial jobs (OPCS, 1984). Male manual workers are also more likely to define breadwinning as central to their role as fathers (O'Brien, 1982).

Employment patterns of men and women with children are also influenced by the structure of the labour market. Women are found disproportionately in secondary sectors of the labour market and it is here that the increased employment of mothers has mainly occurred. Secondary sector jobs attract women with children because, although they provide no formal recognition of parental responsibilities (e.g. in the provision of child-care or employment rights), they often offer conditions which take into account women's major responsibility for child-care — for instance, part-time hours, evening jobs, home-based work, casual and temporary employment. The price that women with children pay for these conditions is low earnings, poor prospects, less security, and minimal training and promotion opportunities. As a consequence, the postwar growth in employment rates among women with children has reinforced, rather than reduced, occupational inequality.

Women frequently move into these secondary sectors once they have children, while those already there often drop nearer to the bottom, as part of the downward employment process associated with motherhood described earlier in the chapter. This process increases occupational segregation. Seventy percent of women in the WES sample who had part-time jobs reported that 'only women did the same sort of work as them at their work-place', compared to 58 percent among full-time workers.

Increased occupational segregation once children are born, together with low employment rates among women with children, ensures that pressures from those with child-care commitments are diverted away from the primary sectors of the labour market, where men predominate. Primary labour market jobs are relatively well rewarded, skilled and secure, often with opportunities for training and promotion. The 'good' primary sector worker, however, is not expected to let parental commitments influence or interfere with his work. He is expected to follow the same pattern of work, whether or not he has children, a pattern characterized by no breaks in employment, full-time hours and a readiness to work overtime and irregular hours as and when required, and often with little or no notice. The same standards and expectations apply to the minority of women in primary sector jobs. Employers themselves only expect to have to take account of employees' 'family' commitments in exceptional circumstances, and then at their own discretion. Even for an event as exceptional as childbirth, the great majority of men who take time off at or after the birth rely on using annual leave, sick leave, unpaid leave — or making-up the time taken at a later date (Bell et al., 1983).

In professional and managerial occupations, ideas about the 'good' worker and about career are inextricably bound up; the demands of job and of personal advancement mesh. These demands put pressure on men to work long hours and to commit themselves heavily to employment, especially at that stage of their lives when most are likely to have young children. A study of a middle-class housing estate by Cohen (1977), where most of the men worked for large organizations in managerial or professional occupations, illustrates the priority put upon husbands' careerist aspirations, at the expense of involvement in the home: 'their careers necessitated a great deal of mobility, not merely residentially, but within the job itself . . . even those who did not have to travel abroad and to other parts of the UK rarely saw their children during weekdays'.

The effect of fathers' employment on men

Nearly half the fathers in O'Brien's study 'expressed high or fairly high' levels of work–home conflict. These were mostly middle-class men, who articulated beliefs in shared family and child-care responsibility, yet actually did relatively little, while at the same time being heavily involved in their paid work. Such 'work–home' conflicts felt by fathers cannot be assumed to be comparable to those felt by women who go out to work. Fathers who work full-time do so in an ideological context that fully legitimates their activity. Mothers in full-time employment do not; even though they may not consciously subscribe to the dominant ideology, they still live in a society where most people accept it, and must to some extent be influenced by this. Men may feel they should do more in the home, yet most accept that their role is subsidiary to that of women and know their wives will assume responsibility for what they do not do. Employed women, however, cannot rely on husbands assuming responsibility for tasks in the home that they may not feel able or willing to do.

In the TP study, over two-thirds of the fathers said they did not feel they had enough time with their 12-month-old child, and over half said they would ideally have liked to work fewer hours during their child's first year. Yet, only one in ten thought that the ideal arrangement in this period would have been for their wives to have worked. Moreover, less than a fifth of the men felt that they were not giving enough child-care help. This suggests that the essence of the work–home conflict for many men is a wish to spend more time in the company of their child, rather than any desire to assume equal responsibility for child-care and domestic work.

Such limited evidence as exists suggests that some men find their present level of involvement in employment at particular life cycle points unsatisfactory — in relation to the time they feel they should be spending at home. It is an area that requires more study, as does the consequences for children of the employment patterns of fathers. Some children, as in Cohen's study, go days without seeing their fathers at all. More usually, there is contact, but not much of it. In both TP and DC studies, fathers of 10–12-month-olds, with *non-employed* wives, averaged 2¾ hours per day at home in the week at times when their children were awake; and two-thirds also spent some period away from their children at the week-end. Not all of this 'at home' time was actually spent by men with their children, and most child-care work was done by the mothers even when men were not at work. Even less time was spent by men in sole charge of their children: at 12 months of age, children in the TP study had been left on average 1.5 times in their father's care in the preceding 2 weeks — and half these times were evenings, when children were often asleep.

The effects of fathers' employment on women

The most obviously problematic aspect of fathers' employment is its effect on women. It has a bearing on how much child-care and domestic work they have to do — though as Pleck (1985) concludes in his time budget study 'while differences in paid work hours account for some of the family time disparity between the sexes, a large husband–wife gap (in family work time) remains even when (paid) work has been taken into account'. In other words, the disparity between men's and women's involvement in the domestic division of labour is not only a matter of the time spent by men in paid work.

Equally important, men's patterns of employment set standards and create expectations which affect all who are members of, or aspire to join, primary sectors of the labour market. To achieve equality with men means conforming with their working habits, which take little account of outside responsibilities. This raises a crucial question. Must or should the way to equality for women be through the emulation of men's current employment behaviour? Or should it occur through women and men finding new and common ways of working in employment, ways that recognize the existence and importance of parenthood and other unpaid work?

Fathers' employment and social policy

We have described some of the salient characteristics of employment among men with children and considered the ways in which dominant ideologies and the stucture of the labour market reinforce and legitimate these characteristics, and lead most people to take them for granted — as we pointed out at the beginning, fathers' employment is not a contentious issue in the way mothers' employment has become. This situation is, however, unlikely to continue. Increasingly, the organization of employment in relationship to the child-care commitments of both men and women is being questioned, and this has begun to be reflected in discussions about the role of social policy in facilitating changes in this relationship. A few countries — most notably Sweden — have led the way. International bodies have also shown a recognition, at least in what they say, that caring for and bringing up children should be regarded as a joint responsibility of the father and mother (cf. the United Nations Convention on the Elimination of all forms of Discrimination against Women, adopted 1979; *ILO* Convention No. 156 and Recommendation No. 165

adopted in 1981; declaration adopted at a high level *OECD* confer-
ence on the employment of women, Paris, 1980; and the Council of
Europe Conference of Ministers responsible for Family Affairs,
Rome, 1981).

There is, of course, a considerable gap between the rhetoric and
resolutions of international bodies and national governments, and
action to implement them. However, some proposals for changes in
employment patterns, that would recognize the parental role of both
sexes, have begun to appear on social policy agenda, and some have
been implemented. Maternity Leave was a first step in this direction,
though one necessarily limited to women employees. More recently
consideration has moved to other types of leave, equally appropriate
and available to men and women, and in particular Parental Leave
and Leave for Family Reasons.

Leave for Family Reasons entitles employees to time off — usually
a specified number of days per year, sometimes related to family size
— for important or pressing family reasons. Reasons include: to care
for a child, either because she or her usual caregiver is ill; to attend
medical appointments with a child; or to visit other services such as
schools or nurseries. *Parental Leave* — not to be confused with
paternity leave — entitles an employed parent to stay at home for a
period to take sole or principal charge of his or her child. In a
two-parent household, it can only be taken where the other partner is
back at work or studying — both parents cannot be at home together.
Parents may have some choice about when they can take leave, as
long as it is taken before the child reaches an upper age limit — it
need not therefore be taken as soon as maternity leave ends. Parental
Leave may also include a part-time option, that is all or part of the
entitlement may be taken as part-time leave, with the period of leave
extended proportionately.

An example of a scheme for both types of leave is the proposal
made by the Commission of the European Economic Community
(EEC), in a draft Directive issued in December 1983 and amended in
November 1984. This would require a minimum of 3 months Parental
Leave per worker per child, though member states of the EEC could
choose longer periods. With an employer's agreement, leave could
be taken on a part-time basis. In a two-parent family with both
parents in paid work, this would mean a total entitlement of at least 6
months full-time leave, or at least 12 months half-time leave, to be
divided equally between mother and father, and to be taken up at any
time before the child reaches 2. The leave period may be extended for
single-parent families, who otherwise would be at a disadvantage.
The draft Directive also proposes an entitlement to Leave for Family
Reasons, for all workers with 'family responsibilities', the length of

the leave to be determined by individual countries.

The Directive is intended to set minimum standards for Parental Leave and Leave for Family Reasons in the twelve member states of the EEC. In summer 1986, when this chapter was written, only three of these countries — the Irish Republic, the Netherlands and the United Kingdom — had no form of Parental Leave, though all existing provision fell below the standard proposed in the draft Directive; in five EEC countries, significant legislation on Parental Leave has been introduced within the last 2 years, while the Netherlands has proposals to introduce a scheme. Leave for Family Reasons was less widely established, though some provision is made for at least part of the workforce in a number of EEC member states. Parental Leave was also available in some form in all three non-EEC Scandinavian countries, while Sweden has the most comprehensive Leave for Family Reasons in Europe. Details of the existing provision for both types of leave in the EEC and Scandinavia are summarized in Table 3.1.

Sweden has the longest established and most extensive scheme for Parental Leave in Europe. The Swedes in fact provide no separate postnatal Maternity Leave; all leave in this period is now Parental Leave — available as such equally to men or women. Comparison of Swedish provision, with existing provision in other countries and with the EEC proposal, raises a number of important issues about the operation and role of Parental Leave.

TABLE 3.1
Provision for parental leave (PL) and leave for family reasons (LFR) within the European Economic Community and Scandinavia — summer 1986

Belgium	*PL*: In the public sector, a period of 3 months (unpaid) leave may be taken in the year following the birth of a child, with automatic job reinstatement. A further period of 4 years unpaid leave may be granted, with assured re-employment, but less favourable re-entry conditions. The 1985 'Loi de Redressment' enables employees to take 6–12 months leave for a variety of reasons: a worker on leave whose job is filled by a previously unemployed person is entitled to a monthly payment equivalent to unemployment benefit. Employers may refuse to grant leave on grounds that recruiting a replacement worker would be problematic. *LFR*: 10 days unpaid in the private sector for 'pressing family reasons'. 4 days paid, 2 months unpaid in public sector.
Denmark	*PL*: Since 1985, 10 weeks paid leave (at 90 percent of earnings) which can be taken by either parent. *LFR*: No statutory rights, though provided for in a number of collective agreements.

Table 3.1 continued

Finland	**PL**: Paid leave, which can be taken by either parent, available from the end of maternity leave (11 weeks after birth), to 33 weeks after the birth. Further unpaid leave, introduced in 1985, can be taken by either parent — either continuously or in up to 4 blocks of at least 2 months — until child reaches 3.
	LFR: No information.
France	**PL**: 2 years leave available in public sector or private companies with a workforce of over 100: father may take the leave *if* the mother cedes her right or is unable to take advantage of it. May be taken as full-time or half-time leave. Unpaid unless there are three or more children, where recent legislation provides social security rights and a low flat-rate allowance.
	LFR: 6 days unpaid per spouse for the care of a sick child or 'temporary child-minding'.
Greece	**PL**: Since 1984, a mother and father in a two-parent family are each entitled to 3 months unpaid leave, while a lone parent is entitled to 6 months: leave can be taken at any time until the child is 2½. Only covers employees in private sector companies with over 100 employees.
	LFR: Men and women have the right, when dependents are ill, to take up to 6 days for one dependent, 8 days for two, 10 days for three or more: 4 additional days may be taken in connection with children's schooling.
Ireland	**PL**: No statutory provision.
	LFR: No statutory provision.
Italy	**PL**: Six months leave to be taken between the end of maternity leave and when the child is 1, with the parent receiving 30 percent of normal earnings. Part-time leave is now allowed. Leave is for the mother in the first place, but she can choose to transfer entitlement to the father.
	LFR: 2 months paid leave for the care of a sick child under 3 in the public sector. All workers covered by a law which provides for indefinite but unpaid leave in the case of a sick child under 3.
Luxembourg	**PL**: Public sector employees are entitled to one year's unpaid leave or to transfer to part-time work to look after a child under 4.
	LFR: Paid leave for various reasons (e.g. death of spouse, birth of a child), but not to care for a sick child.
Netherlands	**PL**: No statutory provision, but proposals have been formulated for a statutory scheme and legislation is to be introduced.
	LFR: One day's paid leave 'for family obligations', two days for the birth of a child and up to five days for bereavement.

Norway	*PL*: Parents are 'together' entitled to 3 years unpaid leave before their child reaches the age of 10.
	LFR: No information.
Portugal	*PL*: Since 1984, the mother or father may take unpaid leave of between 6–24 months until the child reaches age 2: part-time leave is also possible, in which case entitlement lasts until the child reaches 12.
	LFR: Up to 30 days a year leave for illness of a child or spouse, covered by social security benefit.
Spain	*PL*: Unpaid leave for up to 3 years — though workers taking leave have only 'preferential rights to vacancies' once leave expires. Workers may also reduce their working day when looking after a child up to age 6.
	LFR: Paid leave of 2–4 days allowed for illness of a child or spouse, or death of a relative.
Sweden	*PL*: 12 months leave, 9 months paid at 90 percent of earnings, 3 months at flat-rate, available until child reaches age 4: may be taken as full-time or part-time leave. In addition, parents of preschool children are entitled to a 6-hour day without compensation for lost earnings.
	LFR: 60 days paid leave per year per child under 12 to care for sick children, or to take children to clinics. 2 days paid leave to visit nurseries or schools.
United Kingdom	*PL*: No statutory provision.
	LFR: No statutory provision.
West Germany	*PL*: From 1986, 10 months leave, rising to 12 months in 1987, with low flat-rate payment. The public sector allows 3 years unpaid leave.
	LFR: All employees entitled to leave on full pay 'for relatively insubstantial periods of time': details are often settled via collective agreements. Parents taking time off to care for a sick child below 8 may claim up to 5 days sick pay per year.

Should parents be compensated for lost earnings while on leave? In most European countries already providing Parental Leave, either no payment is made for the leave period or else payment is made at a low flat rate; this is in contrast to Maternity Leave, where the usual practise is to pay an earnings-related benefit. The main exception on Parental Leave is Sweden, where a substantial leave period is largely covered by a benefit payment fixed at 90 percent of earnings. No payment or payment at a low rate will deter take-up for both parents, but particularly for men, whose earnings are usually higher than their partner's and the loss of which would usually remove more than half of household income.

What period should be covered by Parental Leave? In general, Parental Leave has been envisaged as a short-term measure, for the period of early infancy, when child dependency is greatest. Some see it as an alternative to the provision of child-care services, eventually developing to bridge the gap between the end of Maternity Leave and children starting nursery provision at around 2. For others, Parental Leave is but one child-care option for under-2s — an alternative, not a substitute, for child-care services.

Parental Leave can however serve a longer-term function. Children make demands on parents well beyond the first year or two of life. Events or circumstances can occur after this age when it would help parents if they could take time off paid work, or work shorter hours for a period. Such needs might be met by extending the period during which Parental Leave could be taken — for instance until a child started school or moved into junior school — and by extending the amount of leave available. In Sweden, Parental Leave can be taken until a child reaches the age of 4. Whenever taken, leave is covered by social insurance benefits, and may be full-time or part-time. Parents are also entitled to a 6-hour working day for the period until their children start school which is not covered by Parental Leave — though with no compensation for lost earnings.

How much flexibility should parents have over the use of Parental Leave? A main area of potential choice concerns how Parental Leave can be used. Should parents be allowed to choose when they take leave, up to an upper age limit for their child? Or should they be required to take it at a specified time, for instance immediately after Maternity Leave? Should there be a part-time option? If so, should this be an employee right or depend on the agreement of the employer?

Another dimension of choice concerns *who* uses Parental Leave. Parental Leave must be equally available to mothers and fathers. The draft EEC Directive proposes that each worker should have his or her own entitlement, which may *not* be transferred to their partner. An alternative approach, adopted in Sweden, is to have a household entitlement, which may be taken by either parent in its entirety, or else shared between parents in any way they choose. This approach might be more flexible and responsive to the needs, circumstances and preferences of individual households. Transferability of leave could, however, encourage men not to take their share; the Equal

Opportunities Commission (1984) has urged that the proposed EEC
Directive not be changed in this respect because 'it is essential that
fathers are encouraged to take (leave) up themselves rather than
transfer their leave entitlement to the mother'.

Prospects for change in a broader context

The introduction of Parental Leave is unlikely by itself to produce
major changes in men's employment behaviour, any more than the
introduction of Maternity Leave has had a major effect on the number of women resuming employment after birth. This is not an
argument against legislation. Legislation has an important and necessary part to play — but it is not a sufficient requirement of change.
That will require, among other things, successfully challenging existing dominant ideologies and employment expectations and practices.

Measures such as Parental Leave need to be set in the context of
broader debates about changes in the overall restructuring of employment. Such debates are being stimulated by a number of social
and economic changes, including the introduction of new technolo-
gies, the decline of old industries and, perhaps above all, the massive
increase in unemployment in recent years. Ideas are being floated
about shortening the working week, breaks in employment for a
variety of reasons, more flexible working patterns in all forms of
employment and so on. In Europe, the unemployment problem has
already had some impact on the development of Parental Leave. The
Belgian 'Loi de Redressement' is not in fact a Parental Leave scheme
as such; rather, it offers workers the opportunity to take leave for a
variety of purposes, and is specifically linked to the reduction of
unemployment. Similarly, the recent German Parental Leave
scheme has been introduced, in part, as a means of reducing unemployment.

Locating Parental Leave within the context of these broader discussions, especially about ways to reduce unemployment, carries a
risk of abuse. Leave schemes may be devised, the main aim or
consequence of which is to remove certain groups from the labour
market for a period of time, rather than offer all employees with
children the opportunity for more flexible employment. Schemes
which offer no cash benefits, or only low, flat-rate benefits are, for
instance, likely to become means of encouraging low-skilled women
workers to drop out from employment for the duration of the leave
period; transferability of entitlements from men to women will increase the risk of Parental Leave operating in this way. If, however,
these risks can be avoided, the current context is apposite for considering Parental Leave and other changes in employment patterns

and practice intended to help parents, as part of a general reorganization of day-to-day and lifetime employment for all men and women.

References

Bell, C., McKee, L., and Priestly, K. (1983) *Fathers, Childbirth and Work*. Manchester: Equal Opportunities Commission.
Berger, M. and Wright, L. (1978) 'Divided Allegiance: Men, Work and Family Life', *The Counselling Psychologist* 7: 50–2.
Central Policy Review Staff (1978) *Services for Young Children with Working Mothers*. London: HMSO.
Cohen, G. (1977) 'Absentee Husbands in Spiralist Families: the Myth of the Symmetrical Family', *Journal of Marriage and the Family* 39: 595–604.
Daniel, W. (1980) *Maternity Rights: The Experience of Women*. London: PSI.
Dex, S. (1985) *The Sexual Division of Work: Conceptual Revolutions in the Social Sciences*. Brighton: Harvester Press.
Equal Opportunities Commission (1984). Evidence Presented to the House of Lords Select Committee on Parental Employment. Manchester.
Ferri, E. (1973) 'Characteristics of Motherless Families', *British Journal of Social Work* 3: 91–100.
George, V. and Wilding, P. (1972) *Motherless Families*. London: Routledge and Kegan Paul.
Goldthorpe, J.H., Beckhofer, F. and Platt, J. (1968) *The Affluent Worker: Industrial Attitudes and Behaviour*. Cambridge: Cambridge University Press.
Hoffman, L. (1979) 'Maternal Employment: 1979', *American Psychologist* 34: 859–65.
Hoffman, L. (1984) 'Maternal Employment and the Young Child', in M. Perlmutter (ed.) *Minnesota Symposium on Child Psychology, Vol. 17. Parent–Child Interaction and Parent–Child Relations*. Hillsdale, NJ: Lawrence Erlbaum Associates.
Hunt, A. (1973) *Families and Their Needs*. London: HMSO.
Income Data Services (1985) *Maternity and Paternity Leave Study 351*. London: IDS.
Joshi, H. (1985). *Gender Inequality in the Labour Market and the Domestic Division of Labour*. Paper given at the Cambridge Journal of Economics Conference, 26–29 June, 1985.
Lamb, M. (1982) 'Maternal Employment and Child Development: a review', in M. Lamb (ed.) *Non-traditional Families: Parenting and Child Development*. Hillsdale, NJ: Lawrence Erlbaum Associates.
Martin, J. and Roberts, C. (1984) *Women and Employment: a Lifetime Perspective*. London: HMSO.
Moss, P. (1986) 'Child Care in the Early Months: How child care arrangements are made for babies.' Thomas Coram Reseach Unit Occasional Papers, No. 3. London: TCRU.
Moss, P., Bolland, G. and Foxman, R. (1983) 'Transition to Parenthood: a Report to the DHSS'. Mimeographed report, Thomas Coram Research Unit, London University.
National Board of Prices and Incomes (1970). *Hours of Work, Overtime and Shiftwork: Report No. 161*. London: HMSO.
O'Brien, M. (1982) 'The Working Father', in N. Beail and J. McGuire (eds) *Fathers: Psychological Perspectives*. London: Junction Books.
Office of Population Censuses and Surveys (1984) *General Household Survey, 1982*. London: HMSO.

Office of Population Censuses and Surveys (1985) *General Household Survey, 1983*. London: HMSO.

Pleck, J. (1980) 'Conflicts between Work and Family Life', *Monthly Labour Review* (March): 29–32.

Pleck, J. (1985) *Working wives/Working husbands*. Beverly Hills: Sage.

Rimmer, L. (in press) 'Intra-family Distributions of Paid Work 1968–1981', in A. Hunt and P. Elias *Women and Paid Work: Issues of Equality*. London: Macmillan.

Robertson-Elliot, F. (1979) 'Professional and Family Conflicts in Hospital Medicine', *Social Science and Medicine* 13: 57–64.

Russell, G. (1982) 'Shared-care Giving Families: an Australian Study', in M.E. Lamb (ed.) *Non-traditional Families: Parenting and Child Development*. Hillsdale, NJ: Lawrence Erlbaum Associates.

Russell, G. (1983) *The Changing Role of Fathers*. Milton Keynes: Open University Press.

Tizard, B. (1986) 'The Care of Young Children: Implications of Recent Research.' Thomas Coram Research Unit Occasional Papers, No. 1. London: TCRU.

Werner, B. (1985) 'Fertility Trends in Different Social Classes, 1970–83', *Population Trends* 14: 5–12.

Young, M. and Willmott, P. (1973) *The Symmetrical Family*. London: Routledge and Kegan Paul.

4
Fathers' participation in work, family life and leisure: a Canadian experience[1]

Jarmila Horna and Eugen Lupri

Introduction

Complementary and symmetrical marriage models

Contemporary Canadian parent–child relations are shaped by marital role enactments that fall between two polar ideal types of marriage, defining the daily activities of mothers/wives and fathers/husbands. We call these two ideal types 'complementary marriages' and 'symmetrical marriages'.

In complementary marriages the husband/father and the wife/mother perform interdependent but different tasks. This traditional type of marriage has its roots in the industrial revolution, which brought about a separation of home and work and fostered in turn the ideology of separate spheres for women and men, husbands and wives, mothers and fathers. Women became responsible for domestic work, and men for wage labour outside the home (Young and Willmott, 1975). Parsons' (1955) elaboration of structural–functional theory has lent credence to role complementarity in the family in assuming that sex-role segregation is necessary for family stability. In his development of a functional theory, role allocation in the nuclear family is characterized by role complementarity: husbands and wives perform different tasks (functions) that combine to meet all family 'needs'. The roles of the father/husband are those of provider and protector. His contribution to child-rearing consists largely of providing a solid economic base for the family's survival. As an authority figure he transmits and inculcates broadly defined social norms that shape the child's moral and psychological development. His actual involvement in nurturing and emotional tasks is limited. In complementary marriages, according to Sawyer's (1970) thesis, the two pervasive motivating forces in the male role are stress on achievement and suppression of affect.

The theoretical impact of this model has been impressive and intellectually stimulating, but controversy abounds because the structural–functional image of the family obscures certain aspects of reality (Lupri and Symons, 1982), one of them being the emergence of variant family forms. This has led to another ideal–typical construction: conjugal and parental role symmetry (Young and Will-mott, 1975).

In a symmetrical relationship, the traditionally separate worlds of women and men merge. The partners perform the same roles alternately and share them equally, as instrumental and expressive roles are no longer gender-based. Role interchangeability, rather than role complementarity, is the key to such conjugal or parental role enactment. Unlike their traditional counterparts in complementary marriages, 'androgynous' fathers (Robinson and Barret, 1986: 43) want to relate to their children with warmth, sensitivity, emotion and honesty. Conjugal and parental roles merge as the fathers' emotional involvement with their children contributes significantly to their own need fulfilment. Androgynous fathers socialize their children to become androgynous adults.

Complementary and symmetrical marriages, as well as traditional and androgynous fathers, are 'ideal types' in the Weberian usage. They are not ideal in the normative sense, however; neither are they accurate descriptions of reality. As a heuristic device, ideal types represent logical exaggerations of reality; as such they serve as a basis for comparison and potential measurement of concrete trends. The polar types of 'traditional' and 'androgynous' father serve as a point of reference for the empirical assessment of the social reality: the 'typical' father.

Research objectives
The major objective of this chapter is to articulate the empirical evidence of the Canadian father's role enactment, particularly the extent and degree to which he today represents the traditional or the androgynous type. Within our analytical framework, we conceptualize the parental role as being enacted through a series of tasks that are carried out by either parent or by both. Thus we shall compare mothers' and fathers' performance of specific tasks.

Broader socioeconomic and ideological contexts affect parental role enactments to various degrees. Because of space limitations we can concentrate only on the paid work role in its relation with parental role enactments. These take place inside and outside the household. They occur at various times of the day, week, or over the year, and can be measured chronologically (morning, afternoon, evening, workday, Saturday, Sunday) or according to the prevalent nature of various time blocks (work time, semi-work, semi-leisure, leisure time).

The forms of parental role enactment involve direct or indirect contacts with the child. Tasks are performed for the child's benefit with or without his or her presence and may include the other parent, a friend or relative, or public institutions. We shall compare mothers' and fathers' contacts with their children and the different meanings each parent attaches to role enactments.

In addition to such parental tasks as earning income, providing life necessities, and maintaining the household, we shall examine parental tasks that embrace two basic roles: socialization and child-care. Socialization, in our usage, is limited to the child's social and psychological development. Child-care refers to the physical and psychological maintenance of the child. Behaviourally, these two role enactments overlap considerably, but they are expressed conceptually in distinct activities and tasks. We shall examine whether or how they are segregated according to the individual parent's responsibility for each.

Research design

The setting. A cross-section of couples was selected from Calgary, Alberta, Canada, a city of more than 600,000 inhabitants, which has experienced boom periods of extremely rapid economic and population growth since its founding a century ago. Calgary's riches are founded in agriculture, oil and gas.

Compared with the Canadian national average Calgary has proportionately the same number of married couples (64 percent) and single adults (28 percent); slightly fewer widowed persons (5 v. 6.5 percent in all of Canada), but proportionately twice as many divorced persons (3.5 percent v. 1.8 percent).

In 1981, at the time of the survey, Calgary had a youngish population, composed overwhelmingly of people with English as a mother tongue (83 percent); one-half (49 percent) of the population possessed post-secondary education, as compared to 36 percent for the nation. The labour-force participation rates were very high (64 percent for women v. 52 percent for Canada; 87 percent for men v. 78 percent). Nearly 23 percent of the labour force were engaged in managerial, scientific, and related occupations (v. 15 percent of all Canadian paid workers) and the average income for husband–wife families was one-fifth higher than the national average. As a research locale, therefore, Calgary's social structure presents an excellent testing ground for any changing styles of fatherhood.

Sample description. A systematic random sample was drawn from a telephone directory which represented about 97 percent of the Calgary residents. A letter describing the nature of the research was followed by a personal visit from an interviewer who ascertained whether a heterosexual couple (either married or cohabiting) lived at that address. Because the research design required that information be collected from both members of a couple, it contributed to the refusal rate of about 28 percent. Even so, the sample of 562 couples is believed to be fairly representative of the 133,135 husband–wife families, including couples who live together.

Data collection and measurements. The data were collected by thirty-four trained interviewers of both sexes. While one partner in the couple completed a self-administered questionnaire, the other was interviewed in a separate room; each instrument requiring approximately one hour. The questionnaire dealt with the performance of specific tasks in proportional terms (i.e. by the father always, by the father more than the mother, by both father and mother equally, by the mother more than the father, or by the mother always); decision-making based on the respondent's answers to a series of questions on how final decisions were made in areas deemed important in any marriage; and some potentially sensitive items such as marital power, interspousal conflict, domestic violence, and marital happiness. The interview schedule included background information such as age, employment status and history, and family characteristics. This procedure of simultaneous but physically separate data acquisition by two different methods minimized contaminating responses by either partner.

A third instrument used in our study was left behind, together with a self-addressed and prestamped envelope, to be completed and returned at the respondent's earliest convenience. This procedure yielded completed questionnaires from 367 female and 359 male respondents, including 346 matched couples. This self-administered questionnaire included questions on estimated typical time expenditures (separately on a workday, a Saturday, and a Sunday) for all daily activities including work, non-work and leisure pursuits. The time-budget portion was followed by questions on annual frequencies of involvement in all earlier listed activities, other participants in those activities, reasons for performing them, and several other questions. The particular responses reported in this chapter are drawn largely from the third instrument and from selected parts of the self-administered questionnaire.

Findings

Paid work
The first issue to be addressed concerns the extent to which both parents work for pay outside the home. It has been shown recently that fathers' elevated employment rates begin well before the child is

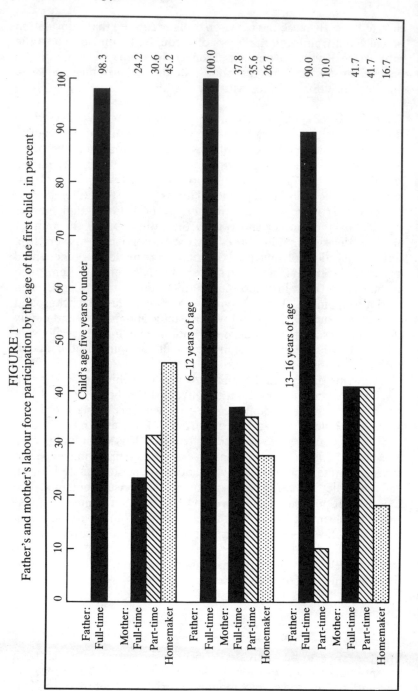

FIGURE 1

Father's and mother's labour force participation by the age of the first child, in percent

born and that the effects of parenthood on men's paid work are much smaller than the effects for women (Waite et al., 1985). The data presented in Figure 1 provide additional support for such a gender-based employment pattern, as well as some unanticipated findings. Mothers' paid work activity is influenced strongly by stage in the life-cycle. Almost half of all mothers with at least one preschool child are full-time homemakers and a further third work part-time. Participation in the labour force rises to 73.4 percent when the child is aged 6–12 and 82.4 percent in the oldest age group. However, half of these employed women continue in part-time employment. The decision to work part-time is not always based on choice and may be related to the unavailability of full-time employment or adequate child-care, or the extent of domestic responsibility (Statistics Canada, 1985: 45).

Despite many young mothers' involvement in the labour force, Figure 1 shows that the vast majority of fathers — particularly those with children of preschool age — still enact the breadwinner role by providing a larger share of the family's total income. In many instances men are the sole recipients of income in husband–wife families. Among our sampled dual-earner parents with small children, fathers earned on average twice as much as their wives (Lupri and Mills, 1987). This wage gap corresponds closely to the national figures, and is due in part to women's concentration in unskilled, clerical, part-time, or seasonal work and low-paying jobs (see Moss and Brannen, Chapter 3). Furthermore, because men hold types of full-time jobs that are more likely to include overtime work, young fathers are much more likely than young mothers to work overtime.

About one father in three reported working overtime often or sometimes (Table 4.1). In contrast, only about one full-time employed mother in ten reported overtime work. Both single- and dual-earner men are caught in what Oppenheimer (1982) calls the 'life-cycle squeeze'. Lupri and Mills (1987) have documented that an increase in family size results in an increase in the amount of time young fathers spend working and that they may be forced to make up the economic loss of their wives' former earnings. According to these data, dual-earner fathers in the early stages of the family life cycle spend even more time at paid work than their childless counterparts, and devote two solid hours more per day to making money than do their employed sexual partners. Working overtime or long hours is one response young families can make when experiencing a 'squeeze' from high child-rearing costs, expensive housing, vacations, and scarce resources. The pressures on families vary over the life-cycle. Men with 6 to 12-year-old children do most overtime, which suggests a heightened 'squeeze' during the middle years of parenting. Later

TABLE 4.1: Frequency of participation in selected activities by mothers' employment status, parents of children 16 years old or younger (in percent)

| Activity | Frequency | Mothers' employment status | | | | | |
| | | Full-time (55)* | | Part-time (57)* | | Not employed (52)* | |
		Fathers	Mothers	Fathers	Mothers	Fathers	Mothers
Overtime	Often	27.3	14.5	30.4	8.6	36.5	—
work	Sometimes	23.6	9.1	32.1	6.9	28.8	—
	Rarely	23.6	21.8	25.0	17.2	13.5	—
	Never	16.4	40.0	8.9	44.8	15.4	—
	Does not apply	9.1	14.5	3.6	22.4	5.8	100
	Total	100	100	100	100	100	100
Cooking	Often	40.0	80.0	32.1	94.6	7.7	100
	Sometimes	36.4	14.5	30.4	5.4	25.0	—
	Rarely	16.4	5.5	25.0	—	51.9	—
	Never	5.5	—	12.5	—	7.7	—
	Does not apply	1.8	—	—	—	7.7	—
	Total	100	100	100	100	100	100
Housework	Often	40.0	90.9	32.1	96.6	13.5	100
	Sometimes	41.8	9.1	37.5	1.7	40.4	—
	Rarely	16.4	—	26.8	1.7	40.4	—
	Never	—	—	3.6	—	1.9	—
	Does not apply	1.8	—	—	—	3.8	—
	Total	100	100	100	100	100	100
Maintenance	Often	41.8	12.7	56.1	10.9	46.2	21.2
	Sometimes	45.5	23.6	31.6	50.9	42.3	32.7
	Rarely	10.9	43.6	10.5	21.8	11.5	30.8
	Never	—	18.2	1.8	7.3	—	11.5
	Does not apply	1.8	1.8	—	9.1	—	3.8
	Total	100	100	100	100	100	100
Child-care	Often	50.9	72.2	45.6	84.2	32.7	94.2
	Sometimes	29.1	18.5	36.8	14.0	42.3	3.8
	Rarely	16.4	7.4	12.3	1.8	19.2	—
	Never	1.8	1.9	3.5	—	3.8	1.9
	Does not apply	1.8	—	1.8	—	1.9	—
	Total	100	100	100	100	100	100
Games with	Often	27.3	35.2	44.6	55.2	44.2	69.2
children	Sometimes	41.8	38.9	48.2	36.2	42.3	26.9
	Rarely	21.8	18.5	7.1	8.6	13.5	3.8
	Never	5.5	3.7	—	—	—	—
	Does not apply	3.6	3.7	—	—	—	—
	Total	100	100	100	100	100	100

* Figures in parentheses represent number of cases.

when we examine time allocations to other family activities, we should keep in mind this difference in fathers' and mothers' daily paid work commitments.

Perceptions of work and family
It might be argued that the fathers' work patterns reflect a greater commitment to work than to family. While we would not question such commitment, we find few fathers who claim that work is their central interest in life. Like Dubin (1963), we found that the overwhelming majority of fathers consider not work but the family to be the most important domain in their life: 86.4 percent when their children are 12 years old or younger, and 70.0 percent when their children are between 13 and 16 years old (Horna, 1985b). The corresponding figures for mothers are even higher: over 90 percent in each group consider their family more important than other domains of life.

This orientation, however, has an interesting twist. When asked which is more important to them — housework, job, or both equally — fathers do not hesitate to name work as more important than housework, or equally important. Almost three-quarters of fathers of younger children and 90.0 percent with children between 13 and 16 find their jobs more important; the remainder indicate that jobs and housework are of equal importance; practically no one chooses housework as more important. Their wives, on the other hand, find housework far more important, or housework and jobs equally important; those with children in the two younger age groups are divided almost equally three ways in their preferences, while mothers of older children shift their preferences from housework to job. These findings are further corroborated in parents' explanations for alterations in their work patterns over the past five years. Whether fathers' employment time increases or decreases, they attribute such change to their work in eight out of ten cases, while only 10 percent mention their family. In contrast, over 80 percent of mothers in each age group attribute new work patterns to change in family responsibilities.

Domestic work
The household division of labour is central to a fuller understanding of the changing roles of parents in contemporary society. The question of domestic work and its relation to gender role *a*symmetry has been at the centre of recent debates between feminists and other scholars in both capitalist and socialist countries (Lupri, 1983). Unlike work done outside the family, domestic work is unpaid. Traditionally, women's economic contribution to the family has been

devalued and ignored by experts and lay persons alike. The very nature of work in the home, its variability and discontinuity, makes domestic tasks difficult to assess in economic terms or even to define. Our measures include time devoted to household chores, cooking and household maintenance. Child-care will be considered in a subsequent section because it is qualitatively different from domestic work.

Measured in proportional terms, fewer than one-third of fathers with children in the two younger age groups report that they cooked often in the past year. Fathers with older children (13 to 16 years of age) are even less likely to participate in this domestic activity: only one-fifth of them report that they cooked often. Not unexpectedly, another fifth of fathers with children in each of the three age groups never cook. In sharp contrast to their husbands, however, an overwhelming majority of mothers prepare meals. Fathers' nonparticipation in cooking is paralleled by nonparticipation in housework: only one-quarter of all fathers do housework often, compared with close to 95 percent of all mothers with children in all three age groups.

Young fathers, however, are not completely insensitive to their wives' participation in paid work. As Table 4.1 shows, there is a statistically significant inverse relationship between maternal employment status and the fathers' contribution to meal preparation (40.47 v. 32.12 v. 7.7 percent in the three, full-time, part-time, not employed groups respectively: chi-squared = 14.01 [d.f. = 2] $p < 0.0001$). The same pattern exists for housework: fathers whose wives work full-time for pay contribute a somewhat greater share to housework than fathers whose wives work part-time or are full-time houseworkers (40 v. 32.1 v. 13 percent: chi-squared = 7.17 [d.f. = 2] $p < 0.05$).

When the proportional measures are contrasted with actual time estimates for these activities, however, fathers' contributions to meal preparation and household chores appear even more modest and delimited. Of those men who report that they cooked at all on an average workday, 29.8 percent worked less than 15 minutes, 21.3 percent up to 30 minutes, and 36.2 percent between one-half hour and one hour in the kitchen. On Saturdays and Sundays, their participation in cooking increases only slightly. When fathers engage in meal preparation, they do so jointly with their wives: only 15 percent are solely responsible for this task (Figure 2). Unlike fathers, the vast majority of mothers report between one and one-half and three hours on both week-days and week-ends as the most usual amount of time spent in the kitchen.

Lupri and Mills (1987), who compared time budgets of single-earner and dual-earner couples, found similar patterns. Whether or

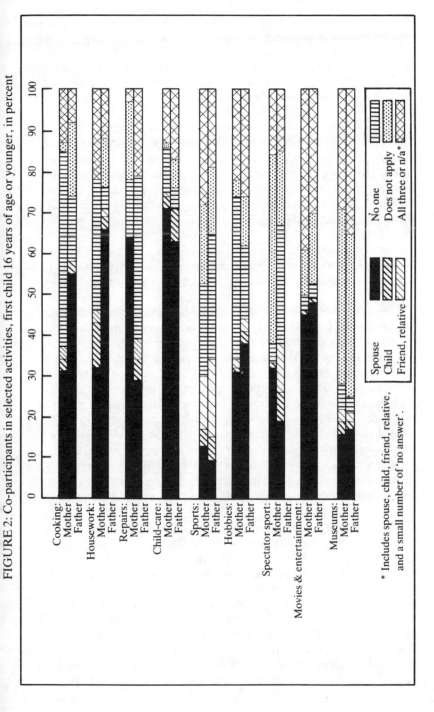

FIGURE 2: Co-participants in selected activities, first child 16 years of age or younger, in percent

not they have children, dual- and single-earner men spend only about 20 minutes at cooking on a regular workday, even when family-related time demands are greatest (one or more children under the age of 6 at home). In contrast, young employed mothers were found to be particularly over-burdened, as they must allocate about two hours to preparing meals, approximately three to four times as much as their partners (Lupri and Mills, 1987).

Fathers' participation in housework chores is somewhat greater than in meal preparation. About one-half report doing more than 30 minutes of housework on Saturdays, more than other days of the week. However, almost twice as many of their wives report doing housework on any day of the week; moreover, wives report longer time periods. Apart from Sundays one-quarter does housework over three hours each day — equivalent to the work of only 2 percent of husbands.

A distinct pattern that we observed for fathers in meal preparation reemerges in housework: if fathers participate in any housework at all, the vast majority (66 percent) do it jointly with their wives (Figure 2).

The low involvement of fathers in housework is confirmed by Lupri and Mills' (1987) findings based on summary measures for the actual time women and men spent in housework and child-care tasks. Men, whether or not they are fathers, report spending about one half-hour at housework on week-days. Mothers, whatever the age of their children, are forced to expend more than two hours per day at housework. One might expect that the fathers whose wives are employed would contribute significantly more time to housework than their traditional counterpart, but they do not. Whether or not their wives work for pay or whether or not they have children, the men's contribution does not differ greatly. Lupri and Mills found that this gender-segregated housework pattern persists on week-ends: though fathers increase their help, mothers increase their share of housework even more.

Such traditional division of labour in the family is complemented by the main responsibility for house maintenance, repairs, and garage and yard work, which is traditionally assigned to fathers. Half the fathers in our study are involved often in these activities, and another one-third to 41.7 percent sometimes; furthermore, they frequently do this work alone (39.7 percent against 13.6 percent of women). Differences according to the wife's work status are insignificant, further documenting men's prevalent responsibility for repairs and maintenance (Table 4.1). More nonemployed mothers do some repairs (21.2 percent) than their full-time (12.7 percent) or part-time (10.9 percent) working counterparts. Such a gender-based division of

FIGURE 3

Individual perceptions of selected activities, in percent

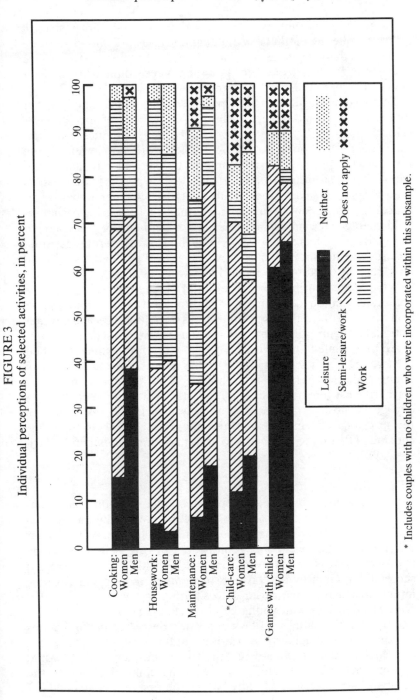

* Includes couples with no children who were incorporated within this subsample.

tasks gives the advantage of greater time flexibility to husbands/ fathers; while the mothers' cooking and housework chores must be performed daily, even several times a day, the fathers' maintenance chores may be carried out at irregular times according to his convenience (Meissner et al., 1975; Lupri and Mills, 1987).

The asymmetrical division of parental roles is illustrated further by the mothers' and fathers' different perceptions of specific tasks (Horna, 1986). When asked to define their daily activities as leisure, semi-leisure/semi-work, work, or neither work nor leisure, more husbands than wives perceived domestic tasks, child-care, and games with children as leisure (Figure 3). While 35.7 percent of husbands, for example, view cooking as leisure, only 14.3 percent of their wives share this view. Likewise, over twice as many husbands regard household maintenance and repairs as leisure or semi-leisure (76.8 percent husbands v. 35 percent wives). Only housework represents little leisure, whether for husbands or wives; as 60.7 percent of wives and 46.4 percent of husbands define housework as work.

What stands out in these differential perceptions is the father's greater inclination to view many of his domestic and paternal tasks as something intrinsically leisure-like, at his own discretion and perhaps optional, thus affording him a greater sense of freedom than his wife.

All told, while fathers with wives who work for pay increase their relative share somewhat in domestic tasks, and while the presence of young children alters the household division of labour in limited ways, role asymmetry persists in domestic work and young mothers engage in most of the onerous household activities. A review of recent changes in sex roles and the division of labour in the home concluded that there is 'much ado about nothing' (Miller and Garrison, 1982: 242). We agree.

Child-care
No single family activity is as deeply embedded in traditional values and norms as child-care, and no tasks are potentially more time-consuming and onerous than those related to child-rearing. Gender differences in the enactment of child-care roles are well-documented in proportional as well as absolute terms, notwithstanding the recent successful attempt by the 'fathers' movement' to help some willing fathers to discover their caring selves through closer and more satisfying relationships with young children (Fein, 1974).

In light of the patterns of task allocation described in the sections on paid work and domestic work, it should come as no surprise that the chief portion of child-care falls to the mother. As we would expect, child-care is related directly to the child's age and to the number of children in the family. When the first or second child is 5 years old or younger, over 90 percent of mothers are involved in child-care *often*. Only when the second child is aged 13 to 16 does this involvement decrease to 62.5 percent. At the same time, only 50 percent of fathers with younger children and fewer than 30 percent of fathers with older children participate often in child-care. Fathers assume some responsibility for taking children to various activities; about one-quarter do it more often than the mother (Table 4.2). Only 5.0 percent, however, report caring for the child alone, while 62.5 percent do it with the wife, and 15.8 percent with her and another child (when data for the first child are analysed; Figure 2). Interestingly, mothers also report a high rate of child-care with the spouse (70.6 percent) and only 11.8 percent do it alone. Unfortunately, our data do not allow us to separate child-care carried out jointly by both parents at the same time from child-care performed by either the father or the mother.

In spite of the relatively high degree of participation by fathers, mothers still assume a greater part of child-care tasks, documented by the fathers' and mothers' time budgets: the most usual length of time allotted to child-care by mothers is four or more hours per day, reported by 61.6 percent of mothers for workdays, 77.6 percent for Saturdays, and 80.2 percent for Sundays. Meanwhile, 52.8 percent of fathers spend up to one hour per day and only 10 percent spend over four hours. At week-ends the number of fathers who report doing four hours rises to 28.3 percent on Saturdays and 36.4 percent on Sundays.

As in other tasks, the frequency of the father's involvement in child-care reflects his wife's employment status. Husbands of women working full-time with children under 16 years of age in the home participate in child-care often in 50.9 percent of the cases; husbands of part-time workers in 45.6 percent, and homemakers' partners in 32.7 percent (Table 4.1). These rates still fall below the mothers' rates: full-time working mothers care for their children often in 72.2 percent of the cases, part-time working mothers in 84.2 percent, and nonemployed mothers in 94.2 percent.

Child-care — aside from meeting the physical needs of the child — involves a great deal of social interaction and the consideration of time and activities that are essential for the child's social, moral, and psychological development. Thus child-care tasks often overlap and converge with leisure pursuits, which we will now discuss.

Leisure with children
Similar to Kelly's (1983) original proposition, we argue that play and games with children are role-determined, i.e. they stem from the parental role. The frequencies of play and games with children show

variations accordingly. Firstly, they are consistently lower for fathers than for mothers. For example, 56.7 percent of the fathers of young first children play with them often, while 75.8 percent of mothers do so. Secondly, the child's age is important. When the firstborn is in the third age category, 33.3 percent of mothers are still involved in games and play with them, but only 10.0 percent of fathers. The presence of the second child influences the frequency of play and games with children; the greatest amount of play seems to occur when the second child is still in the youngest age category.

When examining the influence of the wife's employment status, we find a pattern opposite to those typical for the four previously reported tasks (Table 4.1). More husbands of houseworkers play often with their children than husbands of full-time working mothers (27.3 percent); husbands of part-time workers are close in frequency to houseworkers' spouses (44.6 percent). Mothers outdo their spouses in each employment group (35.2 percent of full-time working mothers, 55.2 percent of part-time workers, and 69.2 percent of houseworkers play often with their children). Because nonemployed mothers are at home mostly with the youngest children, who need more attention (since teenagers break away from family leisure pursuits), it is possible that these different rates are more a function of the child's age than of the mother's work status.

Do fathers deprive themselves of leisure time with their children? We might assume that their diminished role in play is the price men must pay for their extended paid work activity. On the other hand, it is quite possible that fathers play and spend leisure time with their children as much as they wish; this conclusion is indicated clearly by the fathers' stated desires and preferences for leisure activities. Games and play with children do not appear on the list of the five most preferred or desired activities; sports and physical exercise (17.1 percent), relaxation with the spouse (12.1 percent), and hobbies (11.3 percent) appear at the top of the list of activities fathers would like to pursue more than they do at present (Horna, 1985a).

The lack of involvement in the child's games might be compensated somewhat by involving the child in some of the adult's leisure activities. We do not find much support for this proposition, however, since fewer than 10 percent of fathers take their children along to active sports and physical exercise, spectator sports, or movies and other commercial entertainment, or involve them in hobbies (Figure 2). Some fathers prefer to be involved in those leisure activities as a family unit and to participate with their spouses and children. In contrast approximately one-quarter to one-third of men report being involved without other family members whether in sports and physical exercise (31 v. 22 percent of mothers), spectator sports (29.2 v. 5

percent of mothers), or hobbies (17.5 v. 39 percent of mothers); when there is a second child younger than 16 the corresponding numbers are similar.

Socialization and decision-making

Parental tasks directly involving socialization or decision-making about children are distributed between fathers and mothers in patterns similar to task allocations mentioned above. It is worth noting that spouses seldom agree on their own and their partners' degree of contribution. As Linda Haas (1981) found in Sweden, Canadian fathers also consistently claim greater involvement than their wives give them credit for and underrate the extent of their wives' participation. In some instances the discrepancy is considerable: 'usually the father' and 'father more than mother' disciplines the children in 13.7 percent of cases according to the husbands, but only in 4.1 percent of cases according to the wives; 'usually the mother' tells the children what to do at home in 33.8 percent of cases, according to the wives, but the husbands give wives credit for only 14.1 percent. These

TABLE 4.2
Parental task distribution, mothers and fathers reporting separately
(in percent)

Task Who:	Reported by	Usually father or father more than mother	Both equally	Usually mother or mother more than father	Other person	Total
Gets children to bed						
Mothers		1.8	28.8	68.3	1.1	100
Fathers		5.6	33.5	60.9	0.0	100
Tells children what chores to do						
Mothers		1.9	36.5	51.0	0.8	100
Fathers		8.3	37.0	43.1	0.4	100
Helps children with schoolwork						
Mothers		11.2	37.0	43.1	0.8	100
Fathers		13.9	42.6	42.1	0.4	100
Teaches children work skills						
Mothers		14.9	52.8	38.0	0.0	100
Fathers		4.1	57.9	24.3	0.0	100
Disciplines children						
Mothers		4.1	57.9	38.0	0.0	100
Fathers		13.7	62.0	24.3	0.0	100
Takes children to activities						
Mothers		25.3	22.9	43.6	1.2	100
Fathers		27.1	44.1	28.8	0.0	100

discrepancies may reveal much about each spouse's perceptions of family life. Yet in spite of them, clearly it is seldom the father who puts the children to bed, tells them what chores to do at home, helps them with schoolwork, teaches them work skills, or disciplines them (Table 4.2). In the overwhelming number of cases these parental tasks are usually performed by the mother, or more often by the mother than by the father.

TABLE 4.3
Division of parental decision-making,
mothers and fathers reporting separately
(in percent)

Final decision on:	Reported by	Father more than mother or father always	Both equally	Mother always or more than father	Total
Spending money for children					
	Mothers	12.8	67.4	19.8	100
	Fathers	6.8	69.6	23.6	100
When children should be disciplined					
	Mothers	9.1	51.5	39.4	100
	Fathers	10.8	60.4	28.8	100
What clothes children should wear					
	Mothers	0.4	15.6	84.0	100
	Fathers	0.0	13.0	87.0	100
What time children should be home at night					
	Mothers	6.2	66.8	27.0	100
	Fathers	4.7	64.9	30.4	100

Similar discrepancies are found in reporting the division of decision-making which concerns children. In spite of obvious disagreements on the specific levels of the father's or mother's authority regarding the child's spending money, clothes, curfew, or discipline, fewer fathers than mothers decide on these matters (Table 4.3). In most couples, both parents decide equally about the child's spending money (69.6 percent or 67.4 percent), discipline (60.4 percent or 51.5 percent), and curfew (64.9 percent or 66.8 percent), as reported by fathers or mothers respectively. However, the category 'both equally', may be open to different interpretation and we cannot say unequivocally whether and how frequently this participatory decision-making is a joint or parallel event. Children's clothes fall mostly under the mother's jurisdiction because mothers decide about clothes always or more often than fathers in over 80 percent of cases.

Conclusion

Given that contemporary Canadian parent–child relations are shaped by marital role enactments that range between complementary marriages and symmetrical marriages, this study found that the transition from instrumental to androgynous fatherhood is far from complete. In fact, the dialectic interplay of parental role enactments inside and outside the household is both varied and complex. The parenting styles described above fall into definite, comprehensive, and interdependent patterns, which are not fixed but varied and fluid depending on the style of parenthood couples choose to employ.

The empirical evidence presented in this chapter documents clearly that specific components of the parental role are disproportionally distributed between fathers and mothers. In one of the crucial instrumental parental tasks — earning the family income — fathers carry the major responsibility. Practically all fathers work full-time while their wives' paid work activity varies according to the age and number of children in the family. Young fathers and mothers respond in different ways, however, to the economic life-cycle squeeze. Many young mothers do not continue to engage in paid work, but become full-time homemakers. This option is seldom extended to fathers because contemporary norms and values still dictate that the man is generally the major income earner with long-term involvement in the occupational sphere. Thus many young fathers whose wives do not work for pay put in longer hours on the job than their counterparts whose spouses are employed. It is not surprising, then, that fathers view their work as their primary obligation towards the family and place it above other kinds of activities such as housework, both in terms of their relative importance and the amount of time spent on domestic tasks. Hence the shift from an instrumental style of fathering to a predominantly androgynous style is beset with inherent contradictions. On the one hand, the ideal father has been described as affectionate, emotionally involved, and willing to play with his children (Robinson and Barret, 1986). On the other hand, his assigned role as breadwinner demands the development of occupational skills and long hours away from home, which often prevent him from becoming androgynous. These contradictory demands are highest in the early stages of the family-life cycle and at a time when job demands may also peak. Thus young fathers are bound to experience role strain not unlike the strain suffered by young full-time employed mothers.

The response of young fathers to these expectations and demands is highly predictable. Not only do they spend less time in cooking and housework; even when they participate, they rarely carry the full responsibility alone. Unlike mothers, many fathers have the fortune to find leisure-like characteristics in those domestic tasks. Men compensate for their lower rate of participation in cooking and housework by assuming the predominant responsibility for the task of maintenance, repairs, and garage and yard work.

Fathers are responsive to their wives' paid work status, and increase their rate of domestic participation somewhat when mothers are employed outside the home, whether full-time or part-time. Child-care is shared by couples more than domestic tasks, but the father still plays a minor part even if the mother is equally employed full-time. Like home maintenance, because the father is more free to participate (or not to participate) in child-care, he finds it more relaxing and leisure-like than the mother.

We conclude that while men who have children 16 years of age or younger do not completely neglect their share of the parental role, they find their role less taxing and time-consuming, less confining, affording more freedom and discretion, and with a more leisure-like nature. Clearly, the paramount element of the paternal role, as found in Canadian society, is still the income-earning obligation. This limited, traditional option continues to act as a barrier to the development of an androgynous style of fathering.

Note

1. The study on which the present analysis is based was supported by a grant from the Social Sciences and Humanities Research Council of Canada. Principal investigators are Jarmila Horna, Eugen Lupri and Donald L. Mills.

References

Dubin, R. (1963) 'Industrial Workers' Worlds: a study in the "Central Life Interests" of Industrial Workers', in E. Smigel (ed.) *Work and Leisure*, pp. 53–72. New Haven: College and University Press.

Fein, R.A. (1974) 'Men and Young Children', in Joseph H. Pleck and Jack Sawyer (eds) *Men and Masculinity*, pp. 54–62. Englewood Cliffs, NJ: Prentice-Hall.

Haas, L. (1981) 'Domestic Role Sharing in Sweden', *Journal of Marriage and the Family* 43(2) (Nov.): 957–67.

Horna, J.L.A. (1985a) 'Desires and Preferences: More of the Same?', *World Leisure and Recreation* 27(1) (Feb.): 28–32.

Horna, J.L.A. (1985b) 'The Social Dialectic of Life, Career and Leisure: a Probe into the Preoccupations Model', *Society and Leisure* 8(2); 615–30.

Horna, J.L.A. (1986) 'The Process of Choosing Leisure Activities and Preferences: an Exploratory Analysis', *XIth World Congress of Sociology*, New Delhi, August.

Kelly, J.R. (1983) *Leisure Identities and Interactions*. London: Allen and Unwin.

Lupri, E. (1983) 'The Changing Position of Women and Men in Comparative Perspective' in Eugen Lupri (ed.) *The Changing Position of Women in Family and Society: A Cross-national Comparison*. Leiden: E. G. Brill.

Lupri, E. and Symons, G. (1982) 'The Emerging Symmetrical Family: Fact or Fiction?' *International Journal of Comparative Sociology*, 23(3–4): 166–89.

Lupri, E. and Mills, D.L. (1987) 'The Household Division of Labour among Young Dual-Earner Couples: The Case of Canada' in *International Review of Sociology*, Vol. XXIII, No. 1. (In press.)

Meissner, M., Humphreys, E.W., Scott, M.M. and Scheu, W.J. (1975) 'No Exit for Wives: Sexual Division of Labour and the Cumulation of Household Demands', *Canadian Review of Sociology and Anthropology* 12(4, pt. 1): 424–39.

Miller, J. and Garrison H.H. (1982) 'Sex Roles: The Division of Labour at Home and in the Workplace', *Annual Review of Sociology* 8: 237–62.

Oppenheimer, V.K. (1982) *Work and the Family: A Study in Social Demography*. New York: The Free Press.

Parsons, T. (1955) 'The American Family: Its Relation to Personality and to the Social Structure', in T. Parsons and R.F. Bales (eds) *Family Socialization and Interaction Process*, pp. 3–33. New York: The Free Press.

Pleck, J.H. (1983) 'Husbands' Paid Work and Family Roles: Current Research Issues', in H. Lopata and J. Pleck (eds) *Research in the Interweave of Social Roles: Families and Jobs*, pp. 251–333. Greenwich, CT: JAI Press.

Pleck, J.H. (1985) *Working Wives/Working Husbands*. Beverly Hills: Sage Publications.

Robinson, B.E. and Barret, Robert L. (1986) *The Developing Father. Emerging Roles in Contemporary Society*. New York: The Guilford Press.

Sawyer, J. (1970) 'On Male Liberation', *Liberation* 15: 33–4.

Statistics Canada (1985) Women in Canada: A Statistical Report. Ottawa: Minister of Supply and Services.

Waite, L.J. and Haggstrom, G.W. and Kanouse, D.E. (1985) 'Changes in the Employment Activities of New Parents', *American Sociological Review* 50(2): 263–72, April.

Young, M. and Willmott, P. (1975) *The Symmetrical Family*. Middlesex: Penguin Books.

5

The negotiation of fatherhood

Kathryn Backett

Introduction

The extent to which fathers are more involved in family life than in previous generations has been the subject of much popular and academic debate over the past decade (Hanson and Bozett, 1985; Russell, 1983). Often however, although important points have been made at the theoretical level, actual empirical evidence has been more limited and sometimes misleading.[1] Any claim that the modern father is significantly more involved must therefore still be treated with considerable scepticism. Feminists have played a major part in criticizing such claims, and have long identified as essential aspects of gender inequality the unequal burden of housework and child-care carried by women (Oakley, 1974; Huber, 1976). There has, however, been much less detailed research into men's involvement in these aspects of family life. Thus we now have detailed analytical knowledge about the structural context of gender inequalities but much less clear understanding of how such inequalities are tolerated and perpetuated in everyday family interactions (Bell and Newby, 1976).

In this chapter I first outline some deficiencies in previous attempts to understand fatherhood, and suggest the value of a different approach. I then focus on how the unequal burden of child-care in particular is lived with as an everyday negotiated 'acceptable' reality. The negotiation of fatherhood is of central importance in this process. Findings of my own empirical work on fathers in two-parent families are described and critically examined.[2] In particular, analysis of how couples construct and sustain belief in the 'involved' father suggests that, paradoxically, this is an important factor in the maintenance of inequalities within the family group.

Critiques of studies of fatherhood

Attempts to understand fatherhood must involve 'taking gender seriously' (Morgan, 1981: 94) and interviewing men about their private as well as public worlds (McKee and O'Brien, 1983). Too often the behaviour and views of men as husbands and fathers have been ignored, inferred, or developed from women's accounts (Safilios-Rothschild, 1969). Additionally, our understanding of paternal behaviour has been obscured by studying fathering within the same conceptual framework as mothering (Richards, 1982). There has also been a tendency in psychology and sociology to neglect the family context within which paternal behaviour was being developed (Lewis, 1982), and the meanings attached by family members to everyday behaviour under study (Backett, 1982; McKee, 1982). Studies of parenting have neglected the interactive effects of family members on one another's behaviour, and only in recent years, for example, has the unidirectional model of socialization been effectively challenged (Bell, 1968; Schaffer, 1977; Lerner and Spanier, 1978). Finally, as has often been the case in family studies, greater insight has frequently come from examining fatherhood in more obviously problematical settings such as lone (O'Brien, 1982) or step parenting (Burgoyne and Clark, 1983). Here, it could be argued, taken-for-granted assumptions about family life and fathering became more salient to respondents, and more accessible to researchers, when men faced special circumstances with which they felt ill-equipped to deal.

Description of present study
The data in this chapter are derived from a qualitative study of accounts of parental behaviour in a group of twenty-two middle-class families. (Fifteen other couples assisted with other preliminary research exercises such as discussion groups and sensitizing interviews.) Each couple had two children, at least one of whom was of preschool age. Both spouses were equally involved in the project and five minimally structured interviews were carried out, individually and jointly, over a period of 15 months. The essence of the methodology was to be guided in data gathering by respondents' accounts. Consequently emerging issues provided some of the framework of later interviews, and themes generated by respondents themselves were explored in depth.

An interactionist approach
The approach I adopt was anticipated by Burgess some sixty years ago when he described the family as 'a unity of interacting personalities' (Burgess, 1926). More recently the perspectives of symbolic interactionism (Blumer, 1969) and phenomenology (Natanson, 1967; Wagner, 1970) provided further theoretical impetus to examining the 'creative' rather than 'given' aspects of family role behaviour.

From these perspectives paternal behaviour can only be fully understood if it is viewed as a social product, continuously being defined and negotiated with other family members. This is not to deny the importance of social structural factors such as class, occupation, gender and family form, many of which are addressed elsewhere in this volume. My own concern, however, is to examine how family members, acting within these varied social constraints, attach meanings to them and negotiate their own particular familial realities. This is treated as a dynamic and extremely problematical process, rife with possibilities for misunderstanding and conflict. As Hess and Handel have pointed out, family members

> are engaged in evolving and mutually adjusting their images of one another. This mutual adjustment takes place in interaction, and it is, in part, the aim of interaction. Since complete consensus is most improbable, life in a family — as elsewhere — is a process ongoing in a situation of actual or potential instability. Pattern is reached, but it can never be complete, since action is always unfolding and the status of family members is undergoing change. (Hess and Handel, 1968: 15)

At the heart of many of these potential conflicts and tensions is the social construction of gender roles. My analysis largely assumes a context of patriarchalism and familialism well dissected by feminists (Gittins, 1985; Barrett and McIntosh, 1982), and examines the everyday negotiation and perpetuation of the consequent inequalities at the basis of family life. For many of the study couples the continuous striving to negotiate mutually acceptable examples of 'fairness' in the development of parental behaviour could be seen as their attempts to cope with the often deeply contradictory reality which they faced.[3] This is the background against which paternal behaviour must be studied and its problems viewed. To a great extent this chapter will show that notions of fairness and equity in modern-day parenting have provided a smokescreen for continuing basic inequalities. For example, one instance of 'progress' often cited in research, which was certainly also stressed by study families, was the fact that the fathers were willing to help out when necessary. It can be argued that this does not necessarily provide evidence of great advances in fathering, but rather the continued retention by the man of powers of choice over involvement in domestic responsibilities. The role of helper, by definition, abdicates the assumption of true responsibility.

The familial context of fathering
The basis of the interactionist approach is that, in studying two-parent families, the behaviour of one spouse is only properly understood in the context of the other. Equally, the effects of the children themselves should also be taken into account. An important aspect of this is how parents form understandings of their children. I made detailed study of such 'images', and briefly outline them later in this

section. As I have argued elsewhere (Backett, 1980) these images of children provided underlying assumptions crucial to the negotiation of parenthood. First, however, I shall describe how being a mother was seen by these couples.

(a) *Being a mother*. Analysis of respondents' accounts of family life indicated that the development of the mother role was much less problematical than that of the father. This does not mean that motherhood was regarded as 'easy', it most certainly was not (see Backett, 1982: 65–72). However, motherhood was described as having certain special features, and these defined its parameters and made it distinctively different from fatherhood. In many ways it was these special features themselves which were the basis of the problems of *motherhood!*[4]

Firstly, as indicated also in other studies (Boulton, 1983; Oakley, 1979, 1980), there was a fundamental assumption that the mother had the overall ultimate responsibility for organization and care of children and home. Almost all of the women gave up outside employment at least while their children were small. Most envisaged returning to work, and a few did so during the course of the study, but, critically, outside work which would be compatible with child-care responsibilities and husbands' work commitments was always considered. Additionally, almost all necessary arrangements for these eventualities were made by the mothers rather than the fathers.

Secondly, and as a consequence of her greater direct involvement with the children's lives, the mother was perceived as having greater knowledge of the child and its needs. This had some important implications for the context in which *paternal* behaviour was developed as the mother was usually his main source of information about the children. Talking about the children, they claimed, constituted an important element in everyday conversation between spouses. Not only did the mother have more extensive knowledge, but, because this was grounded in *direct* experience, it was also accorded a greater legitimacy, and therefore influence, in everyday child-rearing decisions.

Thirdly, the mother was perceived as being potentially more readily available to the child than was the father. For instance, couples gave many practical examples of their children turning more readily to the mother to satisfy needs and deal with problems, often even when the father was also present. There were also subjective implications whereby the mother *felt* that she herself *should* be available, for example when the child was ill or when a parent had to take time off work because of children's needs. The father was not perceived by couples as experiencing such constraints to the same extent and, for instance, far less concern was expressed about father absence than about mother absence.

(b) *Images of children*. Another important context within which paternal behaviour must be analysed is that of images of children (see also Busfield and Paddon, 1977; Rapoport et al., 1977). Parents are faced with an enormous range of stimuli from their children and, as in all kinds of social behaviour, they form typificatory schemes as part of the process of deciding how to act (Natanson, 1967; Wagner, 1970). A guiding assumption for the couples in my group was that children should be 'understood'. Thus, negotiating parental behaviour with one another involved developing, exchanging and sustaining images of the child and its world which could be used as subjectively satisfactory bases for action.

Parents developed images of children both from their social stocks of knowledge ('abstract' images) and from their ongoing biographical experience ('grounded' images). 'Abstract' images were invoked to make sense of children in general. Respondents stressed, for instance, that children were learning and developing beings who were different from adults and had variously defined needs for love, security and consistency. 'Grounded' images were attempts to make sense of their own particular child and its behaviour. For example parents developed understandings of the child in terms of its birth order, its sibling relationship, and perceptions of the familial and wider social contexts in which s/he had to act.

Many of these images were regularly invoked by respondents to explain what for them was the importance of a father's involvement with his children. As previously indicated, for these couples, the importance of a *mother's* involvement was much more taken-for-granted, and was satisfactorily demonstrated by her more constant presence, overall responsibility and availability.

The negotiation of fatherhood
What then did being a father mean to these couples? A basic assumption was that fatherhood entailed a direct involvement and active interest in the children. A father should get to know his children and not be a stranger to them. This assumption was frequently legitimated by referring to images of children. As Maureen Rankin explained:

> I think fathers should be very involved with the children, and I think the time for them to be involved is right from the word go. I think, if they're going to get on well with their children when they're older, they've got to start right from the beginning and develop a relationship at the same time as the mother develops a relationship.

Diane Hemingway added a further dimension when she said:

> If there are children I think it's very important that he shows them lots of love and plays with them, takes an interest in all their doings. It's important for the children, it's also important for the wife if she knows that he's taking an equal part in their upbringing, not just providing the money.

Such broad assumptions were frequently expressed in this way by respondents. Much more problematical, however, was their practical implementation. It was evident from my analysis that spouses aimed to negotiate with each other mutually satisfactory arrangements which enabled them to maintain belief in the *direct* involvement of the father. In terms of *actual* behaviour this involvement varied both between couples and within each family over time. The crucial factor in the process of belief maintenance was the ability to draw on various spheres of behaviour at different levels, all of which provided 'proof' of involvement. Importantly, it was *not*, however, perceived as necessary for the father to participate fully and constantly in *all* of these spheres. Rather, it was a matter of his participating sufficiently regularly in those particular spheres which spouses had identified as relevant to their own family situation. In other words, for father involvement to be subjectively satisfactory it did not tend to be measured against some abstract set of behavioural ideals. It was negotiated and evaluated in terms of the paternal behaviour perceived as appropriate by the spouses within their own special situation at any one point in time.

I identified three principal overlapping areas within which spheres of paternal behaviour were being developed. These were: (a) dealing with general domestic and family matters; (b) negotiating acceptable parental behaviour in relation to the mother; and (c) developing a direct relationship with the child. The first and second are progressively further removed from the situation to which, in theory, the couples attached the greatest importance. This was that being a parent was a learning situation characterized by direct personal experience (see discussion in Backett, 1980). Even though couples stressed the overwhelming importance of (c), most paternal behaviour was directed towards (a) and (b). For the majority of the men, time limitations and personal choice lead them *in practice* only to be minimally involved in the third area.

(a) *Dealing with general domestic and family matters*
This was the widest area of paternal behaviour which, it could be claimed, demonstrated involvement. Here, being a father meant sharing overall responsibility for the administration of domestic matters such as finances; care, education and development of children;

and the organization of family leisure activities. Madeleine Harris, who felt that Jeff was very much involved, said to him:

> Yes I think that we in general share the whole notion of teaching them, you know, playing with them. I mean, just taking care of emotional and intellectual and cultural development [Jeff agreed], and everything else. That it's nobody's function to do any one thing in particular.

This area of overall administrative activity was extremely broadly defined by respondents. In practice, however, there was considerable variation between couples in the kind, amount and regularity of such activity undertaken by the fathers. Also, and of relevance to the social construction of fatherhood, there was often only a fine subjective distinction between *passive* and *active* involvement. All of the husbands were kept 'informed' by their wives, and claimed an interest in this everyday administration. The couples sustained belief in this *passive* level of paternal involvement by claiming, for example, that domestic matters, especially those pertaining to the children, constituted a major part of their 'mundane' conversation.

The variation amongst the couples lay in the extent to which husbands played an *active* part in making decisions, allocating priorities and general organization. Compare for example the following statements from two fathers whose views illustrated the extremes within the group. Patrick Hislop spoke of 'being a mother' as follows:

> Being a provider of a stable home life and, much more so, influencing the children by example, much more so than the father.
> K.B: Why do you see it as being much more so than the father?
> Patrick: Because the mother will inevitably be in much closer contact with the children. And this is obviously just because of my particular job, not just *my* particular job, many fellows in my position because of the demands of their job, they are not in as close contact with the children as they could be or should be so that your presence is required only *in extremis*.

Philip Barber, however, said he had come to view fatherhood as requiring considerable practical involvement, he explained:

> I think it's one's parental responsibility to *spend* time with one's children, and to sort out priorities like this in the early years in particular when the child's development is progressing at a *very* rapid pace and so much of the basic pattern is being set. That it's a *father's* responsibility as well as a *mother's*, to give the *time* that is required for looking after the children in a very practical way.

The wives of these two men expressed similar views in their own interviews and it was a crucial feature of negotiation that *both* spouses believed such active involvement to be more or less necessary. For example, the man's involvement remained more on the passive level if the woman regarded him simply as a 'sounding board' for decisions which she had already made. In fact, the woman's response was always vital, since it was *her* everyday existence which tended to be most affected by these administrative and organizational decisions. Also *her* greater direct time commitment to the children gave her considerable power over the choice of those activities or routines which were actually put into practice.

The most typical pattern was a fluctuation between passive and active involvement. General spheres of behaviour considered appropriate to their own family set-up were negotiated on a hypothetical level by spouses. Often then the actual behaviour was, so to speak, held 'in reserve', and only minimal practical applications were required to maintain beliefs. It was subjectively satisfactory simply to maintain that the father 'would if he could' or 'could if he *had* to'.

Good illustrations of these points came from Alan Hemingway. He initially maintained that parenthood was a shared administrative responsibility, but later went on to allocate the major part of initiative in these spheres to his wife. He said about 'being a mother':

> ... very much the same [as being a father] I would think, in our case. These areas are very definitely the problems that we share, em, the children. We don't slot one aspect of their well being into my area and another in Dianne's, em, they're very much *ours* in terms of these kinds of decisions. And that's one thing we talk about a lot.

But later he said:

> Dianne's sphere of things, em, involves very much more the children, in terms of doing things with them and, er trying to be original in what we do, and doing the things we ought to do. And these are very much her areas of initiative, because she will always say before I ever get round to it, 'we ought to do such n'such with the kids', and we *do* it.

(b) *Negotiating acceptable paternal behaviour in relation to that of the mother*

Belief in father involvement was also sustained through the relationship with the mother. This was expressed by (i) adopting a generally supportive attitude towards her child-rearing activities, (ii) relieving her of practical and psychological pressures when both parents were present and (iii) acting as substitute when she wished to have time away from home and family.

The interactive complexities of the social construction of fatherhood are particularly evident in this area. The father relied heavily on the mother's information about herself and the children for cues to his own behaviour. He was vulnerable in his personal evaluations of everyday family events since he was, in fact, absent from a great deal of the child-rearing activity. The mother's account was his prime source of information but he could never be certain that he had grasped 'the total picture' since, inadvertently or deliberately, her account was bound to be selective.

(i) As previously outlined, respondents described the mother as having overall responsibility for child-rearing, and fulfilling a greater direct share of its everyday requirements. A consequence of this was that the mother also took on a greater share of the direct emotional pressures and constraints of child-rearing. All of the couples acknowledged that becoming parents had affected the woman's daily life much more than that of the man. They described her as having less freedom of action, and often being less intellectually satisfied by her daily life than was the man.

Such views were somewhat contradictory to their other stated beliefs that parenthood should be a 'fairly' shared reality. One response to such contradictions was for the husband to adopt a supportive and understanding attitude to his wife's child-rearing activities and problems. During the course of the interviews any critical comments from the men were usually couched either in an acknowledgement either of the arduousness of the mother's situation, or that his own inferior knowledge might have led him to make a wrong assessment. A typical example came from Roy Vaughan when he said:

> I wouldn't like to do that every day you know, and so I can understand how she feels when I come in at night, you know. It's quite a job for a woman really, two children. So I wouldn't condemn her at all, you know, just she maybe gives them a row but they must be due or she wouldn't give it.

Thus, in the interviews, greater legitimacy was accorded to the mother's child-rearing decisions and behaviour. This often found expression in the mother being critical of the father's activities, for example if she assessed *his* disciplining of the children as being too lenient or too strict. The father, however, usually muted or qualified any criticism, and expressed *his* involvement by acting in a generally supportive capacity.

(ii) This second area, that of demonstrating father involvement through relieving perceived child-rearing pressures on the mother, when both parents were present, provides ample illustration of the varying amount of 'practical proof' required for belief maintenance. For some couples such relief was little more than an extension of supportive statements; for others, it entailed the father working alongside the mother in a well defined range of activities. All couples, however, coped with contradictions, such as fluctuations in the availability of the father, by emphasizing the voluntary aspects of his domestic activities and stressing that 'help' was always given when really needed. An example of this came from Carole Burns who commented:

> I think he's very good really, em, he comes in and sometimes he's whacked cos he's had a very brain-filled day, which can be much more exhausting than pick and shovels. And, er, they [children] just crawl all over him like ants, and he puts up with it, which I think is quite good.

Significantly, however, even at times such as weekends when the father was perceived as equally available, emphasis on 'voluntarism' and 'opting in' continued to operate. Also, weekends generally provided a different context for parenting, as most families tried to minimize the mundane tasks typical of the weekday domestic routine. Thus, whilst the husbands might be 'involved' at weekends, this was usually as part of a different range of activities with relaxation often as an important aim. Barry Coulson's remarks were particularly illuminating; he said:

> And, em, I mean, if you've got children, that's it, it's non stop work. I mean *I* participate when I feel like it, but if I feel like burying my head in the newspaper I *do*, or if I feel like ignoring the disturbances that are going on, then I can do it. Jean sometimes will call upon, em, will say, 'can you help me out?', or something, and I can do it. *And I don't want her to feel that she has to do all the work* (my emphasis). I usually help her more at weekends.

(iii) Finally, father involvement was expressed by the husband deputizing for his wife if she wished to leave the children or in an emergency. When family life was defined as a situation of 'fairness' and mutual responsibility for children, it was important to maintain a belief that, just as the father could 'escape' from domestic commitments, so also could the mother. As Maureen Roberts said:

> The main thing is that he's quite prepared to take charge and give me freedom if I want to go, if there's anywhere special that I want to go, I know he doesn't mind me going.

However, although one component of being a father was deputizing for the mother, this activity did not need to be regular, frequent, or of an equivalent standard to be subjectively satisfactory. Men were only expected to substitute for *part* of the woman's usual activities, the main requirement being child-minding. Many stories were related of things left unattended to when fathers were 'in charge'. Also, child-minding standards were not expected to approximate to those of the mother. Adequacy of parental behaviour was defined differently if it was carried out by the father.

(c) *Being a father in relation to the child*

The final area of father involvement, and that perhaps most stressed by the couples, was that the father should have a *direct* relationship with the child. There were two key aspects of this direct involvement. Firstly, many respondents stressed the importance of the *potential* involvement of the man in *all* practical aspects of looking after the children, even if this was only to a limited extent and sporadic. It was felt that such activities not only fostered a good relationship with the child but also kept good faith with the mother by sustaining beliefs in 'fairness'. Thus, Andrew David commented:

> I think a direct involvement with your children, you know, none of this shunning responsibilities and shouldering it on to your wife, or the mother, I think it's, it's unfair.

Secondly, direct involvement was seen as a crucial way of building a relationship with the child. The predominant way in which such involvement was expressed was in playing with the children, or otherwise keeping them occupied. However, whether through practical care or play, the more the man participated the more he gained that direct knowledge about his children which was so valued in the parental negotiations. Barbara Johnson highlighted some of these feelings when she said:

> If you've got *no* relationship with the child as it's developing, I don't think you're ever going to understand it. So I feel that men ought to be prepared to muck in with the babies in *all* the sordid details. I mean there's nobody better at changing nappies than Ian. But em, I think it creates a relationship which is valuable.

This then was an area of involvement which was accorded great importance. It was also perhaps the most problematical in terms of 'practical proof' since, compared with the mother, the father could invest much less time in such activity. Equally, even when he *was* directly involved with the child, such interaction tended in any case to be mediated through the indirect understandings provided by the mother. For example, the mother might inform the father about the day's events to 'put him in the picture' as to the child's mood when he arrived home in the evening.

Elaborate coping mechanisms were developed to sustain belief in the reality of a direct father–child relationship. For instance, great emphasis was laid on claims that the father *valued* the direct relationship with the child, and derived pleasure from it. The implication was always that, in the future or given more time, a greater involvement would be desired. Shirley Jackson's view of 'being a father' was typical. She said:

I think, em, loving, really very much the same as what a mother involves. Er, loving your children, playing with them, spending time with them, I think Edward would like to be able to spend *more* time with the children, but unfortunately he isn't in, em, you know, he isn't sort of nine to five.

In fact only two fathers said they *would* like to be at home all day with the children. Even these men, like most of the others (and the women too!) nevertheless admitted that prolonged periods of direct involvement with the children were a strain. Implicit in such statements were images of children as demanding and potentially oppressive.

Issues of the meanings attached to 'time' and its implications for paternal activity had particular potency in this area. The father had the problem of making time to 'get to know the child' in a way in which the mother did not. As the mother was, at this stage, more constantly available to the child, she was perceived as being able to 'get to know' him/her through the whole variety of everyday interactions. The father, on the other hand, had more deliberately to set time aside, or organize his other commitments, in order to sustain belief that he was achieving this *direct* knowledge. In addition, underlying assumptions that parenthood was a process of learning, and images that children needed consistency, implied that time had regularly to be 'made' for them. Also, the context of his relationship with the child was different from that of the mother, since she often played a significant part in organizing the times when father and child could be available to one another. All of these elements behind the father's time with the child resulted in mechanisms to sustain belief that he frequently and actively 'spent' some of it on him/her.

One such mechanism was the situation of the father being left in total charge of the children and household while the mother went out. This mechanism needed only to be implemented irregularly or even, in two extreme cases, to be a 'possibility' which was mostly held in reserve, for it to be subjectively satisfactory. Being left in total charge was, however, 'practical proof' of involvement and also supported the validity of that other important coping mechanism, voluntarism. It also meant that the father 'spent time' directly with the children and thus *had* to learn about them, and how to deal with them, directly through his own experience.

Respondents' accounts also indicated that the fact that the father spent less time with the children affected how *they* in turn viewed *him*. Many parents, for example, emphasized that the child saw the father as 'refreshment' from the mother and might therefore choose *his* company when *both* parents were available. Such claims could, however, be analysed as constituting further mechanisms for sustaining belief in father involvement. The success of a *direct* relationship could be seen as undeniably 'proven' when the *child* chose to spend time with the father.

This leads on to the final sphere of involvement, and the one most frequently stressed by respondents, that of the father as a source of fun and pleasure. Helen Moffat said, for instance:

> I think fathers *should* be fun, I think they should be light relief. But I think because he's such fun and he's so precious, I think what he does, actually *does*, with the children makes more impression.

And Jean Coulson commented of her elder son:

> If we're both here he tends to go for Barry [husband]. But I think that's because I'm here all the time and it's great to have Dad at home sort of thing.

Playing with children and being a source of pleasure were thus highly meaningful ways of demonstrating father involvement. This was an area of activity which the father could carry out spontaneously and voluntarily with the minimum of specific knowledge or consultation with the mother being necessary. It could also be carried out regularly when little time was available, for instance a routinely told bedtime story. Finally, the emotive salience attached to this area of paternal involvement also meant that it could be accomplished to the satisfaction of both spouses, even with a relatively small input of time.

Discussion

The study of power relations within families is highly complex principally because of the confounding effects of emotional attachments. Undoubtedly, traditional patriarchal values continue to structure the framework for decision-making in most two-parent families. For the middle-class couples I studied this was evidenced primarily by the woman continuing to assume overall responsibility for home and family, and organize her outside employment and commitments accordingly, whilst the man's principal responsibility was to provide earnings.[5] I therefore agree with Barrett and McIntosh (1982: 65) when they said:

> Despite the contemporary rhetoric of the 'egalitarian family' and the 'sharing marriage', despite the disappearance of the more obvious formalised manifestations of paternal power and manly authority, modern families are still deeply unequal affairs. The principle of the wage-earner and his dependents, of the husband who contributes cash while the wife contributes household labour, is not a division of labour between equals, but an unequal exchange in which the man's interests predominate.

My analysis has, however, highlighted the woman's hidden power in the family. On an everyday level it appeared that the woman exercised considerable power domestically, particularly over child-rearing, since her direct involvement imbued her opinions with a greater legitimacy than those of the man. This, however, must be seen as a double-edged sword which, in fact, simply reinforced her perceived greater responsibility in domestic matters. Even couples whose domestic organization before children was, they claimed, equally shared, soon found this situation altered by the kind of parental division of labour they adopted. The father spent far less time on home and family matters than did the mother, and consequently was soon judged to be not so 'in touch' or 'competent' in these matters. Directly acquired knowledge and ability were valued in child-rearing, and the man's overall competence in these respects was rapidly perceived to be inferior to the woman's. I would suggest that this pattern, which is most obvious when the children are young, continues to be dominant whilst there are dependent offspring. Many feminists have argued that it is as imperative for women consciously to bring men into the domestic arena as to fight for equal rights in the world of work (see for example, Huber, 1976). I would also emphasize that a greater awareness of the processes involved in the negotiation of fatherhood must lead women to allow men to develop paternal competences which are accorded equal weight and validity.

In an important theoretical contribution, Bell and Newby (1976) argued that it was important to investigate male–female relationships within the family as one way of further understanding continued sexual stratification in our society. They suggested that researchers should study the ways in which males continued to maintain their traditional authority over women and 'to explore the necessary strategies they employ in attempting to ensure the stability of their power'. Some of these processes were evident in my study. For instance, it could be argued that, in sustaining beliefs about 'fairly' shared child-rearing and 'involved' fatherhood, couples are in fact impeding progress towards any real changes in parenting. My data showed, for example, that respondents perceived frequent contradictions between beliefs in such fair and mutual parental involvement, and what actually happened. Acknowledgement of such discrepancies was made most obvious by various 'coping mechanisms' implemented to deal with resultant difficulties. In the joint interviews, for instance, spouses frequently reassured one another that they *were* adopting the 'fairest' solution possible in the prevailing circumstances. Such beliefs were further sustained by stressing that the father was (a) *willing* to do things for the children when necessary (b) *able* to do things for them *if* necessary and (c) *had* demonstrated such voluntarism and ability on previous occasions. This final point is of crucial importance, as such 'practical proof' did not have to be regularly demonstrated, or achieve the same standards as that of the mother, for it to be judged adequate by the couple.

Popular belief in the more 'involved' father must therefore be seen as something of an illusion. My respondents, by invoking notions of 'fairness' and 'sharing', were attempting to take only small strides towards 'equity' (and in no way towards equality). Even such limited change appeared constantly thwarted, however, as long as the men were still given and took the very special freedom of 'opting in' to child-rearing, and the women continued to tolerate their minimal opportunities to 'opt out'. Until the existence of these fundamental inequalities is fully appreciated, and the processes revealed, proper understanding of the nature of fatherhood in our society and its true potential for change will not be achieved.

Notes

1. See, for example, influential early work by Newson and Newson (1963, 1968), and Gavron (1966). In their studies the Newsons asked only very general questions which were unlikely to obtain an accurate assessment of the actual quantity of child-care by the father. Gavron simply asked if the father *would* do things with or for the children. Along with other researchers, such questions perhaps led them to document how their respondents, like mine, sustained a belief in the 'involved father'. And, of course, there could well be a wide discrepancy between beliefs of this kind and the *fact* of regular practical participation by the father in child-rearing.

2. All names have been changed to protect the anonymity of respondents.

3. This is one of many sets of 'coping mechanisms' which are discussed in Backett (1982, Chapter 4).

4. These taken-for-granted assumptions about motherhood do appear to be an important aspect of the social construction of parenthood in popular culture (Rapoport, et al., 1977), although many experts have expressed considerable doubt about, for example, biologically based gender differences in bonding, nurturing and, by extension, child-care (Berman, 1980; Lamb and Goldberg, 1982; Lamb et al., 1981).

5. Such fundamental assumptions were also evident in my later study of working-class family planning practices. Many more of these women worked whilst their children were small. Usually, however, they worked part-time on early morning or evening shifts when their husbands were available to childmind. The father's willingness to 'help out' in this way was frequently put forward by the woman as proof of his 'involvement' (McGlew and Backett, forthcoming).

References

Backett, K.C. (1980) 'Images of Parenthood', in Anderson, M. (ed.) *Sociology of the Family*, 2nd edn. London: Penguin.

Backett, K.C. (1982) *Mothers and Fathers: A Study of the Development and Negotiation of Parental Behaviour*. London and Basingstoke: Macmillan.

Barker, D. and Allen, S. (eds) (1976) *Dependence and Exploitation in Work and Marriage*. London and New York: Longman.

Barrett, M. and McIntosh, M. (1982) *The Anti-social Family*. London: Verso/NLB Thetford Press.

Bell, C. and Newby, H. (1976) 'Husband and Wives: the Dynamics of the Deferential

Dialectic', in D. Barker and S. Allen *Dependence and Exploitation in Work and Marriage*. London and New York: Longman.

Bell, R.A. (1968) 'A Reinterpretation of the Direction of Effects in Studies of Socialisation', *Psychological Review*: 81–95.

Berman, P.W. (1980) 'Are Women More Responsive than Men to the Young? A Review of Developmental and Situational Variables', *Psychological Bulletin* 88: 668–95.

Blumer, H.S. (1969) *Symbolic Interactionism: Perspective and Method*. Englewood Cliffs, NJ: Prentice-Hall.

Boulton, M.G. (1983) *On Being a Mother*. London and New York: Tavistock Publications.

Burgess, E.W. (1926) 'The Family as a Unity of Interacting Personalities', *Family*, 7: 3–9.

Burgoyne, I. and Clark, D. (1983) *Making a go of it: A Study of Step Families in Sheffield*. London: Routledge and Kegan Paul.

Busfield, J. and Paddon, M. (1977) *Thinking About Children*. London: Cambridge University Press.

Gamarnikow, E., Morgan, D.H.J., Purvis, J. and Taylorson, D. (eds) (1983) *The Public and the Private*. London: Heinemann.

Gavron, H. (1966) *The Captive Wife*. London: Routledge and Kegan Paul.

Gittins, D. (1985) *The Family in Question: Changing Households and Familiar Ideologies*. London: Macmillan.

Hanson, S.M.H. and Bozett, F.W. (1985) *Dimensions of Fatherhood*. Beverly Hills and London: Sage.

Hess, R.D. and Handel, G. (1968) 'The Family as a Psychosocial Organisation', in G. Handel (ed.) *The Psychosocial Interior of the Family*. London: Allen and Unwin.

Huber, J. (1976) 'Towards a Sociotechnological Theory of the Women's Movement'. *Social Problems*: 371–88.

Lamb, M.E. and Goldberg, W.A. (1982) 'The Father–Child Relationship: A Synthesis of Biological, Evolutionary and Social Perspectives', in R. Gandelman and L. Hoffman (eds) *Parental Behaviour: Its Causes and Consequences*. Hillsdale, NJ: Lawrence Erlbaum.

Lamb, M.E., Frodi, A.M., Hwang, C.P., Frodi, M. and Steinberg, J. (1981). 'Attitudes and Behaviour of Traditional and Non-traditional Parents in Sweden', in R. Emde and R. Hannan (eds) *Attachment and Affiliative Systems: Neurobiological and Psycho-biological Aspects*. New York: Plenum.

Lerner, R.M. and Spanier, G.B. (eds) (1978) *Child Influences on Marital and Family Interaction a Life-Span Perspective*. London: Academic Press.

Lewis, C. (1982) 'The Observation of Father–Infant Relationships: An "Attachment" to Outmoded Concepts', in L. McKee and M. O'Brien (eds) *The Father Figure*. London: Tavistock.

McGlew, T.J. and Backett, K.C. (forthcoming) *Fertility and Family Planning in a Working Class Population* (provisional title). London and Basingstoke: Macmillan.

McKee, L. (1982) 'Fathers' Participation in Infant Care: A Critique', in L. McKee and M. O'Brien *The Father Figure*. London: Tavistock.

McKee, L. and O'Brien, M. (1983) 'Interviewing Men: Taking Gender Seriously', in E. Garmarnikow, D.H.J. Morgan, J. Purvis and D. Taylorson (eds) *The Public and the Private*. London: Heinemann.

Morgan, D.H.J. (1981) 'Men, Masculinity and the Process of Sociological Enquiry', in H. Roberts (ed.) *Doing Feminist Research*. London: Routledge and Kegan Paul.

Natanson, M. (ed.) (1967) *Alfred Schutz: Collected Papers Vol I*. The Hague: Martinns Nijhoff.

Newson, J. and Newson, E. (1963) *Infant Care in an Urban Community*. London: Allen and Unwin.

Newson, J. and Newson, E. (1968) *Four Years Old in an Urban Community*. London: Allen and Unwin.

Oakley, A. (1974) *The Sociology of Housework*. Oxford: Martin Robertson.

Oakley, A. (1979) *Becoming a Mother*. Oxford: Martin Robertson.

Oakley, A. (1980) *Women Confined*. Oxford: Martin Robertson.

O'Brien, M. (1982) 'Becoming a Lone Father: Differential Patterns and Experiences', in L. McKee and M. O'Brien (eds) *The Father Figure*. London: Tavistock.

Rapoport, R., Rapoport, R.N. and Strelitz, Z., with Kew, S. (1977). *Fathers, Mothers and Others: Towards New Alliances*. London: Routledge and Kegan Paul.

Richards, M.P.M. (1982) 'How Should We Approach the Study of Fathers?', in L. McKee and M. O'Brien (eds) *The Father Figure*. London and New York: Tavistock.

Russell, G. (1983) *The Changing Role of Fathers*. Milton Keynes: The Open University Press.

Safilios-Rothschild, C. (1969) 'Family Sociology or Wives' Family Sociology? A Cross Cultural Examination of Decision Making', *Journal of Marriage and the Family*: 290–301.

Schaffer, H.R. (1977) *Studies in Mother–Infant Interaction*. London: Academic Press.

Wagner, H.R. (ed.) (1970) *Alfred Schutz: On Phenomenology and Social Relations*. Chicago: University of Chicago Press.

6

The experience of grandfatherhood

Sarah Cunningham-Burley

SCB: Is it different being a father and being a grandfather?
GF: I think there is something different, don't ask me to put it into words, but I think there is something different about it. I think you try to bring up your own in a certain, under certain rules, and that, with your own grandchildren it'll be different. (Pat GF, 2bi)[1]

Introduction
Grandfathers have long been neglected in family studies. Much work on grandparenthood has either focused only on grandmothers or has not been gender specific in its analysis (Bengston and Robertson, 1985; Burton and Bengston, 1985; Robertson, 1977). This has led to assumptions about the grandparenting role and its significance to men (Cavan, 1962; Huyck, 1974). We know little about the experience of grandfatherhood, and existing work does not relate grandfatherhood to fathering (Baranowski, 1985; Russell, 1985). Stereotypically, and in terms of academic research, grandparenthood has been equated with old age. Grandparenting is simply seen as a way of keeping a foot in the social system, or of filling a void (Troll, 1983). However, grandparenthood is something which occurs in middle age, and moreover at a time when one's own child-bearing is likely to be completed. As Baranowski has pointed out, 'grandfathers today may be more specifically identified as grandfathers because they are not simultaneously fathers of young children' (1985: 219). Yet, there are clear parallels between the social institutions of fatherhood and grandfatherhood. In order to examine how grandparenthood is experienced by grandfathers, and to discover in what ways it is meaningful to them, it is necessary to explore the problematical nature of the social institution. Drawing on grandpaternal and grandmaternal accounts, obtained from a qualitative, sociological study of grandparenthood, this chapter will explore how grandfatherhood is socially constructed and understood.

The chapter is divided into six further sections. The first briefly outlines the study. The next section details how grandfatherhood was constructed and displayed in the interview setting. The third section focuses on the dilemmas experienced by the grandparents in defining an appropriate role for themselves. The following section examines the grandfathers' role within the context of perceived social change: the conflicting views of grandmothers and grandfathers are discussed. The penultimate section describes the experience of grandfatherhood from the grandfathers' point of view. Lastly, as a conclusion, the implications which this study has for our understanding of grandfatherhood will be discussed, and suggestions made for future research.

The study

The study aimed to examine the meaning and significance of grandparenthood, in depth, from the point of view of people becoming grandparents for the first time.[2] A sample of eighteen couples were interviewed over a period of one year, once before and twice after the birth of their first grandchild. The couples all lived in Aberdeen, and had their families either living within the city or its environs. They were aged between 42 and 55 years, except one couple in their mid-sixties. Most were working class, with only two couples having middle-class occupations. All the grandfathers were in full-time employment. All but one of the grandmothers were working, at least part-time. Contact was made via the daughter or daughter-in-law while she was attending the antenatal clinic. This prospective strategy enabled the process of becoming a grandparent to be explored, from the early anticipations of the first interviews, through the excitement of the birth itself, to the routines developed by the time the child was 6 to 9 months old.

The study was exploratory, and intensive techniques were employed in order to allow the respondents as much scope as possible in talking about their experiences, and in defining what was important to them. A mixture of semi-structured and unstructured interviewing techniques were used: the interviews became more informal as I, the researcher, got to know the grandparents better, and as grandparenthood itself became something more tangible. The interviews were tape-recorded and transcribed. In addition, ethnographic notes were taken on the interview setting to provide contextual data on the interviews in particular, and the research process in general. The analysis reflected the principal aims of the research study. The focus was on the procedures used by the grandparents to construct an appropriate role, and the background assumptions and common-sense knowledge underlying such processes. The analysis included an appraisal of how they talked about their personal experiences of family life, and the subjective meanings which they attached to grandparenthood. These techniques differ from previous work in this area which has tended to be more structured both in terms of data collection and analysis. The methods used in this investigation allow for in-depth study of a small sample. The findings presented here are suggestive, and do not attempt to offer a definitive account of the experience of grandfatherhood.

Constructing grandfatherhood

An analysis of the grandfathers' role in the interview setting showed that it would be easy to discount men in family research, or to construct their role in families only from a woman's point of view. The grandmothers certainly spoke much more in the interview setting. They also seemed to be much more involved in speaking about grandparenthood on other occasions as well. For them, much of the experience was something tangible, and amenable to verbalization:

> e.g. Mrs. Lawson: . . . I speak about it more. It's different for a man, a man's nay (not) so emotional, do you see, ken (you know)? Ken, maybe underneath, er, er he doesn't speak about it much like I do. (Mat GM, 4aiii)

The grandfathers, however, were much less involved in such verbal interchanges, and treated the interviews very differently. They laughed and joked, came and went, and tended to be somewhat peripheral to the proceedings. In short, the interviews were rather dominated by the grandmothers. It is important to understand this difference between the grandmothers and grandfathers, for it informs how grandfatherhood is socially constructed. On the whole the grandfathers did not seem to find it so easy to express how they felt about grandfatherhood. However, one should not interpret this as a lack of involvement in grandparenthood. As I have noted elsewhere,

> Grandfatherhood was in some ways made invisible in these interviews. They (the grandfathers) talked less about grandparenthood in the interview setting, they lacked an obvious role in the early months of grandparenthood, and tended to define both these as women's activity. Yet enough was said by both grandmothers and grandfathers to tell me that this did not necessarily constitute an accurate portrayal of grandfatherhood, for they did seem to enjoy being a grandfather. (Cunningham-Burley, 1984: 333)

Becoming a grandfather involves a transition from parenthood to grandparenthood, or more specifically from fatherhood to grandfatherhood. Neither of these states is static: they change across an individual's life span and between different generational cohorts. Both the grandmothers and the grandfathers in this study talked differently of their experiences, both past and present, in a way which illuminates their perceptions of family structures, and how they define and re-define roles such as grandmother, grandfather, father and mother to accommodate both change and continuity.

The respondents discussed the changing nature of grandparent-hood, the differences between grandparenting and parenting both at a general level, and for themselves in particular. They also talked about the differences between parents past and present, and especially the changing role of fathers. The complexity and contradictory nature of these accounts makes generalization difficult. The substantive views of the respondents differed: some saw change where others did not. Others did not readily or spontaneously recall past experiences. Those who talked about change did not necessarily find it reflected in personal experience; others recounted their personal experience as symptomatic of broader change. Yet, whether drawing on personal experience or general knowledge, how the people interviewed perceived or accounted for change and continuity across the generations sheds light on how they located their own experience of the role of grandfather within this wider framework. Prior experience, generalized typical knowledge and the construction of grand-fatherhood are interrelated. To study the impact of both personal biography and cultural change, it is necessary to investigate how both are managed by, and represented in the accounts of the respondents.

Dilemmas of grandparenthood
Both the grandmothers and grandfathers recollected past experience, and from this made an assessment of both the differences between grandparents past and present, and between parenting and grandparenting. The grandfathers were more likely to stress the different environment of today and how this meant that you had less grandchildren, and more time to spend with them. The grandmothers were more likely to say that people had more resources these days, especially money: grandparents were able to do more today.

> e.g. Mrs Cormack: Of course you couldna give, in them days, you had to it took you all yer time to look aifter yoursel', I think they get lot more nowadays. (Pat GM, 6biii)

Many respondents used recollections of their own parents as grandparents to illustrate what they felt that one should or should not do as grandparents. Rather than producing a clear definition of the grandparental role, the grandparents' recollections seemed to high-light some inherent dilemmas in the grandparental role.

The grandfathers were more likely than the grandmothers to talk about arguments which they had had with their own parents and parents-in-law about their role with the grandchildren. This tended to make them seem more sceptical. While agreeing that grandparents today could do more, they did not think this was wholly positive in the way that the grandmothers did. While grandparents were able to do more than before, they were also constrained. Both the grandfathers and the grandmothers said that they should not interfere with the new family, or spoil the grandchild. They should not impose their desire to grandparent on the young couple (Cunningham-Burley, 1985).

> Mr Innes: I've no doubt, if they said no you dinna give it this you dinna di that. I would never go against their wishes, no 'cos I think it's wrong for the youngster to do a thing like that. (Pat GF, 2bi)

The grandfathers particularly seemed to be aware that by the very nature of their role they may end up making the same mistakes as their own parents as grandparents did sometimes. Learning from past experience seemed to be important. However, the grandparents thought that there may be a certain inevitability to their actions. While all said that they should not interfere, they also realized that grandfatherhood was something new to them, so that they would not be sure how they would react. One grandfather noted, when recalling arguments he had with his own mother-in-law:

> No, I, I, I, think Mark (respondent's son) will be like I was with Nora's mother (respondent's mother-in-law) . . . you know when I was a father. I'm going to be a grandad now — I might be the same as what they were. (Pat GF, 1bi)

As a father, the grandfather in this example became annoyed with the grandparents of his children. Yet, as a grandfather he felt that he may behave in that same annoying way. In many ways the differences between fathering and grandfathering seemed to be very pertinent. Through making this comparison, the grandfathers were able both to make sense of and describe the experience of grandfatherhood. Grandfatherhood today was seen as something new, and different from the experience of the respondents' own parents or grandparents.

In order to express what grandfatherhood was like, the grandfathers would liken it, in one way or another, to fatherhood.

> e.g. 1. Mr Anderson: It's like starting all over again only you're the eldest ones. (Pat GF, 2bii)

> e.g. 2. Mr Angus: It makes you feel younger I think . . . like starting all over again, in a way. (Mat GF, 5aii)

The accounts of the differences between grandfathering and fathering reflected both change and continuity. These contradictory components pertained both to the grandfathers' experiences and to the meanings which they attached to grandfatherhood. There was an important variety in the grandfathers' accounts, which should not be lost in the search for general patterns. While at one level grandfatherhood was like 'starting all over again', it was also different from fathering.

> SCB: Is it very difficult being a father and being a grandfather?
> GF: Oh-oh-yes definitely. Having said what I said you try to bring your own up in a . . . in the way I believe is right, whether it be right or wrong, you know, but I think a grandchild's different. He's just a . . . something to love, I suppose, have a bit of fun with, it's up to him (the son) to bring it up, him or her, whatever you like. You haven't got the same pressure on you that to see that it goes on the right path, you know, just here for fun. (Pat GF, 4bii)

Although the grandfathers did not seem to find it easy to express how they felt about grandfatherhood, when they talked about the differences between their fathering and grandfathering, a sense of their enjoyment and type of experience would be elicited. The grand-mothers, and in one case a daughter who happened to be present at the interview (see below) joined in reinforcing some of the grand-fathers' tentative statements. In this way, they too were part of the process through which grandfatherhood was constructed.

The grandfathers' recollections of their own fathering were domin-ated by the experience of not having the time to be with their young children. As grandfathers they felt that they would be able to spend more time with their grandchildren than they did with their own children, and enjoy their development. As one grandfather ex-plained:

> Mr Anderson: The first four years we were married. I was away, the first four year, well, Mark (son) was very strange . . . well . . . I think it's being close together — you can see the bairn (grandchild) and not feel strange. (Pat GF, 1bi)

Although most of the grandfathers did not have such a period of separation from their families as fathers, they were all working long hours, which meant they did not have as much time to be with their families as they had now. Mr Henderson's daughter noted :

> That's what Dad says . . . he's got more patience with his grandchildren than he ever had for us. That's what he ay (always) says to me.

Mrs Henderson then went on to explain why this was the case:

> Mrs Henderson: He'd nay (no) time, he did na (not) have the patience with you, as we've tried to tell you before. When you were a baby your father had to work three nights a week overtime to get money. (Mat GM, 4aiii)

Having more time seemed to constitute an essential difference between fathering as it was then, and grandfathering as it is now. Having more patience also was significant. This was related to having more time but also to having less 'parental' responsibility for the child, and to being older and more lenient oneself. The responsibilities of fathers and grandfathers were seen as quite different:

> e.g. 1. Mr Henderson: I'll even give my grandchildren more scope than I gave my son. I dare say. (Mat GF, 2ai)

> e.g. 2. Mr Gilbert: If it starts screaming, take it from me. I dinna hae to walk the floor at night. (Mat GF, 3aii)

In many ways then, grandfatherhood could be enjoyed more than fatherhood, although one grandfather noted that 'it's not as exciting as your own children' (Pat GF, 4bi), making it difficult to generalize. While a difference between being a parent and being a grandparent was often expressed by the respondents, the essence of these differences remained ill-defined. Some said that they could not remember what they felt like becoming or being a father, or speculated that they must have felt about the same. Thus, comparing fatherhood and grandfatherhood was one method through which the grandfathers expressed what becoming a grandfather was like. Yet such comparisons also demonstrated the dilemmas of grandfatherhood: they had the opportunity to do more, yet were restrained by not wanting to interfere or spoil the child.

> e.g. 2. Mr Anderson: It's their life — they're trying to bring up the child, not us, 'cos I think that grandparents get very selfish, do you know what I mean? You spoil it and then when you're tired o' it, cheerio. (Pat GF, 1bi)

Grandfathers and social change

The grandfathers often worked long hours when they were fathers, and both the grandmothers and grandfathers generally said that the grandfathers were not very involved in child-care because of this. However, the grandmothers also felt that the role of fathers had changed since then. As will be noted below, there were exceptions to this, namely, those grandfathers who were 'involved' fathers. Both the grandmothers and grandfathers had a lot to say about the changing role of fathers across the generations. This is of interest to a fuller understanding of the grandfathers' experience of grandfatherhood, and the constraints and contradictions within it. It also highlights some interesting gender differences, which underlie how family life is accounted and described by men and women.

The respondents' own recollections of early married life reflected a harder time, with less help from relatives. Wages did not go far. The respondents told of how, as young parents, they could not afford to go out, and that life was a struggle. This was not the case for the younger generation: life had changed, and was easier. The grandparents themselves contributed to that change by providing material goods for the new family, and helping out in various ways. They would do all these things because they knew it was hard bringing up a family whatever the circumstances. They were glad of the opportunity to help out, and the impact of these changes was generally seen as good.

Within this broad consensus about the changing social environment of family life, the grandmothers and grandfathers differed greatly in their assessment of the role of grandfathers. Although the respondents did discuss the role of mothers, it was the role of fathers which came under greatest scrutiny. It was within these discussions that diverse assessments were made of the grandfathers' fathering, and reference made to their grandfathering. In this way it is interesting to see how the grandmothers and the grandfathers account for change differently, and locate the role of fathers, and grandfathers within divergent perceptions of social change.

For the grandmothers, particularly, certain noteworthy features of fathering today served to represent underlying differences between the generations, yet at the same time they also amounted to these very differences. In this way the grandmothers' discussion of fathering provides an insightful example of what Garfinkel (1967) has termed 'the documentary method of interpretation'. An actual appearance is treated as ' "the document of " as "pointing to" as "standing on behalf of " a "presumed underlying pattern" ' (1967: 78). Evidence of an underlying change in the role of fathers did not have to be produced: the grandmothers thought that they could see it all around them. This provides a useful framework through which to understand the grandmothers' responses: it offers an account of how the fathering role appears to them to have changed, rather more than it may in fact have changed. Research has shown that the fathering role has altered less than is popularly assumed (Backett, 1982).

The most common symbol of the changed role of fathers used by the grandmothers was the highly visible activity of 'pushing the pram'.

> e.g. 1. Mrs Sinclair: You see young fathers now walking out with their prams, and that, which you never would have seen before. (Pat GM, 4bi)

> e.g. 2. Mrs Cookson: Oh yes, I mean prams, they go out with the pram. (Mat GM, Aii)

This was the most remarkable feature of fathering today, perhaps because it was so visible, and external to the private domestic scene. As such it was used by the grandmothers to describe the new fathers' role, without actually having to go into more detail. Underlying change was taken-for-granted. Although the grandfathers would not dispute that one saw more fathers with prams these days, they did not make the same assumptions about the relevance of this. It did not, for them, constitute underlying fundamental change in the way it did for the grandmothers.

The grandmothers also remarked on the fact that the new fathers went shopping, something again which could be seen easily, and used to account for 'real' changes in other spheres:

> e.g. Mrs Rae: I think they just sort o' all muck in together. This sort of thing . . . all help.
> Mr Rae: (laughs) I certainly helped to a certain extent.
> Mrs Rae: Mmm . . . but I don't see you going out to do the shopping—like they do. (Pat GP, Biii)

Within the home, too, the grandmothers noticed certain changes. These were all related to activities involving the baby:

> e.g. Mrs Angus: Well, he (son-in-law) will change nappies, bath her, feed her, nay (not) all the time, but he takes his turn. . . .
> Mr Angus: Mmm. . . .
> Mrs Angus: I don't think you could 'a changed a nappy (to GF)
> Mr Angus: Well. . . .
> Mrs Angus: *You* never did, and *he* does. (Mat GP, 5aiii)

As some of these examples show, by implication if not by direct comparison, the grandmothers thought that the grandfathers, when they were fathers of young children, did not do as much as their sons or sons-in-law are perceived to do.

A few of the grandfathers were described as being exceptionally good fathers, by the grandmothers, because they went beyond what they considered to be the then accepted role, and became involved with their children. They played and had fun with their families, and it was expected that they would be the same as grandfathers. For example, Mrs Logan said of her husband:

> He was a good father . . . you did, you played a lot, although they were girls he still played a lot with them. (Mat GM, 1ai)

These days, however, 'good' fathers were not just those who happened to be good with children anyway, or who enjoyed being involved: today fathers were expected to help with the baby, and share this new responsibility.

The grandparents also mentioned the fact that fathers now attend the birth of their child or children. This was seen as a new trend which had quickly become the accepted norm. This was totally different from all of the grandparents' experience. Most also said that they would not have liked it themselves, with the grandmothers and grandfathers being in agreement over this. The grandmothers tentatively said that they thought it was a good idea, but it was not something they had considered for themselves.

> e.g. Mrs Davis: I don't think I would hae got my man . . . it wasn't popular then but no, I think they kinda insist that the fathers be there and that.
> SCB: Do you think it's a good idea?
> Mrs Davis: Well, I suppose it is, in a way, it just lets them see. On the other hand I wouldna hae forced my man, you ken, it's something you hae to go ahead and do yourself. (Pat GM, Eiii)

Unlike the other changes which were noted, the grandfathers were not in any way criticized for not being involved with the actual birth of their children. Because the grandmothers too were somewhat ambivalent about this new development, and did not seem to wish that their own childbirths had been different, the opposing views of the grandmothers and grandfathers were not troublesome. However, the differences in their views on fatherhood generally were more marked. This gave rise to considerable controversy during the interviews. By implication discussion of the new fathers or of fatherhood today, heralded as good by the grandmothers, was critical of the grandfathers themselves as fathers:

> e.g. 1. Mrs Lawson: Aye 'cos *he* (GF) never changed a nappy.
> Mr Lawson: I did so.
> Mrs Lawson: You did not (laughs). He's telling lies, he did not.
> Mr Lawson: I suppose if they're forced to like, they'll di it. (Mat GP, 4aii)

> e.g. 2. SCB: So do you think fathers do more nowadays?
> Mrs Anderson: Oh yes, I mean in his day they thought that they should na di nothing.
> Mr Anderson: Oh I looked after Mark when you went into hospital to hae Alistair.
> Mrs Anderson: Aye but I mean Mark was four, nae a baby, there's no way you'd a looked aifter a six month old baby, I mean changing nappies and feeding. (Pat GP, 1bii)

Some of the grandfathers openly disagreed with their spouse's assessment either of fathers now, or of themselves as fathers:

> e.g. SCB: Do *you* think fathers do more nowadays?
> Mr Angus: I dinna ken, I don't think they do more than before, I don't think so. . . .
> Mrs Angus: Och Jimmy, you never changed a nappy in your life.
> Mr Angus: I'm nae saying about changing nappies, I'm saying. . . .
> Mrs Angus: Well, that's being more involved.
> Mr Angus: The lady asked. . . .
> {Mrs Angus: An' helping
> {Mr Angus: . . . if people were more involved nowadays, I don't think so.
> (Mat GP, 5aiii)

In this example the grandmother cited what for her was concrete evidence of what being more involved meant. The grandfathers did not treat these 'symbols', such as changing nappies, in the same way. For example, Mr Lawson (Mat GF, 4aiii), when asked whether he had ever changed a nappy, said, 'Maybe once or twice'. He then went on to tell me how the new granddaughter loved him, and always went straight to him when she came into the house. This was as if to say that the practicalities of the past or present did not necessarily mean that you were more or less involved, or that the child would not care for you just as much.

The grandparents talked about why things were different these days, drawing both on personal experience and general knowledge:

> e.g. Mr Anderson: I was aye (always) working.
> Mrs Anderson: If you really think back, I think they thought that 'cos we were at home, that we didna need any help.
> Mr Anderson: I suppose we did na think that you'd need any help, everything was aye done, and you're still the same, I come in and get my supper, I'll be sat in here smoking, I ken a' things done, dishes are all washed.
> Mrs Anderson: It's just my way ken. (Pat GP, 1bii)

Each grandfather's experience was different, and accounts for the subtle variety in their expressions about the meaning and significance of grandfatherhood and fatherhood. Those grandfathers who were described as having been 'good fathers' (because they helped out in the home, went shopping, or more especially played with or looked after the infants) could account for their own sons' behaviour as being earned. This occurred in two cases: Mr McCallum said that none of his boys would complain about helping out (Pat GF, 5biii); Mr Sinclair explained that his sons had been taught to help their wives and to be involved with their children (Pat GF, 4bi). Change and continuity could be accounted at a personal level or beyond the immediate family experience. The following example from the second interview with Mr and Mrs Angus showed the difficulties involved in making general claims from personal experience. After Mr Angus said that he did not think that men were more involved nowadays, Mrs Angus replied:

> Mrs Angus: Well, Tim'll be more involved.
> Mr Angus: Tim might but the lady asked if times had changed, well I don't think so, generally.
> Mrs Angus: Well, I da ken, 'boot folks in general, but Tim'll certainly di more than you did. (Mat GP, 5aii)

Others said that times had changed, even when within their own family the trend of increased paternal involvement was seen to have begun with the respondents' own child-rearing. This could be done once individual personal experience was considered atypical.

78174

e.g. Mrs Sinclair: None of my friends' husbands did what my husband did. There's none of their husbands would have gone out and hung out nappies. He really was an exceptionally . . . you know, *good* father. (Pat GM, 4biii)

It was clear from this study that most of the grandfathers had the opportunity to behave differently as grandfathers than they did as fathers, or as their own fathers did as grandfathers. Yet, this was because they were grandfathers, not because fathering as an institution had changed for them. Having more time, money and patience were cited as important. They did not have to worry about bringing the child up or making ends meet. To them grandfatherhood was in many ways totally new: it was different from being a father, yet different from past grandparents' roles. Grandmotherhood was perhaps more taken-for-granted: they saw the family during the day more, since most of the grandmothers worked part-time rather than full-time. However, the grandfathers certainly spent time with their grandchildren, and many activities were joint activities in the evenings or at weekends. Only one grandfather said that he felt left out, although as I have noted elsewhere lesser grandparental involvement in the early months of grandparenthood was perhaps taken for granted (Cunningham-Burley, 1984). Yet, the grandfathers did seem to enjoy grandfatherhood, and through comments made both by them and the grandmothers, an understanding of the experience of grandfatherhood can be developed.

The experience of grandfatherhood
In the early stages of grandfathering, the grandfathers' role was not clear cut. They did not become immediately involved in helping out, in knitting, or in talking about their grandchildren to friends — all activities which the grandmothers spoke about frequently. Not only were these activities associated with grandmothers but also with babies. Some of the grandfathers said that they would wait until the child was older:

e.g. Mr Douglas: Well, er, I think er probably the grandmothers'll be probably more closer to them when they're younger but once they get, er, they grow up a bit, I think the grandfather just takes as much part o' them as the grandmother. (Mat GF, 7ai)

As noted earlier, many of the grandfathers had not been involved with their children as babies. However, it was also recognized that they might end up being more involved with their grandchildren as babies than they had anticipated. This was because they had, for example, more time now than they had as fathers. Grandfatherhood brings with it the potential to do things differently. As one grandmother pointed out:

e.g. Mrs Henderson: He really wants the baby all the time — he's showing a greater love for her than any of his own. At least it seems that way — may be it isn't. (Mat GM, 2aiii)

In the case of those grandfathers who had been involved as fathers, grandfatherhood brought with it the chance to do things again. The constraints which the grandfathers felt affected their fathering (that is not having enough time), coupled with ageing effects (having more patience) were the very enabling features of grandfathering. They could be different, and enjoy their grandchildren in a different way from their own children.

Grandfatherhood did seem to be important to the grandfathers in the sample, they just found it difficult to express how they felt:

e.g. Mr Henderson: Everybody asks you, 'How do you feel being a grandfather?' But you can't say ... I don't feel any different yet it is a different feeling. Don't ask me to put it into words for you. (Mat GF, 2aii)

The grandmothers talked easily and effusively about what they did, and how they felt: the grandfathers did not. Grandfatherhood was both new and nebulous. Some of them joked about it rather than saying how they felt:

e.g. Mr Sinclair: After all it's more a woman's time isn't it, when kids are born, especially it's not so bad — father, but grandfathers — who wants to be a grandfather? I'm too young. (Pat GF 4bii)

Here the grandmother, worrying that I had taken the remark seriously said that her husband was only pulling my leg, and that he loved his grandchild and played with her all the time:

Mrs Sinclair: He's dotty about her really, he adores her, and he thinks there's no one like her. (Pat GM, 4bii)

The significance of grandfatherhood was thus difficult to explore, because of the grandfathers' difficulty in expressing their feelings (Cunningham-Burley, 1984). As the following example demonstrates, this does not mean that the experience of grandfatherhood was not something meaningful to them:

e.g. Mr Findlay: I would not show it as much as my wife. I never show my feelings outwardly — but inwardly I'll probably be just as excited or more excited. (Pat GP, 7bii)

In addition to grandfatherhood being a chance to be involved with children either again or for the first time, becoming a grandfather held other meanings. Although the grandfathers did not talk about doing very much in terms of grandparental activities at this early stage, they still described grandfatherhood as important, in a symbolic way. It is part of life, and thus both significant and important:

e.g. Mr Davis: It's part of life ... your child growing up, you having children, them having children ... it's er a part of life itself. (Pat GF, Di)

Conclusion

Although we do not know very much about grandfatherhood, this study has demonstrated that it is important to those becoming grandfathers. A sensitive approach to collecting data from men is needed to explore the meaning and significance of the family, or in this case grandfatherhood, in more depth. Existing work has tended to try to impose categories on to grandfathers in order to describe different grandparenting styles. There is a need for a more individually based, developmental perspective. An individual grandfather may have quite different experiences with different grandchildren, as his grandchildren get older, or as he himself ages. The research reported here has shown that each grandfather has a unique history of family relationships, although there were common threads across the sample. Grandfatherhood is bound up with experiences of fatherhood past and present. Its special features are that it is different from parenting, because of having more time, money and patience, yet different from grandparenting in the past because today's grandparents can do more for and with the family and child. Future work should explore these changes across an individual's life course, investigating cohort and period effects in more detail. This study produced some interesting data on the changing role of fathers from the grandparents' perspective. The fathering role was seen to have changed much more than the mothering role. Although this was welcomed by the grandmothers, it caused some trouble for the grandfathers: their own parenting was implicitly called into question, and they had to develop a role for themselves in a new family setting. Unlike Russell (1985) I did not find that the grandfathers regretted their own fathering, but saw it as appropriate for the time, and within the constraints of their working lives. The grandmothers, it seemed, could take much more for granted in developing their grandmaternal roles. In spite of these difficulties the grandfathers were enjoying the experience of grandfatherhood, not only in the practical sense of being with their grandchildren, but at a symbolic level as becoming a grandfather was part of the way life developed and progressed.

Notes

1. The notation used to identify a respondent couple, or respondent, makes reference to whether the couple or respondent are maternal or paternal grandparents, grandfathers or grandmothers (e.g. Mat GP or Pat GF), and also to the couples number (main study: 2a, 3b etc.), or letter (pilot study: A, B etc.), and to the interview number (i, ii, iii). The names are pseudonyms.

2. The study was conducted under an SSRC studentship (1979–82), at the Medical

Research Council Medical Sociology Unit, Institute of Medical Sociology, University of Aberdeen.

References

Backett, K.C. (1982) *Mothers and Fathers. A Study of the Development and Negotiation of Parental Behaviour*. London: Macmillan.

Baranowski, M.D. (1985) 'Men as Grandfathers', in S.M.H. Hanson and F.W. Bozett (eds) *Dimensions of Fatherhood*. Beverly Hills: Sage.

Bengston, V.L. and Robertson, J.F. (eds) (1985) *Grandparenthood*. Beverly Hills: Sage.

Burton, L.M. and Bengston, V.L. (1985) 'Black Grandmothers: Issues of Timing and Continuity of Roles', in V.L. Bengston and J.F. Robertson (eds) *Grandparenthood*. Beverly Hills: Sage.

Cavan, R.S. (1962) 'Self and Role Adjustment During Old Age', in A.M. Rose (ed.) *Human Behaviour and Social Process: An Interactional Approach*. Boston: Houghton Mifflin.

Cunningham-Burley, S. (1984) ' "We Don't Talk about it . . ." Issues of Gender and Method in the Portrayal of Grandfatherhood', *Sociology*, 18 (3): 325–38.

Cunningham-Burley, S. (1985) 'Constructing Grandparenthood: Anticipating Appropriate Action', *Sociology*, 19 (3): 421–36.

Garfinkel, H. (1967) *Studies in Ethnomethodology*. Englewood Cliffs, NJ: Prentice-Hall.

Huyck, M.H. (1974) *Growing Older*. Englewood Cliffs, NJ: Prentice Hall.

Robertson, J.F. (1977) 'Grandmotherhood: A Study of Role Conceptions', *Journal of Marriage and the Family*, 39, 165–74.

Russell, G. (1985) 'Grandfathers: Making Up for Lost Opportunities?' in R.A. Lewis and R.E. Salt (eds) *Men in Families*. Beverly Hills: Sage.

Troll, L.E. (1983) 'Grandparents: The Family Watchdogs', in T.H. Brubaker (ed.) *Family Relationships in Later Life*. Beverly Hills: Sage.

II

ATTEMPTS TO CHANGE PATERNAL ROLES

As we indicated in Chapter 1, there is a strong contemporary belief that men are becoming more active in family life. However, authors in this field have also noted that couples find the change to more equal roles exceedingly difficult. The chapters in this section highlight, firstly, the changes which some couples attempt to effect in their division of domestic labour, and secondly the problematic nature of such change.

In the first contribution, Lamb, Pleck and Levine (Chapter 7) draw upon a large body of mainly American literature to examine the influence of a change to more egalitarian parental and occupational roles upon the family. They consider the losses and gains for men and women in such positions and present the reader with a broad spectrum of issues which must be considered when attempting to understand, or instigate, greater paternal involvement.

Lamb, Pleck and Levine emphasize the need to look beyond the father's own reasons for, and perceptions of, increased involvement. Brannen and Moss (Chapter 8) follow their lead by focusing upon women in dual earner families who break with tradition and resume full-time employment when their babies are young. In such families fathers may be expected to become increasingly participant in infant care. However, despite apparent equality in their roles at work, Brannen and Moss find that couples do not radically alter their division of labour in the home. Indeed working mothers appear not to expect an increase in participation at this time. Brannen and Moss account for this disparity by revealing the lower status attributed to the wife's job (even when 'objectively' it is a higher status than the husband's). The authors claim that women place more emphasis upon the husband's emotional support than his practical participation in domestic work.

No country has made a more concerted effort in recent times to increase paternal involvement than Sweden. Sandqvist (Chapter 9) explains why this is the case, before detailing the major legal innovations in the Swedish Parental Insurance scheme, which has unfolded over the past fifteen years. As other commentators have noted, men make little use of important parts of the scheme and overall are less likely than their wives to take part in its operation. However, Sand-qvist's examination of the literature on parental involvement suggests that there have been modest, but significant, increases in fathers' participation in child-care over the past forty years, although she notes that this cannot be attributed solely to recent social policy changes.

The very existence of, and commentary upon, 'role reversed' families (where men take on the major responsibility for child-care) gives the impression of a shift in parental roles, despite the absence of adequate historical data with which to compare contemporary studies. However, Russell's discussion in Chapter 10 shows that we cannot assume that all couples who reverse roles make lasting and easy transitions into a new life-style. He describes the complexities and contradictions of reversed roles in a longitudinal study of Australian families. Both partners express reservations about their own and their partner's new roles and a large number of couples revert to what is termed the 'traditional' family form, having experimented with role reversal. Russell traces the strategies which couples use to return to the status quo and suggests social and psychological mechanisms which might halt this process.

7

Effects of increased paternal involvement on fathers and mothers[1]

Michael E. Lamb, Joseph H. Pleck and James A. Levine

For a variety of sociopolitical, economic, scientific and clinical reasons, considerable interest in the study of father–child relationships has emerged in the last decade. In the last few years, the focus has narrowed to concern about the effects of increased paternal involvement. Interest in, and concern about, the latter seems to be especially prominent among social service providers and clinicians — the major audience for this volume. For this reason, and also because the voluminous literature on paternal influences on children has been scrutinized quite extensively (e.g. Lamb, 1981a,b), we shall focus in this chapter on evidence concerning the effects of increased involvement on mothers and fathers.

Contrary to those who have argued for or against increased paternal involvement on the grounds that it will have generally positive or negative effects on children, mothers, and/or fathers, we believe there is little evidence that, and no coherent reason to expect that, increased paternal involvement in itself has any clear-cut or direct effects. Our argument is that increased paternal involvement must be viewed and can only be understood in the context of the family, circumstances, values, and the reasons for the increased paternal involvement. To be sure, paternal involvement and the attitudes/values associated with it *can* have positive consequences when it is in accord with the desires of both parents. However, consequences are likely to be mixed when either or both parents view the changed paternal role as an unfortunate temporary circumstance that flies in the face of their values and better judgement. Because of this, we think it is misguided to see increased paternal involvement as a universally desirable goal. Rather, we believe that attempts should be made to increase the options available to fathers, so that those who want to be can become more involved in their children's lives. Families tend to do best when they are able to organize their lives and responsibilities in accordance with their own values and preferences, rather than in accord with a rigid, socially determined pattern. As a result, we disagree with those who extol the advantages and benefits of increased paternal involvement. While there is evidence that fathers do have significant effects — both positive and negative — on their children's development, none of the evidence reviewed in this chapter suggests that increased paternal involvement *necessarily* has beneficial consequences for children, fathers or mothers. Instead, it seems that paternal involvement *can* have such consequences *when it is the arrangement of choice for the family concerned.* The goal of this chapter is to review the evidence supporting this conclusion.

There are, we believe three sorts of arguments that can be used to support the introduction of increased options for mothers and fathers. The first, and most common, is to focus on the effects of increased paternal involvement on at least *some* mothers, and fathers. The review of such arguments and studies occupies most of this chapter. Second, there are considerations of equity, which essentially hold that it is unfair for mothers to be expected to fill the roles of parent/homemaker *and* breadwinner, while fathers, focused nearly exclusively on breadwinning, have a markedly less onerous total workload. Third, there are arguments that stress the beneficial effects of choice — the notion that families that are free to make their own decisions about paternal involvement are, as a result, characterized by more harmonious relationships between contented parents who thus have positive effects on their children's development.

It is in relation to the effects on mothers and fathers that considerations of equity and the freedom of choice are most pertinent. Changes in levels of paternal participation are likely to produce major changes in the experiences and responsibilities of all family members, and since changes in the psychological status of any family member may affect his or her behaviour toward the others, indirect effects on child development and adjustment may result. These indirect effects could be as significant as the direct effects with which psychologists are typically concerned. For example, one of the best established findings is that when parents are satisfied with their lives and marital relationships, their children are more likely to be well-adjusted. Thus effects of increased paternal participation on mothers and fathers are interesting both in their own right and because they may in turn yield differences in the way these adults interact with their children. Unfortunately, we know little about such 'indirect effects', so we are only able to speculate about their importance.

What's in it for the mothers?
Many discussions of paternal involvement argue that paternal participation either is increasing or must increase in the future because this is necessary to ensure the satisfaction of mothers (e.g. Hoffman, 1983). These arguments often lay great stress on the well-known fact that an increasing number of women, including mothers, are now

permanent participants in the paid labour force. By 1978, 50 percent of the women in the US and 44 percent of the married women with husbands present were in the paid labour force, and the number of employed women is expected to rise to at least 57 percent by 1995 (Glick, 1979).

Employment rates are not substantially lower for married mothers in intact families than for women in general: in 1979, 52 percent of the married mothers of school-aged children and 36 percent of the married mothers of infants and preschool children were employed (Glick and Norton, 1979). For obvious economic reasons, employment rates are even higher among single mothers and Black mothers, both single and married (Glick and Norton, 1979). In other words, *most* American children now grow up in families in which both parents, or the single resident parent, are employed outside the home.

It is in relation to such families that considerations of equity have been used to justify the need for increased paternal involvement. Commentators such as Lois Hoffman (1977) and Lamb and Bronson (1980) have argued that levels of paternal involvement should increase and are increasing as a result of increasing rates of maternal employment. This occurs, suggests Hoffman, because it is unfair for employed women to be burdened with the demands of two roles — those of breadwinning and homemaking/parenting — while their husbands must deal with only one — that of breadwinning. This argument implies that role strain will be reduced, and marital satisfaction enhanced, when fathers are more involved. This is expected to be desirable not only for the women themselves, but also for their children, since contented parents tend to be better parents. Unfortunately, while arguments such as these have a common-sense plausibility, the empirical evidence suggests that they are not generally true.

Do mothers — especially employed mothers — want more help from their spouses?

There has been substantial controversy about whether or not maternal employment does lead to increased paternal participation in home and child-care (Hoffman, 1981 and 1983 *v*. Pleck, 1983). However, all agree that the *relative* involvement of men certainly increases in either case simply because their wives have much less time to devote to child-care, and that women seem to feel overloaded when employed (Pleck, 1983). It is also worth noting that because we do not have any longitudinal data available, we do not know whether maternal employment actually affects levels of paternal participation, whether paternal participation potentiates maternal employment as Sagi (1982) suggests, or whether some third factor (e.g.

liberal attitudes) affects both paternal participation and maternal employment. In the present context, we need simply note that whereas it is plausible that the life satisfaction of women may be enhanced by increased paternal participation, there is little evidence that appreciable changes in paternal participation have taken place in response to increases in women's total (family plus paid) workload. Furthermore, the argument that employed women would be substantially more satisfied if their husbands played a greater role in family and child-care is weakened by evidence indicating that only a minority of women seem to desire increased participation by their husbands in child-care, and that the rates are not appreciably higher for employed than for unemployed women (Pleck, 1983). If these expressed desires can be taken at face value, increased paternal participation may not have a desirable effect on life satisfaction in many families.

In fact, Baruch and Barnett (1981) found that women whose husbands did more child-care were less satisfied with their own role-pattern than were women whose husbands participated less. Of course, we do not know whether the low satisfaction precipitated increased paternal participation, rather than having been caused by it, as we have only correlational data available. However, Bailyn (1974) found that, whether employed or not, women were more satisfied when their spouses were 'family-oriented'.

If it is true that many women do not want their partners to become more involved in family work and child-care, the question is: 'Why?' The answer may lie in traditional patterns of female power and privilege. Some women may fear losing their traditional power and domination over home activities if they allow men to relieve them of even part of the home and family work which has always been their responsibility (Polatnik, 1974).

Does role overload affect the mental health of women?

Although there is only equivocal evidence that role overload (total of paid and family work demands) affects the mental health of women (Hauenstein et al., 1977; Pearlin, 1975; Radloff, 1975), there does appear to be a relationship between amount of family work for which women are responsible and reported marital adjustment. In a sample of dual-worker British families, Bailyn (1970) found that lowered marital happiness occurred when women had higher family workloads. A similar relationship was not found by Gross and Arvey (1977) but unfortunately the latter researchers used relative rather than absolute measures of family work. A large US survey conducted in 1973 reported that for employed wives with children, wives' marital happiness increased in proportion to increases in their husbands' absolute involvement in home and child-care (Staines et al., 1978). The relationship was not significant for unemployed women and their husbands. Analyses of data gathered in two surveys conducted in 1975–6 reveal somewhat different results, with the findings obtained in the study employing absolute measures showing different effects of increased family work on the reported marital satisfaction of men and women. Men who engaged in more family work reported better family adjustment, whereas when women did more, worsened family adjustment was reported. In the other study, time in family work had positive effects for both men and women. Unfortunately, the analyses reported did not indicate whether increased involvement by fathers increased mothers' satisfaction, which is our major concern here. However, it is significant that when employed mothers reportedly wanted their husbands to be more involved than they were, family adjustment and well-being were substantially lower. In other words, increased paternal involvement seemed likely to have desirable consequences when it was valued by mothers, whereas the failure of fathers to be more involved only had adverse consequences when it was desired by the women concerned.

This appears to indicate that the effects of increased paternal participation vary depending on the attitudes of the women concerned. Whatever burdens accrue to women who are both breadwinners and primary housekeepers and caretakers may be offset by the increased satisfaction obtained from employment or pursuit of a career. Further, individuals who find both parenthood and employment gratifying may maximize their total satisfaction by pursuing both, even if this increases their total workload (Baruch and Barnett, 1979; Owen et al., 1982; Stewart, 1978; Verbrugge, 1980).

As we emphasize repeatedly in this chapter, these results point to a need for recognition of the variability among families. There appears to be a substantial minority of families in which increased paternal involvement would alleviate a source of stress and dissatisfaction, and there appears to be another, perhaps larger, group of families in which this would not occur. Perhaps this is because many women are employed seasonally or part-time and because the amount of work involved in home and child-care has decreased as smaller families and labour-saving devices have become more common. In any event, the implication is that equity is not sufficient grounds for urging increased paternal involvement, because these considerations do not apply to many families. However, since at least some families would benefit in this way, there is reason for broadening the options that would allow some families to adjust levels of paternal involvement to suit their individual preferences.

Does paternal participation enhance wives' satisfaction?
It also seems possible that extensive paternal involvement would facilitate career advancement in their wives and thus contribute to an enhancement in their overall satisfaction. Both scholarly and popular analyses (e.g. Bird, 1979; Levine et al., 1981) have repeatedly noted that women with young children are considered employment risks because of the work–family conflicts that are likely to arise. These prejudices are likely to remain as long as women employees alone take time off to care for sick children, to attend parent–teacher conferences, and to supervise children during school holidays, for example. If male employees requested time off for these reasons, too, it might go a long way towards relieving the scepticism and prejudices concerning female employees in general, whether or not the individuals themselves had ever allowed work–family conflicts to interfere with their performance as employees. From this perspective, increased paternal participation may have important implications for the attainment of equal employment opportunities. At the very least, it may permit individual dual-career or dual-worker families to share and thus limit the adverse effects of work–family conflicts on either career.

As Russell's (1982, 1983, see Chapter 10) study of highly involved Australian fathers revealed, however, there are some potential costs. Many of the wives in his study expressed dissatisfaction about the quality of the fathers' home and child-care performance, and this in turn was a source of marital friction. Since most of the families did not choose their non-traditional life-style, but had it thrust on them by economic circumstances, one wonders whether similar concerns would arise in families where the unusual distribution of responsibilities was chosen on ideological grounds. Interestingly, Baruch and Barnett (1981) found that women were more dissatisfied when their husbands were less involved.

As mentioned earlier, many women claim not to want their husbands to be more involved in home and child-care (Pleck, 1983). Presumably, what motivates this is not simply a love of household and child-care chores, but a concern about marital power relationships and the assumed association between relative involvement in caretaking and relative affective importance to children. Although multiple interpretations are possible, these findings may reveal a concern on the part of many women that increased paternal participation would involve a loss of domination in the family arena and would bring about a dilution of exclusive mother–child relationships. These concerns are reasonable ones; it is hard to believe that mothers would feel the same sense of crucial importance to their children's development when child-rearing is shared with another person with equal investment and commitment. As long as motherhood remains a central aspect of self-definition for many women and as long as prospects for fulfilment in the employment arena remain uncertain, many are likely to fear the abdication or partial abdication of responsibility for parental care. Those who do so may experience ambivalence, regret and guilt. Further, mothers will no longer be able to count on obtaining custody of their children after divorce, because fathers who have been more involved in child-care may have established close relationships to their children, and may thus legitimately claim full or joint custody for themselves.

Summary
Increased paternal participation evidently will not bring equivalent and unambiguously positive effects for all women. While the sharing of responsibilities that have hitherto been the exclusive province of wives and mothers may relieve the total work overload of employed mothers and may facilitate their increased commitment to work roles, this will be achieved only at the expense of the exclusive, close relationships to children that mothers have traditionally enjoyed, and at the expense of the mothers' traditional domination of the home. Given the extent of 'socialization for motherhood' which most women experience, it is unlikely that these costs will be insignificant to many women. This underscores again that increased paternal involvement necessarily involves major changes in family responsibilities and roles and more specifically requires that women share power in the one arena in which their domination has hitherto been sacrosanct. In exchange for this, they obtain greater flexibility to pursue success and fulfilment in the occupational sphere, although attainment of either success or fulfilment is quite uncertain. At the very least, therefore, many women are likely to feel ambivalent about increased paternal involvement because increased involvement, while increasing the woman's opportunities and flexibility, also threatens her prerogatives in the one area where her domination and power has been assured. Whether a reallocation of parental responsibilities is desirable in any individual case depends on the relative evaluation of the costs and benefits, and this in turn will be influenced by the family circumstances as well as the attitudes and aspirations of the two parents. Further, even when the benefits on balance exceed the costs, some disadvantages and some misgivings are inevitable. Evaluation of the costs and benefits depends on the individuals' evaluations of the relative importance of factors such as career, motherhood, etc. Since this evaluation will vary from one family to the next, we believe that it is flexibility, rather than prescribed levels of paternal involvement — whether high or low — which is desirable.

What's in it for fathers?

However beneficial for mothers (i.e. wives/partners) and children, fathers are unlikely to change their life-styles radically so as to become more involved in child-care unless they feel that the changes are desirable and beneficial for themselves. In this section we consider what fathers stand to gain or lose from assuming a more extensive direct involvement in the lives and rearing of their children. Essentially, the issue here has to do with the choice between career and paternal involvement and this choice depends on the relative evaluation of the two.

Traditionally, fulfilment for men has been defined in terms of occupational and economic success (e.g. Cazenave, 1979; Benson, 1968; Pleck, 1983). Within the family, a 'good' father is one who is a reliable economic provider, and one who buffers other members of the family (especially mothers) from concerns about economic stresses. Of course, to the extent that their jobs permit them to play a more active role in the family — doing things with their wives and children — men have usually been lauded for direct involvement. However, economic provision has always been the sine qua non of the paternal role. Furthermore, although national statistics show that an increasing number of couples are now delaying child-bearing, most young families still have their children at a time when the career-oriented male is trying to establish himself and 'get-ahead'. As mentioned in Chapter 3, these circumstances exert a powerful brake on paternal involvement as there is little doubt that fathers devote time to child-rearing at the expense of the time devoted to their jobs. In many studies of role-sharing or role-reversing families, fathers have reported that their career advancement was adversely affected, or that a lack of concern with this made the changed life-style viable (e.g. Radin, 1982; Russell, 1982, 1983). In addition, many of Russell's highly involved fathers only adopted their roles when unemployment or underemployment made it a viable option. Even if they are able to maintain their productivity and professional skills while devoting additional time to their families, highly-involved fathers are likely to be perceived as less committed or less serious by colleagues and superiors, and thus their professional status and future prospects are deleteriously affected. As long as these factors are of central importance to men's evaluations of their success, increased paternal involvement would seem to be an unattractive proposition.

Thus far, there is no empirical evidence available concerning the effects of increased paternal participation on career advancement and income. As noted in the previous chapter, concerns about adverse effects of this sort appear to constitute one of the barriers to increased paternal involvement, and the fears certainly appear well-founded. The experiences of employed mothers indicate that when family responsibilities impede the ability to work long uninterrupted hours or go on business-related trips, the opportunities and promotions go to others, even when the individual is performing well within the range of contracted responsibilities. Bailyn's (1974) data suggest that the same is true for fathers, since family-oriented 'accommodators' seemed to be confined to lower status positions than their non-accommodative peers. Increased paternal participation is inimical with overtime and moonlighting as means of supplementing family income. Further, professional responsibilities are often at their maximum at precisely the time that family workloads are heaviest, which maximizes the cost of increased paternal involvement to career-committed men. As Veroff and Feld (1970) point out:

> at this point in the life cycle, work represents their attempt to solidify their career for the sake of their family's security. They are torn between their desire to establish a close relationship with their children and their desire to establish financial security for the family (p. 180).

The situation is also complicated by the fact that male employees continue to earn much more than female employees; this means that the reduced earnings of a father are offset only by disproportionate increases in the workload of their partners. Taken together, these considerations suggest that increased paternal participation may often entail a decrease in the family's present and future earning power. As long as this remains the case, increased paternal participation will be economically intolerable for many families. It will not become an acceptable option for others unless there is a radical change in the relative evaluation of career advancement and family involvement as determinants of individual male fulfilment.

Why might some men want to become more involved?
There is some reason to believe that young men today are less willing than their fathers or grandfathers to define personal success solely in terms of occupational and economic success. Many men today (such as those interviewed by Rubin, 1982), report dissatisfaction with the relationships they had with their fathers. This leads on to expect that these men will strive to be more involved than their fathers were, and indeed this is what some attitude surveys seem to suggest. In an admittedly unrepresentative sample of 'close to 2000 men', most of whom were *Esquire* readers willing to complete a questionnaire, Gail Sheehy (1979) found that many young men considered satisfying personal relationships — especially those with spouses and children — to be of great importance. Many commented that if it was neces-

sary to retard their occupational progress in order to have sufficient time for family relationships, they would be willing to do this, because fulfilment for them required some measure of success in close relationships as well as occupational achievement. These data thus suggest that at least some men are redefining 'success' in a way which might make increased paternal involvement attractive. Further evidence that fathers may be willing to increase their involvement in child-care and family roles more generally comes from a national survey reported by Pleck (1983). Pleck reported that the majority of fathers have a greater interest in, and derive more satisfaction from, their families than from their paid work. Of course, it is not clear from these data just what aspects of their family roles are most satisfying, and it cannot simply be assumed that these fathers are expressing a desire to become primary or even equal participants in child-care. For example, a 'traditional' man may express his commitment to family in the form of increased effort at the work place, since increased earnings enhance the quality of life he makes possible for his family. Thus, although there are clear historical trends, average levels of paternal involvement have risen surprisingly little (given the level of rhetoric) in the last two decades (Juster, in press). One reason for this may be that the effects of involvement on the quality of father–child relationships are more complex than many initially hoped.

Do closer relationships follow when fathers are more involved?
For this changing definition of male fulfilment to produce increased paternal involvement, increased involvement would have to facilitate closer, richer personal relationships and/or be intrinsically enjoyable. There is some reason to believe the first proposition to be true although we should view the data cautiously, since we do not have adequate data to conclude that involvement produced sensitivity and competence rather than that the more competent and sensitive fathers chose to become more involved. In a longitudinal study focused on the relationships among maternal and paternal attitudes about work, parenting and child-rearing, for example, Owen et al. (1982) found that men who valued parenthood highly were more involved in child-care and found parenthood more satisfying than did those for whom parenthood was less intrinsically important. Similar relationships were found by Frodi et al. (1982) in a study of Swedish mothers and fathers. Further, Russell (1982, 1983) and Kelly (1981) in Australia, Radin (1982) and Hood and Golden (1979) in the United States, Gronseth (1975) in Norway, Hwang (1982) in Sweden, and Sagi (1982) in Israel all found that highly involved fathers spoke favourably of their family arrangements. When dis-

satisfaction was mentioned, it was usually expressed by men who were not as involved in child-care as they would have liked. In each study, a common reason for the positive evaluation by highly involved fathers was that it allowed the fathers to become closer to their children, observe and participate in their development more closely, and feel more intrinsically important to their children. Thus the evidence supports the assumption that increased paternal involvement does make for closer, richer, relationships with one's children — at least when the men concerned opted for increased involvement when they wanted it and circumstances made it possible.

What are the other possible rewards of increased paternal involvement?

There is another way in which increased paternal involvement can be rewarding. As Goldberg (1977) and Lamb and Easterbrooks (1981) have argued, parents' sense of accomplishment and fulfilment is enhanced when they feel that they are competent and effective caretakers. One factor affecting caretaking competence is experience. For many traditional fathers, early uninvolvement by fathers allow mothers to develop their skills while fathers remain unskilled. Later, the perception that mother is more competent serves to limit fathers' involvement because he feels incompetent. The perception of personal incompetence serves to limit further involvement and thus the father does not have the practice and experiences that would give him the self-confidence needed to make active parenting a rewarding experience. By contrast, fathers who are involved in child-care rapidly realize that they can be just as competent and effective as their spouses, and thus fathering becomes an increasingly rewarding and enjoyable experience.

Consistent with these notions, two-thirds of the role-sharing Norwegian fathers included in Gronseth's (1975) small study ($n = 16$) reported that they understood their children better as a result of being home with them. Similarly, a quarter of the highly participant Australian fathers studied by Russell (1982) reported that their increased participation led them to a better understanding of their children and their everyday needs. Interestingly, they explicitly identified sole responsibility, rather than amount of time together, as the critical factor. Furthermore, the fathers reported that their increased competence and sensitivity made them feel more self-confident and more effective as parents. Finally, in Sagi's (1982) analysis of variously involved Israeli fathers, nurturance was highly correlated with the degree of paternal involvement. The only discordant findings were reported by Radin and Sagi (1982) and Radin (1982) in a study of highly involved American fathers whose behaviour was no more sensitive or nurturant than the behaviour of traditional fathers. It is not clear whether these discordant results reflect a cultural difference (all the other studies were conducted outside the US), or a difference in methodology, since only Radin and Sagi (1982) assessed nurturance on the basis of unobtrusive behavioural observations. In all other studies, however, highest satisfaction was reported by those fathers who were highly involved in child-care, while dissatisfaction with their current roles was limited to those fathers who were relatively uninvolved. It was the lack of sufficient contact with their children that seemed to result in dissatisfaction (e.g. Sagi, 1982).

How does increased paternal involvement affect the father's personality and feelings about himself?

While there is reason to claim that increased paternal involvement can be rewarding for fathers, it is important not to romanticize fathering or exaggerate the joys of parenting. In addition to the undeniable economic costs mentioned earlier, there are also personal and emotional costs the extent of which may vary depending on the reasons why fathers have chosen to be unusually involved in child-care. In other words, the costs and benefits will differ depending on whether fathers are involved because they cannot find paid work, because they are committed to sexual equity, because they enjoy children, or because their wives insist on greater paternal involvement. In the only long-term follow-up of men who had been primary caretakers, Russell (1982, 1983) found that many of the families returned to more traditional divisions of family roles. In retrospect, many of the men who had been primary caretakers had a fairly negative perception of their experiences, and these perceptions were frequently shared by their wives. The men's complaints sound familiar to those who have been monitoring the concerns of traditional mothers: they felt deprived of adult contacts and they found their lives boring and repetitive. In addition, many reported that neighbours, family and friends were consistently unsupportive and rather critical of the unusual divisions of family responsibilities. For their part, the mothers felt distanced from their children. Both parents in the role-reversing or role-sharing families felt that their lives were chaotic and rushed — a familiar complaint among dual-career families. Consequently, when the fathers were able to obtain well-paying jobs, they returned to paid work and reverted to more traditional roles within the family. In many of Russell's families, the non-traditional lifestyle was originally precipitated by economic circumstances (i.e. the fathers' inability to find jobs) rather than ideological commitment and we do not know whether the same negative evaluations would have been reached by fathers who had chosen increased involvement for ideological reasons. Further, while dual-career families inevitably experience more chaos, overextension, and stress than traditional single-career families, the question is whether that chaos is likely to be more or less when both parents share in breadwinning and parenting instead of having mothers fill these two roles while their traditional partners devote themselves exclusively to breadwinning. Interestingly, Gronseth's (1978) Norwegian subjects reported far more positive effects on the marital relationship than did Russell's (1982, 1983) Australian respondents. Perhaps this was because *none* of Gronseth's subjects worked full-time, whereas in Russell's study at least one, and often (50 percent) both, of the parents in each couple were employed full-time. Role overload would thus be more predictable in Russell's study.

Another source of marital conflict reported by Russell (1982), DeFrain (1979) and Lein (1979), had to do with the mothers' dissatisfaction with the quality of the fathers' child-care and housework. According to Russell, one reason for this was that the mothers felt threatened by their husbands' participation in traditionally female domains. However, in 30 percent of Russell's families, the increased conflict occurred mainly during a brief adjustment period beginning right after the non-traditional roles were adopted.

Bailyn's (1974) study of highly educated businessmen showed that the family-oriented accommodators had more negative self concepts — such as reduced self-esteem, and less confidence in their creativity or problem-solving ability — than did men who were more single-mindedly committed to their jobs. The accommodators were also more professionally passive and less successful professionally. They also tended to be in less prestigious jobs within their organizations, although it was not clear whether this was a cause or an effect of the family-oriented accommodative strategies.

Another adverse consequence of increased paternal involvement was described by Russell (1982, 1983) and Kelly (1981) in studies of Australian families. In both studies, highly participant fathers had more conflicts with their children than did less involved fathers. Similarly, Radin and Sagi (1983) found that highly involved fathers were perceived as more punitive by their children. As Russell (1982) suggests, these findings mean that highly participant fathers had more realistic (i.e. less romanticized) relationships with their children, which was seen as a positive consequence of paternal participation by mothers, but not by fathers!

Summary
Increased paternal involvement promises both advantages and disadvantages to fathers themselves. Among the costs are the likelihood

of diminished earnings and career prospects as well as retarded promotion, marital friction, dissatisfaction with the boring tedium of day-to-day parenthood, and social isolation from disapproving friends, relatives and colleagues. Among the advantages or benefits are the potential for personal fulfilment through closer, richer relationships to one's children, along with the opportunity to witness and influence their development more thoroughly. As in the case of mothers, the relative evaluation of the costs and benefits must depend on the individual's values and aspirations as well as both economic and social circumstances. Thus many men and many couples may find increased paternal involvement an undesirable option, just as their values and circumstances may make increased paternal involvement desirable for other couples. The fact is, however, that the number of men currently willing to sacrifice their careers and wage-earning roles in order to achieve greater involvement with their children is very small. The group is certainly not large enough to justify advocating increased paternal involvement for all.

Conclusion
The evidence reviewed in this chapter is sketchy, inconclusive and at times contradictory. This makes it difficult to make clear-cut defensible conclusions. As far as mothers are concerned, increased paternal involvement should reduce the total (combined family and paid) workload of employed women, although the empirical evidence suggests that maternal employment has not in the past substantially affected paternal involvement in housework or child-care and that, on average, many employed women today do not have a larger total workload than their husbands. On the negative side, increased paternal involvement will diminish, and perhaps eliminate, maternal domination in the child-rearing domain, and at least some women may resent this both because of its effect on marital power balance as well as because it may dilute and make less exclusive mother–child relationships. To the extent that fathers have less experience with home or child-care skills, mothers may find these responsibilities being fulfilled by others less vigorously (or at least differently) than they would like. Agreeing to share family work may facilitate women's advancement in the employment sector but there is always the risk that if the latter sector proves disappointing, women will find themselves without any arena in which they dominate.

For men, finally, the advantages of increased involvement in child-care may consist primarily of closer, richer and more realistic relationships with their children, coupled perhaps with the fulfilment of the desire to express nurturant feelings and behaviour. The costs are the retardation of career advancement, in terms of both money and status. As in the case of women, the relinquishment of domination in one arena brings the attendant risk of ending up between a rock and the proverbial hard place.

Individual characteristics and circumstances obviously determine whether the net costs exceed the benefits — at least in the eyes of the particular parents concerned. Effects on the children may well vary depending on the parents' evaluation of the changes, because if there is one general truism in developmental psychology, it is that contented, adjusted parents tend to have contented, adjusted children. Stated another way, we have to consider the effects of changing family roles on all family members even if our real interest is only in the psychological status of only one member. Since parents are most likely to be satisfied and contented when they feel fulfilled and actualized, the flexibility to divide family and breadwinning responsibilities in accordance with their individual preferences is of maximum importance.

The fact that increased paternal involvement may have both beneficial and detrimental consequences for mothers and fathers precludes us from concluding that changes in paternal involvement would necessarily be *either* 'good' or 'bad' in themselves. Clearly, each couple must weigh the potential costs and benefits in the light of their own values, attitudes and aspirations. Each decision about the distribution of child-care, household and paid work must represent an individual couple's appraisal of what arrangement appears best in the light of personal considerations and socioeconomic circumstances.

Note

1. This chapter is an abridged version of a chapter entitled 'The Role of the Father in Child Development: The Effects of Increased Paternal Involvement' which was published in B.B. Lahey and A.E. Kazdin (eds), *Advances in Clinical Child Psychology* (Vol. 8). Reprinted by permission.

References

Bailyn, L. (1970) 'Career and Family Orientations of Husbands and Wives in Relation to Marital Happiness', *Human Relations* 23: 97–113.

Bailyn, L. (1974) *Accommodation as Career Strategy: Implications for the Realm of Work*. Working Paper 728–74, Sloan School of Management, Massachusetts Institute of Technology.

Baruch, G.K. and Barnett, R.C. (1979) 'Fathers' Participation in the Care of their Preschool Children', Unpublished manuscript, Wellesley College.

Baruch, G.K. and Barnett, R.C. (1981) 'Correlates of Fathers' Participation in Family Work: A Technical Report', Unpublished manuscript, Wellesley College.

Benson, L. (1968) *Fatherhood: A Sociological Perspective*. New York: Random House.

Bird, C. (1979) *The Two-paycheck Marriage*. New York: Rawson, Wade.

Cazenave, N. (1979) 'Middle-income Black Fathers: An Analysis of the Provider Role', *Family Coordinator* 28: 583–93.

DeFrain, J. (1979) 'Androgynous Parents Tell Who They Are and What They Need', *Family Coordinator* 28: 237–43.

Frodi, A.M., Lamb, M.E., Frodi, M., Hwang, C.-P., Forsstrom, B. and Corry, T. (1982) 'Stability and Change in Parental Attitudes Following an Infant's Birth into Traditional and Nontraditional Swedish Families', *Scandinavian Journal of Psychology*, 23: 53–62.

Glick, P.C. (1979) 'Future American Families', *COFU Memo* 2 (3): 2–5.

Glick, P.C. and Norton, A.J. (1979) 'Marrying, Divorcing, and Living Together in the U.S. Today', *Population Bulletin* 32: whole no. 5.

Goldberg, S. (1977) 'Social Competence in Infancy: A Model of Parent–Infant Interaction', *Merrill-Palmer Quarterly* 23: 163–77.

Gronseth, E. (1975) 'Work-sharing Families: Adaptations of Pioneering Families with Husband and Wife in Part-time Employment', Paper presented to the International Society for the Study of Behavioral Development, Surrey (England), July.

Gross, R.H. and Arvey, R.D. (1977) 'Marital Satisfaction, Job Satisfaction, and Task Distribution in the Homemaker Job', *Journal of Vocational Behavior* 11: 1–13.

Hauenstein, L., Kasl, S. and Harburg, E. (1977) 'Work Status, Work Satisfaction, and Blood Pressure among Married Black and White Women', *Psychology of Women Quarterly* 1: 334–50.

Hoffman, L.W. (1977) 'Changes in Family Roles, Socialization and Sex Differences', *American Psychologist* 32: 644–57.

Hoffman, L.W. (1983) 'Increased Fathering: Effects on the Mother', in M.E. Lamb and A. Sagi (eds) *Fatherhood and Family Policy*. Hillsdale, NJ: Lawrence Erlbaum.

Hoffman, M.L. (1981) 'The role of the Father in Moral Internalization', in M.E. Lamb (ed.) *The Role of the Father in Child Development* , revised edn. New York: Wiley.

Hood, J. and Golden, S. (1979) 'Beating Time/Making Time: The Impact of Work Scheduling on Men's Family Roles', *Family Coordinator* 28: 575–82.

Hwang, C.-P. (1982) 'Attitudes to Paternity Leave', Presentation to the Bank Street College Research Colloquium.

Juster, F.T. (in press) 'A Note on Recent Changes in Time Use', in F.T. Juster and F. Stafford (eds), *Studies in the Measurement of Time Allocation*. Ann Arbor, MI: Institute for Social Research.

Kelly, S. (1981) 'Changing Parent–child Relationships: An Outcome of Mother Returning to College', Unpublished manuscript, University of Melbourne (Australia).

Lamb, M.E. (1981a) 'Fathers and Child Development: An Integrative Overview', in M.E. Lamb (ed.), *The Role of the Father in Child Development*, revised edn. New York: Wiley.

Lamb, M.E. (ed.) (1981b) *The Role of the Father in Child Development*, revised edn. New York: Wiley.

Lamb, M.E. and Bronson, S.K. (1980) 'Fathers in the Context of Family Influences: Past, Present, and Future', *School Psychology Digest* 9: 336–53.

Lamb, M.E. and Easterbrooks, M.A. (1981) 'Individual Differences in Parental Sensitivity: Origins, Components, and Consequences', in M.E. Lamb and L.R. Sherrod (eds) *Infant Social Cognition: Empirical and Theoretical Considerations*. Hillsdale, NJ: Lawrence Erlbaum.

Lein, L. (1979) 'Male Participation in Home Life: Impact of Social Supports and Breadwinner Responsibility on the Allocation of Tasks', *Family Coordinator* 28: 489–96.

Levine, J., Harlan, S., Seligson, M., Pleck, J.H. and Lein, L. (1981) *Child Care and Equal Opportunity for Women*. Washington: US Commission on Civil Rights.

Owen, M.T., Chase-Lansdale, P.L. and Lamb, M.E. (1982) 'Mothers and Fathers' Attitudes, Maternal Employment, and the Security of Infant–Parent Attachment', Unpublished manuscript.

Pearlin, L. (1975) 'Sex Roles and Depression', in N. Datan (ed.) *Lifespan Developmental Psychology: Normative Life Crises*. New York: Academic.

Pleck, J.H. (1983) 'Husbands' Paid Work and Family Roles: Current Research Issues', in H. Lopata and J.H. Pleck (eds) *Research in the Interweave of Social Roles*, Vol. 3, *Families and Jobs*. Greenwich, CT: JAI Press.

Polatnik, N. (1974) 'Why Men don't Rear Children: A Power Analysis', *Berkeley Journal of Sociology* 18: 45–86.

Radin, N. (1982) 'Primary Caregiving and Role-sharing Fathers', in M.E. Lamb (ed.) *Nontraditional Families: Parenting and Child Development*. Hillsdale, NJ: Lawrence Erlbaum.

Radin, N. and Sagi, A. (1983) 'Childrearing Fathers in Intact Families in Israel and the U.S.A.', *Merrill-Palmer Quarterly*, 28: 111–36.

Radloff, L. (1975) 'Sex Differences in Depression: The Effects of Occupation and Marital Status. *Sex Roles* 1: 149–65.

Rubin, L. (1982) 'The Search for Reunion', *Psychology Today*, June: 23–33.

Russell, G. (1982) 'Shared-caregiving Families: An Australian Study', in M.E. Lamb (ed.) *Nontraditional Families: Parenting and Child Development*. Hillsdale, NJ: Lawrence Erlbaum.

Russell, G. (1983) *The Changing Role of Fathers?* St Lucia, Queensland: University of Queensland Press.

Sagi, A. (1982) 'Antecedents and Consequences of Various Degrees of Paternal Involvement in Child Rearing: The Israeli Project', in M.E. Lamb (ed.) *Nontraditional Families: Parenting and Child Development*. Hillsdale, NJ: Lawrence Erlbaum.

Sheehy, G. (1979) 'Introducing the Postponing Generation', *Esquire* 92 (4): 25–33.

Staines, G., Pleck, J.H., Sheppard, L. and O'Connor, P. (1978) 'Wives' Employment Status and Marital Adjustment: Yet another Look', *Psychology of Women Quarterly* 3: 90–120.

Stewart, A. (1978) 'Role Combination and Psychological Health in Women', paper presented in the Eastern Psychological Association, New York, March.

Verbrugge, L. (1980) 'Women's Social Roles and Health', paper presented at 'Women: A developmental perspective: A conference on research'. National Institute of Child Health and Human Development, Bethesda, MD, November.

Veroff, J. and Feld, S. (1970) *Marriage and Work in America*. New York: Van Nostrand Rinehold.

8

Fathers in dual-earner households — through mothers' eyes

Julia Brannen and Peter Moss

Many studies of husbands' support in dual-earner households concentrate on routine participation in housework and child-care, drawing on a list of stereotypical tasks which are assumed to be appropriate and central to all types of households (see Pleck, 1985). There are, however, activities peculiar to the life stage and life-style of dual-earner households which are equally, if not more, important. These activities include the search for child-care; the servicing of child-care once found; and taking time off work to care for sick children. Husbands' involvement in these tasks form an important part of the support necessary to these households.

Other equally important forms of support need also to be considered. In addition to participation in *practical* activities, support involves social and emotional dimensions which range from the purely social to the profoundly personal. We refer here to individuals' needs for opportunities to discuss their decisions and situations with concerned and sympathetic 'significant others' and to express their feelings freely, including doubts and anxieties (Weiss, 1969; Caplan, 1974).

Returning to work soon after childbirth is a deviant course of action for women in Britain today, contravening the dominant ideology that mothers are the best persons to care for young children. For women who do return to work, social support in the form of services and entitlements is poor. Child-care provisions for infants and young children are very limited; qualifications for statutory maternity leave are so restrictive that only half of women giving birth are eligible (Daniel, 1980); those who do qualify must return on a full-time basis; and there is no parental leave or leave for family reasons. Not surprisingly, given this context, very few women return under the maternity leave provisions — an estimated 5 percent (Daniel, 1980). Altogether, including women who do not qualify for leave but resume employment, only 7 percent of women are back full-time within 8 months of first time childbirth.

For these reasons, those relatively few women who make the decision to stay in the labour market when they have children are likely to require support — emotional and social, as well as practical — in making that decision and in pursuing what is frequently a lonely and disapproved of enterprise. Men as husbands and fathers are most closely implicated in women's decisions to stay in the labour market. The nature of their support is therefore likely to be critical in shaping women's experiences.

In the first part of the chapter we review the nature of the support provided by husbands in households where women resume full-time employment after maternity leave, drawing on data from a longitudinal study being conducted at the Thomas Coram Research Unit. Next we discuss some of the possible explanations as to the extent to which men play, or fail to play, an equal part in the domestic division of labour. Lastly, we discuss the disjunction between an egalitarian ideology and the actuality of the domestic division of labour and why this does not necessarily lead to overt dissatisfaction with marriage on women's part. We present two cases from the study which bring together some of the themes of this argument. First, however, it is necessary to give some details of the study.

The study

The study is based on a sample of 188 two-parent households in which women said they intended to resume full-time employment within 9 months of the birth of their first child. The households were situated in the Greater London area, and the sample was first studied in 1982 and 1983. Women were interviewed on four separate occasions: before the return to work (5 months after childbirth) and again three times after the return when their children were 10, 18 and 36 months: the material presented in this chapter is drawn from the first two of these interviews. The children were also assessed and observed on three of the four occasions.

The research was intended to explore a number of quite distinct questions concerning the progress of young children in dual-earner households and women's experiences of combining full-time employment with motherhood. The study was not primarily concerned with men's participation in the domestic division of labour. Our initial interest in this issue was subsidiary to the question of *women's* experiences of the return to work after childbirth and was restricted to *women's accounts* of men's involvement and to their feelings about the support husbands provided or failed to provide. We therefore make no claims to represent men's perspectives. We would, however, argue that the dominant paradigm which assumes that women have major responsibility for children and housework is reinforced by theoretical and methodological approaches which continue to spotlight women as mothers and housewives and treat men as subsidiary to women in caring and servicing roles. A complete account of these issues is long overdue.

The decision to return

Before they returned to work, women were asked about their husbands' attitudes towards their return and also about the ways in which they found them helpful and unhelpful in making their decisions. Over the whole sample, the proportion of husbands thought to be in favour of their wives resuming work (41 percent) was almost equal to those thought to be opposed (44 percent). Within these overall figures, there were clear occupational differences; more husbands of women in professional and managerial occupations were reported as being in favour than husbands of women in lower status occupations (non-professional white collar and all blue collar workers) (57 percent as against 27 percent). The replies given by many of the women were tentative, because they were not wholly clear about their husbands' position: a number of women actually said that they had no idea what their husbands 'really' thought.

A qualitative analysis of a subset of interviews ($n = 48$) indicates why this apparent lack of knowledge is the case. Husbands' views were typified according to four main themes. Sometimes these occurred singly in women's accounts; sometimes they were found in combination. Frequently husbands' reported views and messages to their wives emerged as highly ambiguous. At one extreme husbands were reported as encouraging or instructing their wives 'to go back for the money', but also as saying that they would really prefer them to remain at home. According to a second theme, husbands acknowledged that their wives had no option but to return and yet at the same time voiced the view that 'It's entirely up to you'. The third theme applied to a group of husbands who were said to have expressed no views on the subject, thereby waiving responsibility for the decision altogether. Finally, a fourth theme concerned a couple of husbands who were reported as participating with their wives in the decision to resume work: one of these rare examples is described in more detail in the second case study later in the chapter.

Even though most women did not dissent from the view that they should be the ones to decide, they were not all happy with the responses of husbands, and especially those who 'sat on the fence', a strategy which enabled husbands to hide their own ambivalence. Moreover, by failing to express a clear, unequivocal view, men could abdicate responsibility both from the decision and from its consequences. However, reporting a particular stance as unhelpful did not necessarily lead women to criticize their husbands directly.[1] Criticism was often implied or muted, or it was balanced out by positive statements: 'He's very good really'. (See also Backett (1982) for the notion of 'balance' as a coping mechanism in marital disagreements.)

Taking responsibility for the decision to return implies further participation and responsibility once women are back at work. The kinds of responses from husbands which women reported as helpful bear this out. The *promise* of future responsibility for an involvement in the care of the child and the domestic chores was most likely to buoy women up before they went back to work. For example, support lay in knowing that a husband, who was a teacher, was prepared to look after the child at home throughout the school holidays.

Making child-care arrangements
Only a handful of child-care arrangements were described as being made by fathers alone (4 percent), or by both parents together (14 percent). Husbands appear largely to have limited themselves to a discursive role; only a quarter were reported as having done anything practical to help, mainly visiting the proposed placement to give a 'second opinion'. Though most men (88 percent) were reported as being involved in discussions with their wives, the extent of this varied and did not necessarily lead to a joint decision, as the following comment indicates:

> I had to make the decision. My husband and I talked it over and tried to make a list of the pluses and minuses . . . I think in the end he just wanted me to do what I felt happiest with.

In only a third of cases did the women describe the final decision about the child's care as 'joint'. Even those men who were substantially involved in discussion 'sounded' distant.

By abrogating responsibility for these decisions, husbands implicitly reinforced the perspective that child-care is ultimately women's responsibility, and women's resumption of work is 'their choice' rather than a household or couple decision. Yet, despite this limited involvement of fathers in the choice of the actual care arrangements for their children, three-quarters of the women, in response to a direct question, reported their husbands as supportive. Again women showed a marked reluctance to be overtly critical of their husbands. However, reflecting back some two-and-a-half years later on the experience of finding child-care for her young baby, Mrs Mason's account indicates what a lonely and unsupportive experience it can be. A person with whom to share the experience might have proved very helpful at the time:

> It's quite a daunting thing to do when you've got a little one in a pram. You've to 'phone all these people up and say 'Will you take my child? I don't know who you are but will you take him?' It was very hard. I

wouldn't like to have gone back and done that again. And you do all that on your own because you haven't got the support. That was the one time I could have done with my husband's support to be with me then and to go round and do that. (Did you ask him?) It was impractical because of work ... And the only time I could have gone with my husband was the evening and I thought that was a bit silly — just to go and see her and the house. It was a bit false! (Ann Mason, aged 29, a teacher, married to a college lecturer)

Participation in routine child-care and housework
At our second interview — some 10 to 11 months after childbirth — we asked women if their husbands' participation in child-care and housework had changed since their return to work. A third reported no change and a few (5 percent) a reduction. In most cases (55 percent) women said their husbands' participation had increased. Even so, equality in the domestic division of labour was far from being the case. Women were asked to complete 'forced choice' questionnaires upon which they recorded the proportions of house-work and child-care tasks they performed. On total scores women were clearly doing well over half of the tasks covered and men well under half.[2] The differences were more marked for housework, with 80 percent of husbands scoring less than half marks.[3]

In a 'typical' working day, in the time between the child waking in the morning and being put down for the night, women spent on average 1.6 hours more than their husbands with their child. This was partly because husbands spent longer at work (Moss and Brannen, Chapter 3, this volume), but also because women were much more likely to take children to and from caregivers: 72 percent of children were taken by their mothers, 14 percent by fathers and 13 percent by both parents. Women were also more likely to take time off work for child-care reasons, though the amount of time taken seems remark-ably little. Since returning to work, 65 percent had had time off for this reason, though only 29 percent had had more than two days; the figures for men were 33 percent and 10 percent respectively. As a final example, at the 10 months interview, 59 percent of the children had woken in the night at least once in the previous week. In just under a third of these cases (31 percent), seeing to the child was described as equally shared: of the rest, 9 percent of fathers did most or all of the getting up, compared to 60 percent of mothers.

Satisfaction with husbands' support and involvement
In our analysis we are essentially concerned with two types of data. The first type is responses to direct questions concerning how women felt about their husbands' involvement in certain areas — such as housework and child-care — or in certain processes — like making

child-care arrangements. Women's replies to these questions were coded and treated quantitatively and statistically for the whole study group. In reply to these questions, women emerged as relatively satisfied. To take several examples, only 15 percent of women felt their husbands had been unsupportive about their decision to resume work, and only 13 percent said they would have liked their husbands to have been more involved in making child-care arrangements. Dissatisfaction was somewhat greater with respect to routine child-care and housework tasks, where just over a third (36 percent) of women were critical of the amount their husbands did. However, criticisms were often muted, qualified or made only after follow-up probes to the direct questions.

The second type of data is qualitative material from women's accounts, where they talked spontaneously about *specific* happenings and circumstances. According to these accounts, women emerged as more dissatisfied with their husbands in the sense of being critical of their specific actions or failure to act. Some of this material will be illustrated later in the chapter.

Commitment to domestic equality

It may be argued that women did not complain a great deal about the unequal division of labour because they did not believe in it. However, questions aimed at exploring whether women subscribed at a general normative level to the notion of equality in the domestic division of labour indicate a high level of overt commitment. Asked whether fathers and mothers of very young children ought to participate equally in child-care and housework when both are in full-time employment, 84 percent approved without qualification.

Significantly, though, women did not comment or elaborate on what an equal relationship might entail. So, while the women in our study agreed in general terms with the notion of equality, there was little evidence either that such equality operated in practice or that women had well developed concepts of what equality would actually entail. This is hardly surprising, given a lack of appropriate role models or of widespread discussion of such issues in British society. The dominant ideology, and the resultant social construction of 'good' motherhood and fatherhood, provide no useful guidelines to dual-earner households seeking a genuinely equal and mutually supportive relationship.

Explaining the lack of equality

Given that men and women in our study were, at least in theory, equally attached to the labour market — why did they not share more equally in the domestic division of labour? Other studies of dual-earner households have proposed a number of explanations.

Whether women work *full-time* rather than part-time is seen to be one of the key determinants of the division of housework and child-care between husbands and wives. In the Women and Employment Survey, for instance, 44 percent of wives who worked full-time said they shared the housework equally with their husbands, compared to 23 percent who worked part-time (Martin and Roberts, 1984). However, as our study and the Women and Employment study both indicate, mothers and fathers in full-time employment were a long way from distributing the work and responsibility equally.

Income equity between the partners has also been proposed as an important precondition of male participation in housework chores (Scanzoni, 1978). The evidence here though is conflicting. A study of 'cross-class' families — that is, women in professional and managerial jobs married to men in manual work — came to the opposite conclusion (McCrae, 1986). Yet another study concludes that income equity leads to men's *refusal* to participate in the domestic division of labour (Paloma and Garland, 1971). In our study, women on average took home 80 percent of their husbands' net earnings, with 25 percent of the women earning the same or more than their husbands. We have so far found no significant relationship between level of earnings and level of performance in child-care and other aspects of the domestic division of labour.

A third explanation suggests that husbands' participation in domestic work is dependent upon how far both partners assume *primary involvement* in their employment roles, with the dual-career marriage representing the epitome of equality. Gowler and Legge (1978) cite here as examples the dual-career marriages from the Rapoports' study (Rapoport and Rapoport, 1976). Gowler and Legge (1978) argue that the employment involvement of the partners affects the nature of the 'work contract' in the marriage. Thus the dual-career marriage (the non-conventional model) is typified by the open or overt domestic work contract, and is contrasted with the dual-earner marriage (the conventional model) where the domestic work contract is hidden or covert. The dual-career marriage is identified as being egalitarian, since the couple has worked out explicit ground rules as to how the various stringent demands upon them should be reconciled. In this respect 41 percent of women in our study said they had not discussed the organization of child-care and housework with their husbands before resuming work, while a further 27 percent said they had discussed, but reached only a vague agreement about how this work was to be organized. This left less than a quarter of women (22 percent) who reported they had agreed a specific arrangement with their partners which had been followed.

In relating the effects of employment upon the domestic division of labour we would argue that it is especially important to take account of men's and women's employment *orientations*. (For a discussion of the concept of work orientation see Dex, 1985.) These are likely to have more explanatory power than simple income or work hours effects. For the importance that men and women attach to their jobs and to their earnings is likely to affect the importance they place upon child-care and housework. Moreover, the social context in which these employment orientations are shaped spans both private as well as public domains — that is, it is not restricted to the labour market.

Despite the fact that both parents in our study were in full-time employment, differences in employment orientation were apparent. For example, we have evidence on the ways in which women viewed their earnings. In response to direct questions, at the second interview just after the return to work, about items of household expenditure almost all the women in the study reported their earnings as contributing to the basic expenses of the household. At the same time, though, many women did not *define* their financial contributions as essential to their household (Brannen and Moss, in press).

Moreover, many women did not envisage staying in continuous and/or full-time employment. Often their resumption of full-time employment after a first child was seen as a temporary measure, or at least as always open to the possibility of change, if circumstances required or permitted. Indeed, by 18 months after the birth, a quarter of the women in our study who initially had returned to full-time employment had stopped work or gone part-time, while over a longer period, the rate is likely to be substantially greater, especially after the birth of second or subsequent children. The Women and Employment Survey illustrates the long-term attrition process: 16 percent of women had returned to work within 6 months of their first child's birth, but only 3 percent of women with more than one birth had returned within 6 months of each birth (Martin and Roberts, 1984).

Many women, therefore, were defining the importance of their jobs and earnings in terms of family and household priorities *at the time* — in their terms as 'luxuries' and 'extras' or as stop-gaps until husbands' pay increased, husbands' job prospects improved, or the households' current financial crises were overcome. In these ways women at this moment in their life often defined their own employment as optional or secondary to their husbands', although in practice their financial contributions to household expenditure were similar.[4] Such definitions of the situation are likely to have profound implications for attitudes to child-care and domestic work and for orientations towards housewife and parenting roles. It is also worth pointing out that women's employment orientations gave no hint that they had considered the possibility that at some stage in their marriages they might become solely dependent upon their own earnings, because of divorce or husbands' unemployment.

In Britain the 'good' husband and father is still one who prefers his wife to take major responsibility for the children when they are young (Lewis, 1986), and the 'good' mother does not 'leave' her children (Oakley, 1974). These normative stereotypes prevailed even in the atypical group of women returning to full-time employment after childbirth. Husbands were reported as preferring their wives to have the choice of leaving rather than continuing in the labour market after childbirth — a kind of 'freedom from' rather than 'freedom to'. Where that choice was not available husbands were said to want their wives to go back to work to alleviate the immediate household financial squeeze.

This particular notion of the 'good husband' is part and parcel of the wider discourse of men's principal role as breadwinners and women's as carers. It is within this set of meanings that women 'choose' whether or not to go back to work. After childbirth only mothers have these decisions to make; fathers take for granted their own employment careers (see Moss and Brannen, Chapter 3, this volume). There is of course a material basis for this, since men's employment and earnings prospects continue to be significantly better than women's. In this sense, women's decisions to return to work are theirs alone.

Explaining women's satisfaction with inequity
Given the fact that husbands and wives were almost equal in terms of their employment attachment — jobs, hours and earnings — it is perhaps surprising that women expressed so little overt dissatisfaction. There seem to be two explanations for this apparent paradox. The first involves bringing together some of the features of the women in our study and of their situation which we have already noted. Many defined their employment as secondary to their husbands; women's resumption of work was widely seen as 'their choice' rather than a household or couple decision; their actions in resuming full-time employment were 'at odds' with the dominant ideology about 'good' motherhood; and equality was supported as a very general ideal, rather than as an elaborated concept supported by an explicit role model. In such circumstances, women's criticisms of their partner's level of involvement and support were restrained, either because the women basically accepted that they should assume primary responsibility for child-care and housework; or because

feeling critical of their partner's contribution to child-care and housework triggered or exacerbated personal doubts and guilt, which in turn muted, qualified or repressed altogether this criticism of others.

The second explanation concerns the expression of marital dissatisfaction. Sociological studies have tended to see marital dissatisfaction as a consequence of conflict between beliefs and behaviour (see McCrae, 1986). We would suggest that the issue is more complex. Certainly our study provides many examples where women expressed a commitment to housework and child-care being equally shared which was at odds with the reality of their husbands' actions. And yet they professed themselves to be relatively satisfied overall with their marriages and with husbands' support. From women's point of view, the viability of a marriage is probably ultimately dependent, not upon what men do (nor how much they 'help'), but upon what aspects of husbands' support are most salient to them.

One of the most significant features of the expressed dissatisfaction with marriage is that it is largely directed to those aspects which are salient to the couple ideology, or what has been called the 'companionate' marriage (Gorer, 1970; Walker and Chester, 1977; Heisler and Whitehouse, 1976; Brannen and Collard, 1982). That is, people get seriously fed up with each other when the symbols that represent their aspirations for the institution are put under threat and the disguise that helps them to pretend that 'everything is fine' no longer holds up. In this context wives complain when husbands no longer make them feel good, when communication, affection and emotional support are lacking. And it is wives, rather than husbands, who appear more likely to be dissatisfied with the absence of these facets of their relationships (Brannen, 1985; Thornes and Collard, 1979). Studies of troubled marriages suggest that women regard communication and affection as of paramount importance in the fulfilment of emotional needs and that they more readily complain when these are transgressed than when other needs are not met (Brannen and Collard, 1982).

This is perhaps the only part of the marital ideology of 'sharing' that has an actual basis. Moreover, many couples may never have held realistic expectations of equality in the domestic division of labour. A study of newly weds suggests that, despite an overt commitment to 'sharing', even within months of marriage couples negotiate a division of labour in which husbands figure as the primary breadwinners and women as secondary earners with the major responsibility for domestic chores (Mansfield, 1982). Furthermore, the couples justified this division of labour in terms of the *anticipation* of parenthood. Such findings are not inconsistent with those of other studies which have found that the onset of parenthood is marked by a clear division of domestic labour.[5]

Thus our argument concerning women's lack of overt dissatisfaction with inequity in marriage is that women are only likely to complain in a global way when their trust in their partners is shaken at a fundamental level and the basis of the marriage is thereby put in jeopardy. Women do not, however, keep totally silent about their husbands' lack of involvement in domestic work. Rather, they express a muted criticism. This emerges in talking about specific incidents and events in their everyday lives which often appear to contradict their general statements about husbands' support (see Wilson, 1986; Brannen, 1986).

This muted criticism arises in a social context in which there are major dominant ideological constraints against revealing to other people the private world of marriage, especially its negative side. In our society a high value is placed upon a 'happy marriage' and the primacy of one's loyalty to one's partner despite, and perhaps because of, the high divorce rate. However, this is not to say that *women* do not talk about their marriages to certain significant others, though it appears the men do not (Brannen and Collard, 1982). As the qualitative material from our dual-earner study suggests, unless marriages were already at the point of collapse women tended to qualify and to draw back from any specific criticisms they made of their husbands or from any admission of dissatisfaction which emerged in talking about incidents in their everyday lives. Such strategies, though not necessarily conscious, allow women to avoid overt conflict and thereby prevent the possible withdrawal of husbands' affective support, which is at the heart of the ideology of the modern companionate marriage. Moreover, this emphasis upon the centrality of affective support in marriage serves to obscure the objective and subjective reality of women's economic dependence upon their husbands. Although this latter issue appears on the surface not to apply to women in our study, the fact remains that women's continuing attachment to the labour market was likely to be considerably affected by having the major responsibility for children.

Two case studies
We turn now to two case histories which may throw some light on the *process* of women's apparent acceptance of the unequal division of child-care and domestic responsibility in dual-earner households. In the interpretation of the interview material we attempted to take into account not only the general substantive meaning conveyed by respondents' words, but also some of the subtleties of expression — such as silences, retractions, contradictions, tentative and muted

responses. These responses are treated not as methodological problems which have inhibited our access to what people are 'really saying'. Rather they are of theoretical significance and are regarded as data which are valid in their own right. The very form of the data is therefore integral to its interpretation (Cunningham-Burley, 1985; Brannen, 1986; Wilson, 1986).

Mrs Dunman left school at 18 after achieving the educational requirements for entry to university. She decided not to take up the university place she had been offered, and instead took a job as a scientific officer in local government. At the age of 21 she married Mr Dunman, a postman, and two years later she resigned from her job because, she said, she had grown 'bored' with it and became a full-time shift worker answering telephone calls for one of the emergency services. Just beforehand, Mr Dunman had started to work nights 'And so the shift work appealed to me'. She became pregnant at the age of 30, 'We drifted into it' . . . it wasn't a conscious decision. We never said "Now is the time".' Her husband was worried about the financial implications of the baby, assuming that Mrs Dunman would give up her job.

> But once we came to a decision that I would try to find a part-time job then he was happy . . . And gradually he came round to the idea that I would probably go back to my old job. And gradually I realized *I* would miss it — that I would miss the money and to be quite honest that I would miss working. Before that I'd felt I *should* give up rather than I wanted to . . . My husband's never expressed any worries about the baby. I think perhaps if we were going to put him with a childminder five days a week instead of his mum having him then it would have been a bit different. But with the shift work (referring to her job only) it's almost like part-time.

Mrs Dunman earns significantly more than her husband, who has ceased to do overtime. However, Mrs Dunman still regards him as the main breadwinner, justifying her beliefs according to the traditional gendered pattern at this time of life, with the man as the main provider and the woman as having main responsibility for children and the home. She returned to her old job with a view to trying to job share if her employer would agree.

Just after resuming work she said:

> I don't see any possibility of him giving up work to stay at home. He is the one that matters. If I lost my job I feel sure I could get some part-time job to fit in with home life. (Because?) Yes, because I'm a married woman and I chose to get married and I suppose I do feel that mothers tend to be closer to their own children than fathers.

Two and a half years after the first interview, and having had a second child, she was still in the same full-time job and her employer still opposed to job-sharing.

In practice Mr Dunman was a moderately participative father, though he did little housework. Before the return he was reported as content with his wife's return to work, though in principle he disapproved of mothers of young children working. Once Mrs Dunman resumed work he changed to an afternoon shift so as to be able to take the baby back and forth to his mother's on the days when Mrs Dunman worked on a day shift. One weekend in four he looked after the baby for a whole day.

Questioned about her husband's participation in domestic work, Mrs Dunman's account displays a number of contradictions. A few months after her return she was asked about specific difficulties connected with going back to work, and she spontaneously mentioned her evident annoyance with her husband 'when he sits there reading the paper and I'm trying to do something'. However, any expressed criticism of her husband was limited to this situated contextual account. Moreover, even here criticisms were moderated by the mention of 'redeeming features': 'But he's generally very good'. Asked later in the same interview about her feelings about her husband's contribution to housework and child-care, Mrs Dunman hardly alluded to her earlier criticism. She says:

> I'm quite happy. I'm happy if he plays with the baby so I can do something else. Yes, I wouldn't expect him to do any more. (What about the housework?) Well, I would like him to do more. (Have you asked him?) Yes, frequently! (What was his reaction?) He said 'Yes' but he doesn't usually.

Mrs Dunman did not comment further and effectively ended the discussion of the topic at this point.

Yet elsewhere in the interview Mrs Dunman was asked her views about sharing child-care and housework equally when the parents of a young child worked full-time. She appeared somewhat ambivalent, shifting between the belief that parents ought to share, the actuality of the situation, and excuses as to why her husband did not participate.

> As far as housework goes he has things to do. He tends to clean the car and look after the garden (which the interviewer had noted was very overgrown!) So it's probably — it's fairly equal, yes. (Do you think parents ought to share or not?) I don't necessarily think equally, it depends on circumstances but I think they should share.

Mrs Dunman regards Mr Dunman as a 'good' husband because he conforms to her expectation of him as the main breadwinner and she sees the home and children as primarily her responsibility. Anything he does over and above these expectations she is 'grateful' for. She therefore chooses to ignore the reality of their situation, namely that they are *both* full-time workers and that she is in fact the higher earner. Moreover, the way in which she carefully refrains from further criticism and her obvious reluctance to express any overt dissatisfaction with her husband's unwillingness to do housework needs to be viewed in the broader context of the way she feels about her marriage and the power relations within it.

We did not explore the emotional aspects of marriage in great detail in this study, though we asked some salient questions which are 'good' indicators of the quality of respondents' marriages. Mrs Dunman described her husband as her only close confidant on 'personal matters' and the person she felt closest to in her life. Asked about her husband's understanding of her situation as a working mother she described him as 'very understanding'. Questioned three years after the birth she numbered him as the first among the three most supportive people in her life since they became parents. Asked in what way he has been supportive she says:

> He'll be quite happy to do anything as required and we can always talk about the children. So in both respects he's very helpful.

What is important to her is that, as a couple, they can communicate well. But also of importance is the *belief* that her husband will help out if necessary, as opposed to actual evidence of practical assistance (which is not to say he had not been helpful). His support is therefore expressed and experienced as *potential* rather than actual and thereby has a *symbolic* ring to it. It is in this context that the ambiguous and contradictory features of Mrs Dunman's account of her husband's failure to contribute to the housework need to be interpreted. Though criticisms are made, they are tentative, low key, and kept well under wraps so as not to threaten one of the bedrocks of the relationship — the belief and the feeling that the relationship is central to Mrs Dunman's identity and to her feelings of security.

The second case presents a number of contrasts. The father is more participative: indeed the couple offer one of the few examples in our study of a genuinely equal relationship within a dual-earner household. Another difference concerns the quality of the account. While Mrs Dunman's account was characterized by ambiguity and contradiction, Mrs Barrett's was marked by a certain terseness or absence of elaboration, even though she was a highly articulate and talkative person. The character of this account reflects the lack of role models in Britain and the absence of an articulated ideology beyond the blanket notion of marriage as a 'sharing partnership' and bald statements asserting egalitarian practice.

Mrs Barrett left school at 18 and took a degree at a polytechnic, where she met her husband. Two years later they married. Both work in local government and they have maintained parallel careers but in different local authorities. Mrs Barrett was 29 when she had her first child. Mr Barrett is two years older than her. At the start of the study they were both on similar administrative grades and earned roughly the same salaries, though Mrs Barrett had just overtaken her husband in the promotion stakes by the fourth round of the study. They decided to try for a baby 6 months before Mrs Barrett got pregnant. Mr Barrett was said to be in favour of Mrs Barrett's decision to return to work:

> He is supportive of what I want to do. He sees it as my decision first but I think he would want me to go back anyway . . . It's something we've talked about before the pregnancy and even before marriage.

Moreover, in terms of practical participation in child-care and domestic work, Mr Barrett was described thus:

> Since the baby was born he's reacted as if I was back at work. He's shared it. He's not really treated me as if I was at home.

Mr Barrett was unable to play an active part in finding the child-care placement because of a serious illness, though he was described as helpful in discussing 'the sorts of questions I was going to ask the childminder'. Once Mrs Barrett was back at work they divided up the household tasks and child-care on an equal basis, both sharing the 'ferrying' of the child to the childminder. Without qualification, she described herself as feeling satisfied with the domestic division of labour.

As to beliefs about equality, Mrs Barrett's replies were unequivocally in favour of equality on all fronts, including all aspects of the domestic division of labour. Furthermore, she regarded her own and her husband's job as equally important, and them both as breadwinners.

Concerning the emotionally supportive quality of their marriage, like Mrs Dunman, Mrs Barrett described her husband as her main confidant on personal matters. Mrs Barrett did, however, mention other people she also felt she could turn to, which perhaps suggests a minor modification to the exclusivity of their marriage. Questioned about the ways in which her husband was understanding of her situation as a working mother, Mrs Barrett significantly described him as not merely 'very understanding', but as sharing the same feelings as herself:

> I think he feels the same. It's something we've talked about. I'm in the situation he was in for the first six months of the baby's life. We talk from similar standpoints. I was seeing to the baby every day and he was going off to work in the morning. Now I'm experiencing what he's already experienced.

As suggested above, Mrs Barrett's account is not just marked by the absence of criticism and qualification, she also failed to elaborate very much upon a model of a shared and equal relationship, and gave little idea of what such a division of labour might look like in practice. The only area about which Mrs Barrett was particularly expansive and articulate concerned emotional support, which is described in terms of the mutually reciprocal experience of 'putting oneself in the place of the other'. However, in spite of this 'reticence', she suggested on a number of occasions in the interview that their *modus vivendi* was one which she and her husband had talked about and worked out together over many years.

Conclusion

In this chapter we have considered key aspects of husband's support for the dual-earner life-style among families with very young children. These have included husbands' participation in decisions and activities peculiar to the dual-earner life-style, in routine housework and child-care, and husbands' emotional support. Where both partners in a household combine parenthood and full-time employment, still a rare course of action in Britain, it may be too easily assumed that men and women will negotiate egalitarian roles in marriage. The analysis of our data thus far suggests that lip service is paid to an egalitarian ideology but women continue to bear the bulk of the responsibility for children, for maintaining the child-care arrangements, and for the housework. Despite a clear gap between beliefs and practice, women tended to play down their dissatisfaction with this state of affairs, and expressed it in a muted form. We have suggested that this strategy is a response to ambivalent feelings about responsibility, as well as being intended to avoid marital conflict. (Bell and Newby, 1976) discuss similar kinds of marital behaviour in terms of the concept of deference.) Women are likely to express dissatisfaction only when their marriages are in serious jeopardy. Overt conflict tends to occur as a result of much more 'serious' infringements of the rules of marriage — the revelation of an affair, for example (Brannen and Collard, 1982). For salient to the ideology of the modern companionate marriage are notions of romantic love, intimacy, and a strong emotional investment. To put the sharing ideology to the test by complaining about inequalities in the domestic division of labour in a society where there are no sanctions guarding against their infringement is likely to be regarded as too slight a cause on its own for threatening the marriage bond.

Notes

1. Women were asked the direct question here — 'Did you find that response

helpful?' Most replied in the negative, but did not elaborate on their answers. The analysis here is of course based on the subset of interviews.
  2. Women scored on average 13.4 out of 20 marks for child-care and 19.4 out of 28 for housework.
  3. Eighty-five percent of husbands married to women in professional and managerial jobs scored less than half compared with 74 percent of husbands married to women in non-professional, white and blue collar jobs.
  4. With the exception of child-care and children's needs (see Brannen and Moss, forthcoming).
  5. See Cowan and Cowan (1981), Moss et al. (1983), Shereshefsky and Yarrow (1973). For example, Moss found that women in early pregnancy (of first children) while they were still in employment did the bulk of housework, and that the arrival of children merely consolidated this pattern.

References

Backett, K. (1982) *Mothers and Fathers: A Study of the Development and Negotiation of Parental Behaviour*. London: Macmillan.

Bell, C. and Newby, H. (1976) 'Husbands and wives: the dynamics of the deferential dialectic', in *Dependence and Exploitation in Work and Marriage*, D.L. Barker and S. Allen (eds). London: Longman.

Brannen, J. (1985) 'Suitable Cases for Treatment? Couples seeking Help for Marital Difficulties', in J. Yoder et al. (eds) *Support Networks in a Caring Community*. The Netherlands: Martinus Nijhoff.

Brannen, J. (1986) 'Taboo Topics: Research Issues in the Study of Marital Problems and Feeling States', paper presented to The Social Research Association Conference 'Researching the Unaskable', 3 April, London.

Brannen, J. and Collard, J. (1982) *Marriages in Trouble: The Process of Seeking Help*. London: Tavistock.

Brannen, J. and Moss, P. (forthcoming) 'Dual Earner Households: Women's Financial Contributions after the Birth of the First Child', in J. Brannen and G. Wilson (eds) *Give and Take in Families: Studies in Resource Distribution*. London: George Allen and Unwin.

Caplan, G. (1974) *Support Systems and Community Mental Health*. New York: Behavioural Publications.

Cowan, C.P. and Cowan, P.A. (1981) 'Couple Role Arrangements and Satisfaction During Family Formation', paper presented at the Society For Research into Child Development. Boston, March–April.

Cunningham-Burley, S. (1985) 'Constructing Grandparenthood: Anticipating Appropriate Action', *Sociology* 19: 421–36.

Daniel, W.W. (1980) *Maternity Rights: The Experience of Women*. London: PSI.

Dex, S. (1985) *The Sexual Division of Work: Conceptual Revolutions in the Social Sciences*. Sussex: Harvester Press.

E.O.C. (1984) Evidence submitted to the House of Lords Select Committee on Parental Leave. Manchester.

Gorer, G. (1970) 'Report on Sex and Marriage', *The Sunday Times* 22 March.

Gowler, D. and Legge, K. (1978) 'Hidden and Open Contracts in Marriage', in R. Rapoport and R. Rapoport with J. Burnstead (ed.) *Working Couples*. London: Routledge and Kegan Paul.

Heisler, J. and Whitehouse, A. (1976) 'The NMGC client, 1975', *Marriage Guidance* 16: 188–93.

Lewis, C. (1986) *Becoming a Father*. Milton Keynes: Open University Press.
Mansfield, P. (1982) 'Getting Ready for Parenthood: Attitudes to and Expectations of having Children of a Group of Newly Weds', *International Journal of Sociology and Social Policy* 2: 28–39.
Martin, J. and Roberts, C. (1984) *Women and Employment: A Lifetime Perspective*. London: HMSO.
McCrae, S. (1986) *Cross-Class Families. A Study of Wives' Occupational Superiority*. Oxford: Clarendon Press.
Moss, P., Bolland, G. and Foxman, R. (1983) *Transition to Parenthood Project*, report to DHSS. Thomas Coram Research Unit.
Oakley, A. (1974) *The Sociology of Housework*. London: Martin Robertson.
Paloma, M. and Garland, N. (1971) 'The Myth of the Egalitarian Family', in A. Theodore (ed.) *The Professional Woman*. Cambridge, MA: Schenkman.
Pleck, J. (1985) *Working Wives/Working Husbands*. London: Sage.
Rapoport, R. and Rapoport, R.N. (1976) *Dual-Career Families Re-examined*, 2nd edn. London: Martin Robertson.
Scanzoni, J. (1978) *Sex Roles, Women's Work and Marital Conflict*. Lexington, MA: D.C. Heath.
Shereshefsky, P. and Yarrow, L. (1973) *Psychological Aspects of a First Pregnancy and Early Post Natal Adaptation*. New York: Raven Press.
Thornes, B. and Collard, J. (1979) *Who Divorces?* London: Routledge and Kegan Paul.
Walker, C. and Chester, R. (1977) 'Marital Satisfaction Amongst British Wives', *Marriage Guidance* 17: 219–27.
Weiss, M.S. (1969) 'The Fund of Sociability', *Transaction* 6: 36–43.
Wilson, G. (1986) 'The Organisation of Financial Management within the Family: Its Effects on Women's Ability to Provide for Domestic Needs'. University of London PhD thesis, unpublished.
Wilson, G. (forthcoming) 'Money Patterns of Responsibility and Irresponsibility in Marriage', in J. Brannen and G. Wilson (eds) *Give and Take in Families: Studies in Resource Distribution*. London: George Allen and Unwin.

9
Swedish family policy and the attempt to change paternal roles

Karin Sandqvist

Swedish fathers have become celebrities in the international father-hood literature by having parental benefits which do not discriminate between mothers and fathers. In so far as Sweden is ahead of other countries in formulating a new role for fathers, our experience is of great interest for social scientists around the world.

A growing body of literature has focused upon Swedish family policy (Berfenstam and William-Olsson, 1973; Liljeström, 1978; Kamerman and Kahn, 1981), its parental insurance (Lamb and Levine, 1983; Hwang, in press), its policy of domestic role-sharing (Haas, 1981), and of women's rights (Wistrand, 1981). These authors have skilfully analysed the ideology and reasoning of the policy-makers. With such an interest they never fail to notice that actual behaviour is more traditional than the official policy: 'Still, policy is one thing, practice another, and the gap between the two is often wide' (Wistrand, 1981: 5).

In this chapter I shall consider why the gap between theory and practice appears to be wide. The first section will examine the histor-ical developments in Sweden leading to the equal provisions for fathers and mothers. The second describes the Swedish family in its societal context. A third section examines how fathers have used the parental schemes available to them. Finally I suggest that, despite the fathers' limited use of these schemes with regard to very young infants, important changes in the nature of parental roles may be occurring.

Family policy in Sweden

Until the 1960s, changes in the structure of the Swedish family closely paralleled similar developments in the western world. In short, pat-riarchal society from pre-Christian times through the nineteenth century valued women less than men, and the family paradigm pre-scribed unequal power and unequal roles for husband and wife. Husband/father was primary, wife/mother was a secondary helper for his benefit. From about 1900, this was gradually replaced by a paradigm of equal power, but unequal roles for the spouses. This is the familiar breadwinner–housewife formula. Now a new paradigm shift is underway, prescribing equal power and equal roles for husband and wife, mother and father: their roles shall be equal both in society and in the home. While evidence of this shift is by no means restricted to Sweden, this nation has developed an unusually clear policy towards it.

These shifts in the family paradigm are, of course, intimately related to other changes in society. Industrialization, democratization and secularization provide the general background, the emancipation of women a more specific force. In Sweden, the first paradigm shift was marked in 1920 by a new marriage law. The husband was no longer superior to his wife, but merely her equal. By doing the housework, she could claim equal share of his earnings and property.

In the following decades, the new family paradigm, which implied an upgrading of motherhood and housework, was manifested in several ways. Motherhood came into the spotlight with the famous *Crisis in the Population Question* by Myrdal and Myrdal (1934), which was inspired by the low birthrate. Studies were made of housework as a profession, with methods taken from the study of industrial work (Boalt, 1983). Sociologists were concerned with the power structure in the family, finding 'equal power' in the majority of the families in the 1950s (Jonsson and Kälvesten, 1964; Kälvesten and Meldahl, 1972). The moves towards a welfare state gave support to mothers via child allowance (1948), a Motherhood Grant to mothers in cash (1950), and 3 months paid maternity leave (1955), a few years later extended to 6 months. Differential roles for parents were clearly the norm: in 1954, a daily paper (*Sydsvenska Dagbladet*) ran a heated reader's debate on the theme: 'Can a Real Man Push a Pram?' But remnants of the earlier paradigm lingered until 1950 when married mothers finally became equal to their husbands as legal guardians of the children.

The period between 1920 and 1960 saw great changes in Swedish society. Economic progress made better living conditions and educational opportunities for the working class possible, which was a central concern of the dominant Social Democratic Party. As a result, the number of domestic servants decreased (Liljeström and Dahlström, 1981). This process of course had its parallels in other western countries, but went further in Sweden. In the 1950s, an employed middle class mother could still find and afford a 'home assistant' (in the Swedish terminology of the period). In the 1960s, this was no longer possible.

Through the 1950s and 1960s, the economy boomed and companies had a shortage of manpower. Practically all unmarried women were already in the workforce and Sweden turned to married women as the labour reserve. Industrial leaders, the ruling Social Democratic Party and women's organizations became allies in opening the working world for women, albeit for very different reasons. This is why 'a wave of concern with sexism, sex discrimination, and the unequal opportunities available to men and women swept the country in the 1960s with an intensity exceeding that manifest elsewhere in the world' (Lamb and Levine, 1983: 41) — a wave which resulted in a family paradigm shift.

At first, the politicians and industrial leaders told women to broaden their interests, but there were enough articulate women to redefine the issues. Their arguments were logical and convincing, and the official bodies could not reject them without appearing backward and hostile to women and parenthood. In 1968 the principles of a new paradigm had clearly penetrated the Swedish Government, which stated in a report to the United Nations Economic and Social Council: 'there must be a radical change in deeply rooted traditions and attitudes, as much among women as among men, and active measures must be taken by society which will stimulate a change in the roles of both men and women (Swedish Institute, 1968: 5).

The economic reward of market work was an immediate concern. Individual taxation, introduced in 1970, can be regarded as the first legal manifestation of the new family paradigm. The roles of husband and wife as income earners now became equal (though mothers of course usually earned less than fathers).

The issues of child-care and housework, less easily solved, were highly emotionally charged and far-reaching. Educated women felt the problems keenly. They could not compete with men at work *and* carry the full load of household responsibilities, and they felt it unfair that women, but not men, were forced to sacrifice either parenthood or careers. The debate was led by those women who wanted to combine careers with parenting.

The necessity for men, especially fathers, to become more active in child-care and housekeeping was recognized as crucial. The laws providing for maternity leave had to be changed into parental leave. When this was effected in 1974, the shift to the family paradigm of equal roles for parents became clear.

Day care and other provisions for children were also necessary. At first part-time employment for women was hailed; but later this became regarded as a trap which keeps women in subordinate positions at work *and* leaves them with full responsibility for the household.

As full-time work for both father and mother obviously puts a strain on family life and parent–child relationships (especially as domestic servants were out of the question), a reduced work-day for all, 'the 6-hour day', became widely regarded as 'The' solution (SOU, 1975). It was thought that this should be introduced without reduction in pay. Although all women's organizations argued for a statutory 6-hour day, the only result, as of 1986, was an unimportant right for parents to work a 6-hour day with reduced pay, which of course is essentially the same as part-time work (Calleman et al., 1984; Sundström, 1983).

The contemporary Swedish family

In the course of one generation, from the 1950s to the 1980s, the family structure in Sweden has undergone significant changes. For example, about 15 percent of families are headed by a single mother, and 3 percent by a single father (SOU, 1983: 51). The highly visible instances of single mothers who cope reasonably well and the decline in formal marriage suggest that Swedish mothers no longer feel a husband necessary for economic security or social status (Eidem, 1983).

Individual taxation has changed the cost-benefit calculations for families drastically. It has become more advantageous for a wife to work, even short hours at a low-paid job, than for her husband to work overtime. This is true also for working-class families, and mothers have gone out to work, mostly part-time, in increasing numbers every year. Although still the primary breadwinners, fathers have generally been kept from moonlighting, and mothers have gained important self-confidence and work experience. Statistics tell the story clearly; in 1960, 17 percent of married women with children under 7 were employed; this rose to 64 percent in 1975, and 84 percent in 1984 (SCB, 1966, 1976, 1985; Official Statistics of Sweden, 1982a).

With the new family paradigm, which prescribes equal roles for the parents in the home, came an interest in the male role. Studies showed that the domestic division of labour was still very sex-typed (men did little housework) and few fathers took advantage of their right to paternal leave from work (Official Statistics of Sweden, 1975, 1981; SOU 1979).

For the first time, 'men' became a research topic (Jalmert, 1984). The nationwide non-profit-making organization for sexual enlightenment (RSFU) made 'men's roles' their theme for 1982–85. Most significantly, the Ministry of Labour appointed a special body called 'Mansgruppen' (The Man Group) to raise consciousness about these issues. This group organized its work around four themes: 'The Father', 'The Worker', 'Feelings' and 'The Male "Breaker"'. However, despite extensive coverage in mass media, men showed little interest in the topic. Books on the male gender role were mostly read by women (Gradin, 1984) and when courses and seminars were arranged, more women than men showed up (Jalmert, personal communication, 1986). The ultimate reason for the lack of male concern with 'male liberation' was probably deeper than economics, but the economic situation in Sweden since the middle 1970s must be commented on.

In the last decade, and especially since 1980, real income has decreased. In addition, certain expenses which once were elective have become necessities. The family car is a prime example. Due to the increased distance between home and work, most families find a car (occasionally two) absolutely necessary. The crowded conditions of the 1950s, when the average Stockholm family home had two rooms only, are no longer acceptable. Thus the average family with children in fact needs two incomes — and even with two incomes, domestic economy is tight (Official Statistics of Sweden, 1982b) and so is the job market. The identity of breadwinner is deeply ingrained in the 'good father' (Pleck, 1983) and when the economic situation of the family is threatened, fathers are not likely to experiment with a decreasing work commitment, even if the mother is also employed.

The breadwinner role is often stressful for the father. In our study,[1] both fathers and mothers rated the work situation of the father as worse than the mother's — despite the fact that the fathers, as usual, were placed higher on the occupational ladder (Andersson, 1985).

From recent studies of family life (Rosengren, 1985; Schönnesson, 1985) and in our study (Andersson, 1985; Lassbo, 1985; Sandqvist, 1985), as well as from statistical information, the following picture of a 'typical' two-parent family emerges: A child-centred family, in which the father is a member, not the head. Both parents are employed. Feelings of togetherness between the parents are taken for granted (unless divorce threatens). A conscious concern with achieving a new father role is quite unusual, but economic stress and work–family conflicts are common.

The Parental Insurance Scheme and its usage
When the Parental Insurance (PI) Scheme was introduced in 1974 it represented an important recognition of parents' rights to equal roles, but in terms of economic support to parents it was an insignificant reform. For decades, employers, co-workers, and mothers had regarded a 6-month 'childbirth' paid leave for mothers as the normal minimum. The world famous Swedish 'Paternal Leave' simply allowed a father to use some of this time, provided the mother went back to work early. The time is allotted per child, and only one parent at a time can use it.

The following account is, when not otherwise noted, based on reports issued by the administrative board (Riksförsäkringsverket, 1984: 6; 1984: 12; 1984: 14; 1985: 4; 1985: 8) and describes the rules in 1986. Three types of leave are available. In principle, parents are paid 90 percent of their usual salary. Its financing by the Riksförsäkringsverket (National Social Insurance Board) means that employers are not directly affected by its cost.

1. *Parental Insurance (PI) at the Birth of a Child* consists of 180 days, usually started a few weeks before delivery.

2. *Special PI* differs from the first type of leave by being deferable for some years, but is usually taken right after it; 90 days with 90 percent pay, plus 90 days with a much lower, fixed sum.

3. *PI for Short-Term Child-Care* is available when the usual care arrangements for children under 12 cannot be used due to illness; parents are allowed 60 days per child, per year. Since 1980, when the previous 10-day limit was extended to 60, fathers have been allowed 10 days at the time of delivery, originally to care for the older siblings while their mother was in the maternity clinic, and recently even when there are no older siblings. This is the only type of leave in which the father does not take days away from the mother while using the scheme. Due to their history, these 'new daddy days' are classified as Short-Term Child-Care.

Table 9.1 summarizes the usage of the PI Scheme by men (with few exceptions, fathers) since its introduction. The percentages are based on the total number of users of the scheme (men *and* women), thus 50 percent means gender equality, not that half of the fathers use the scheme.

As Table 9.1 shows, fathers make very different use of the different parts of the scheme. There are systematic differences related to the age of the child. When the child is less than 6 months old, only about 6 percent of the users are fathers, and they take only 2 percent of the days. Special PI is usually taken when the child is between 6 and 12 months; here more than every fourth user is a father, but men use less than 10 percent of the leave.

Finally, when the child is between 1 and 12 years old, even more men use the scheme. Unfortunately, the inclusion of the 10 extra 'new daddy days' confounds the figures. If they are excluded, the percentages drop to about 40 percent of fathers, using about 35 percent of the days.

The extensive use of the 'new daddy days' (not shown separately in the table) is in stark contrast to the rule that fathers are more involved with older children: 85 percent of fathers take this leave, at an average of 8.5 days each. The fact that these days are not transferable to the mother may possibly explain the fathers' usage, but probably it

TABLE 9.1
Fathers' usage of the Parental Insurance (PI) Scheme

year	I: PI at birth of child (used the first 6 months)		II: Special PI (used mainly when the child is 6–18 months old, occasional use to 8 years)		III: PI for short-term child-care (used when children 1–12 years old are ill, when their regular caretaker is ill, or when a new baby is born)			
	(a) fathers' use (percent of parents' usage)	(b) percent of days used by fathers	(a) fathers' use (percent of parents' usage)	(b) percent of days used by fathers	(a) fathers' use (percent of parent' usage)	(b) percent of days used by fathers	(c) total number of fathers	(d) days taken by fathers (in millions)
1974	2.8	0.5			34.0	39.9	60,000	0.3
1976	5.2	1.4			36.4	40.6	95,000	0.4
1978	6.6	2.1	27.1	10.8	47.8	53.3	215,000	1.3
1980	6.2	2.1	30.4	10.8	47.7	48.4	271,000	1.9
1982	5.5	1.9	28.1	8.7	45.8	46.2	273,000	1.9
1984	5.7	1.9	26.6	9.0	44.6	44.0	285,000	2.0

is the special enrapturing nature of these first days in the life of a new son or daughter which is of greater significance.

Fathers' usage of PI shows the same trend in all three parts of the scheme. A relatively rapid increase between 1974 and 1980 followed by a slow, but steady, decrease. Most likely, the decrease is related to the economic situation. Yet the decline in fathers' (relative to mothers') usage of parental leave should not overshadow the fact that the total numbers in columns c and d tell a different story. In interpreting these, the population structure of Sweden must be kept in mind. With about 8 million individuals there are around 1 million households with children under 16, and a little under 900,000 of these include a father. As column c shows, in recent years almost 300,000 of these fathers have taken Short-Term PI at an average of 7 days per year each. Clearly, at workplaces all over Sweden, the idea of a father's responsibilities to his child taking precedence over his responsibilities at work is becoming commonplace.

Why do fathers use the 'new daddy days' and Short-Term Child-Care extensively, whilst taking up the other forms of the parental insurance rarely? It is notable that the former two imply role sharing and equal roles, the latter role reversal. During the 'new daddy days' both parents take leave from work to share a profoundly vital experience; with Short-Term Child-Care both are expected at work when the routine is broken by the child's illness, and the parents may share responsibility by staying home in turns.

With PI at the Birth of a Child and the Special PI, one parent takes the breadwinner role and the other the homemaker role; thus role reversal is necessary for fathers to take these types of leave. The majority of fathers and mothers approve of fathers taking such parental leave during the first year of the child, which means a temporary role reversal, yet only about 20 percent of the fathers actually do so (SOU 1982).

However, for the first half year, role reversal is out of the question in most families, and the corresponding statistics show very little parental leave taken by fathers. The mother always, for health reasons, has to take the first month and if she breastfeeds the baby this will necessitate longer time off work. It is noteworthy that in the mid-1970s there was renewed interest in breastfeeding, exactly at the time when fathers achieved paternal rights to stay home with babies! (Socialstyrelsen, 1984). It might seem fitting to 'blame' this change on conservative anti-feminists, but it did not seem to originate from those sources. The shift was inspired by the back-to-nature movement, critical of the male 'expertise' guiding hospital routines (Helsing, 1974). Even when breastfeeding fails, Swedish women have become accustomed to their friends and colleagues being on paid leave for half a year after childbirth, a period cherished by feminists and traditional women alike. A mother going back to work 3 months after childbirth would probably have to face a great deal of surprise and covert quizzing.

For the next part of the scheme, the Special PI, the breastfeeding issue is less salient and mother can be expected back at work, but other problems arise. While the first 90 days are compensated at 90 percent of the salary, the next 90 days are paid at a lower, fixed sum. Since women regularly have lower salaries than men, mothers tend to take the days of low pay. If the father is going to take parental leave at all, he will thus aim for a couple of months when the baby is about 5 to 9 months old. In consequence the mother is required to work during these months but also to return home when her partner's leave is finished. Although the legalities are on her side, she is not in a good position to fight for her rights if her employer has objections to this plan, which frequently is the case (Calleman et al., 1984). Thus for the father to take parental leave, his opportunity to be away from work must coincide with his wife's opportunity to go back to work temporarily.

Two studies have investigated fathers who take leave and the reactions of their workmates. The first (SOU, 1982: 36) shows very little negative reaction from superiors and workmates. The second (Hwang et al., 1984), a more thorough project, shows negative reactions from about half of the supervisors and more than a quarter of workmates. It should be noted that the fathers who take leave must be a select group who, by definition, have judged the reactions at work as surmountable. Interestingly workmates in organizations where numerically women dominate are decidedly more in favour of the father taking parental leave than in male-dominated work places (Hwang et al., 1984).

Riksförsäkringsverket (1985: 4) analysed the usage of PI by married fathers during the baby's first year. Of these, 22 percent took parental leave, with an average duration of 47 days. The age and income of the father was shown to have little effect upon his usage of PI. On the other hand, the income of the mother was important. In the highest income group (mainly professional women working full-time) about 50 percent of the fathers took parental leave. Also, when the total length of used parental leave was just 7 or 8 months, about 45 percent of the fathers used the PI; but when the family used the maximum leave of 12 months, only 12 percent of the fathers did so. High income of the mother and short parental leave are probably both related to a strong work motivation of the mother.

A smaller study (SOU, 1982: 36) found that fathers' type of employment was of importance: of those employed by public institutions, 31 percent took parental leave, but of the privately employed, only 19 percent did so. Public institutions (schools, hospitals, central and local governments) usually employ many women, which corroborates Hwang et al.'s (1984) finding that 'female' work places are more supportive of fathers taking parental leave.

In summarizing this section, it is worth noting that while role sharing of parental leave is quite established, role reversal is unusual. The factors shown to facilitate a 'role reversal' usage of PI during the child's first year are in short supply: few wives have high incomes; a minority of families take less than 9 months leave with their new baby; and most fathers are privately, rather than publicly, employed in a highly sex-segregated labour market (Jonung, 1983). In addition, the essence of the new family paradigm is not role reversal, but role sharing.

Fathers' participation in family work
As part of the interest in equal roles for men and women, a fairly large number of studies in the last decade have explored the relative workload of fathers and mothers in child-care and housework (Konsumentverket, 1984; Official Statistics of Sweden, 1981, 1982a, 1984; Sandqvist, 1985; SOU, 1979; Trost, 1983).

In the Swedish debate, the conclusions of such studies usually stress the inequalities between women and men. In other words, the real situation is compared to an ideal state of perfect equality, and the shortcomings are noted. No doubt women still do considerably more child-care and household work than men, but the emphasis on the remaining inequalities may obscure the important changes which have occurred.

A comparison with the situation one generation ago is possible. Boalt (1961) found that 14 percent of fathers 'helped' with the dishes and 4 percent with the cooking in 1957. With the much stricter requirement of sharing equally (or doing more), 40 percent of fathers in 1982 achieved this with dishes and 14 percent with cooking (Official Statistics of Sweden, 1984). In both cases, the samples were national and fairly large.

A 1948 study of child-care (Boalt and Carlsson, 1949) noted the involvement of fathers. Only one father in the sample of 59 families with small children took care of his child at all during weekdays, and only a couple during the weekend. In a study of 100 households in new suburbs (Holm, 1956) fathers seemed more involved, spending almost a daily half-hour on housework and the same on child-care. The discrepancy between these studies could be due to their different definitions of child-care, 'narrow' or 'broad' (Pleck, 1983), but clearly fathers did little child-care.

In recent studies where a comparison between child-care and general housework is made, the results show that fathers participate more in child-care (Konsumentverket, 1985; Sandqvist, 1985; Trost, 1983). Table 9.2 shows the fathers' share of household and child-care tasks in our study of urban families with preschool children in 1982. For researchers in this field it is probably of no surprise that fathers were more likely to play with their young children than to change nappies. Perhaps more surprising was the finding that fathers were more apt to wipe a baby's bottom than to wash the clothes of their family. It is noteworthy that child-care tasks in general are shared quite equally between the parents, while most household tasks are heavily sex-typed.

TABLE 9.2
Rank order of household and child-care tasks, by mean score on Father Involvement Scale (1–5); *n* = 132 (66 couples with independent replies from the spouses)

Household task	mean	Child-care task	mean
Car maintenance	4.7	Playing outdoors	3.2
Household repairs	4.5	Playing indoors	3.1
Paying bills	3.1	Disciplining	3.0
Shopping and errands	2.7	Outings	2.8
Washing dishes	2.4	Keeping an eye	2.6
Window washing	2.0	Reading	2.5
Cooking	2.0	Putting to bed	2.4
Tidying up after people	1.9	Washing and bathing	2.2
Sweeping and dusting	1.8	Feeding	2.1
Scrubbing floors	1.4	Changing nappies	2.1
Washing clothes	1.4	Dressing and undressing	2.0
Ironing	1.2	Caring for sick	1.9

Note: The points on the Father Involvement Scale were:
1 = only mother does task; 2 = mostly mother; 3 = father and mother share; 4 = mostly father; 5 = only father.

The average in Table 9.2 could theoretically be due to almost half of the fathers doing all the child-care, others doing nothing. This was not the case: 'sharing equally' was regularly the most common answer for child-care.

Table 9.2 also shows 'taking care of sick children' to be the child-care task in which fathers are least involved. Yet in usage of parental insurance, fathers are shown to take days from work almost as often as mothers do for this purpose. How can this apparent contradiction be reconciled? In the first place, there are many off-work hours in which mothers may be more active in nursing a sick child, who may need care around the clock. In the second place, parents may include in their judgement not only the actual time spent in the care of a sick child, but also a measure of responsibility for the care. For example, who decides about taking the temperature, calling the doctor, or giving medicine?

Our study found that mothers are much more active than fathers in seeking information when children are ill, and also pay much more attention to issues of child-rearing presented in the media (Andersson, 1985). Mothers are the most important link between the wider society and the family in issues concerning child health and child-rearing.

An analysis of advice networks in families gives further insights into these processes. The advisors in the older generation are of special interest since they provide important role models for parenting. Of 64 studied couples, every second mother had an advisor in her own mother, but fathers with an advisor in their own fathers were clearly exceptional (only 3 percent). Fathers more often turned to their own mothers for advice (30 percent) (Sandqvist, 1985). This is, of course, entirely consistent with the findings that fathers of the previous generation had little to do with child-care.

While Table 9.2 shows that fathers and mothers share child-care quite equally, the mothers' greater attention to child-rearing issues in the media and access to advice from a same-sex parent indicate that the parenting of fathers and mothers is qualitatively different. Probably parenthood is experienced quite differently by fathers and mothers in terms of detailed concerns for the child and in the personal identity of the parent. For fathers, the lack of role models is a handicap.

Findings from national surveys indicate that mothers' workloads are consistently heavier than fathers' (Konsumentverket, 1984). However, as the data in Table 9.3 suggest, when hers is especially high, his is too. This finding implies some attempt to equalize parental workloads.

TABLE 9.3
Total workloads[a] of Swedish parents (in hours per week)

Both parents work full-time:	father 66, mother 74.
Mother works part-time:	father 59, mother 60.
Youngest child under 5:	father 65, mother 70.
Youngest child over 5:	father 55, mother 61.

Source: Adapted from Konsumentverket (1984).
[a] Including hours spent in employment, housework, child-care, car and household maintenance.

Parents' total workloads are worthy of comment. When both are employed full-time they average 140 hours per week together, and about the same amount if there is a small child. The problem of overload is therefore important. Moen (1985) analysed the relevant national surveys from 1968 and 1981. Interestingly she found no increase in reported maternal fatigue, despite increases in maternal employment. There was, however, an increase in paternal fatigue, which Moen attributes to the increase in fathers' child-care responsibilities. Overall though, mothers still reported considerably more fatigue than fathers — which is hardly surprising in view of their workloads.

All in all, there seems to be a good deal of evidence that the new paradigm of equal roles in the home has been influential — to a certain extent. In most homes father is now actively involved in all aspects of child-care, but overall responsibility and routine household work is still mostly done by mothers.

Summary
From the above review of past and present Swedish paternal roles it should be clear that the changing paternal role is a rather complicated phenomenon. Here I will simply summarize the 'problems' faced by participants in and researchers on contemporary Swedish families.

Problems for mothers
The Swedish support system for fathers as equal parents developed as a response to women's difficulties in combining parenting and employment, but career-oriented mothers still feel that 'inevitable' household duties prevent advancement at work. They may also suffer anguish and guilt in leaving the children. In recent years home-oriented women have experienced increasing economic problems and feel forced to work. Even when it is economically possible, her rarity creates problems of loneliness and isolation for the non-working mother.

Problems for fathers
The breadwinning role of the father is still of great importance for the welfare of the family. In an economic climate of unemployment and declining real income, stress at work is not alleviated even if the mother also works. If a father wishes to use his rights to paternal leave, reactions at work may be a problem. If he is not inclined to take an active part in household work and child-care his wife may react negatively and may even divorce him (Eidem, 1983). If he does assume responsibility in these areas, increased fatigue will result. The

father may also worry about leaving the children to be cared for by others.

Problems for policy-makers
Many problems arise in implementing the new family policy, since several forces work against a change in paternal roles. There is the obvious inertia of tradition and habit. The business world is also totally indifferent to the non-commercial needs of children and their parents. Likewise, the majority of the population, which is not in the parenting stage, is not interested in transferring resources to parents, for example, in the form of a 6-hour day with economic compensation. There are also many parents who are not attracted to the new concepts of fatherhood and motherhood implied in the family paradigm of equal roles. For many mothers the labour market is less attractive than their own children. For fathers, and men in general, who seem to show more resistance to change than women, there may be a multitude of reasons, ranging from a reluctance to give up privileges to deep-seated problems of identity and personality.

For policy-makers in other countries, wishing to emulate the Swedish programmes, there may well be a problem in convincing legislators to do so. In Sweden success depended on a combination of factors: (a) a manpower shortage; (b) a view of child-bearers as scarce resources (due to the low birthrate); (c) an extremely limited supply of domestic servants, coupled with a widespread ideological distaste for such an unequal institution; (d) an ideological commitment to gender equality; and (e) a feminist movement in favour of motherhood.

Problems for researchers
Many Swedish studies of paternal roles have been geared to the questions of 'how much' family work fathers do. Much less attention has been paid to the problem of 'under what conditions do fathers adopt an active family role?' What evidence there is points to the importance of the women around the father: his wife, his workmates, and even his mother.

Research on fathers must take the role of his support system into account. Parenting is teamwork, especially for fathers who rarely find themselves in the position of sole caregivers. In addition, the wife is usually the child expert in the family. Within family life, the tasks of child-care and housework and the need for parents to rest often collide.

In the international perspective, the Swedish 'experiment' of equal rights and responsibilities for both parents has attracted a great deal of attention. The results of such specific national programmes cannot be determined by studying a single country, and a comparative study of fathers' involvement in family work is now in progress.

Note

1. Despite a multitude of statistical information, in-depth studies of Swedish families are rare. The study 'Family Support and Development' (The FAST-Project) is uniquely comprehensive, using a sample of 128 working- and middle-class city families with young children who were interviewed and visited over 5 consecutive years. Single-parent families were over sampled. The typical two-parent family had two children, a father working full-time, and a mother working 20–30 hours a week (Andersson and Sandqvist, 1982). As several researchers have reported on the project, in the text I have referred to this project as 'our study'. It is part of a 5-nation research effort, 'The International Group of Human Ecology', with more detailed presentation in the reports.

References

Andersson, B-E. (1985) 'Stress och stöd i fvrdldrarollen' ('Stress and Support in the Parental Role'). Stockholm Institute of Education, Department of Educational Research, Report No. 14.

Andersson, B-E. and Sandqvist, K. (1982) *Family Support and Development: A Presentation of a Swedish Longitudinal Research Project of Families with Small Children*. Reports on Education and Psychology, No. 2, 1982. Stockholm Institute of Education, Department of Educational Research.

Berfenstam, R. and William-Olsson, I. (1973). *Early Child Care in Sweden*. International Monograph Series on Early Child Care. London: Gordon and Breach.

Boalt, C. (1961) '1000 husmödrar om hemarbetet' ('1000 Housewives about Household Work'), *Konsumentinstitutet* 11.

Boalt, C. (1983) 'Hemmens forskningsinstitut' ('The Research Institute for the Homes'), in B. Åkerman (ed.) *Kunskap för ver vardag — utbildning och forskning för hemmen*, pp. 141–95. Stockholm: Akademilitteratur.

Boalt, C. and Carlsson, G. (1949) 'Mor och barn från morgon till kväll. En studie av 80 barns miljö' ('Mother and Child from Morning to Night. A Study of the Milieu of 80 Children'), *Hemmens Forskningsinstitut*, 1948–9, 3: 17–122.

Calleman, D., Lagercrantz, L., Petersson, A. and Widerberg, K. (1984) *Kvinnoreformer på männens villkor (Reforms for Women on the Terms of Men)*. Lund: Studentlitteratur.

Edström, C-G., Holmström, L., Hållberg, B., Lindberg, L-L., Lindberg, R. and Åström, T. (1981) *Ensamförälder 1980 (Single Parent 1980)*. Socialdepartementet Ds S 1981: 18.

Eidem, R. (1983) 'Ekonomiska faktorer' ('Economic Factors'), in C.G. Boethius (ed.) *Varför har det blivit sä svärt att hälla ihop?*, pp. 123–30. Stockholm: Prisma.

Gradin, A. (1984) 'Inledningsanförande' ('Introductory Speech'), in Arbetsgruppen om Mansrollen (eds), *Drömmen om Pappa*. Report from a working seminar, March.

Haas, L. (1981) 'Domestic Role Sharing in Sweden', *Journal of Marriage and the Family*, November: 957–69.

Helsing, E. (1974) *Boken om amning (The Book on Breast Feeding)*. Stockholm: Trevi.

Holm, L. (1956) *Familj och bostad (Family and Housing)*. Enredovisning av fem fältstudier i moderna svenska familjebostäder, Stockholm.

Hwang, C.-P. (in press). 'The Changing Role of Swedish Fathers', in M.E. Lamb (ed.) *The Father's Role: Cross Cultural Perspectives*. Hillsdale, NJ: Lawrence Erlbaum.

Hwang, C.P., Eldén, G. and Fransson, C. (1984) 'Arbetsgivares och arbetskamraters attityder till papaledighet' ('Attitudes of Employers and Colleagues to Paternal Leave'). Psykologiska Institutionen, Göteborgs Universitet, Rapport No. 1.

Jalmert, L. (1984) *Den svenske mannen (The Swedish Man)*. Stockholm: Tiden.

Jonsson, G. and Kälvesten, A-L. (1964) *222 Stockholmspojkar. En socialpsykiatrisk undersvkning av pojkar i skolåldern (222 Stockholm Boys. A Social Psychiatric Study of School Age Boys)*. Stockholm: Almqvist and Wiksell.

Jonung, C. (1983) 'Kvinnors och mäns yrken' ('Women's and Men's Occupations', in M. Lundahl (ed.) *Kvinnan i ekonomin*, pp. 53–63. Malmö: Liber.

Kälvesten, A.L. and Meldahl, G. (1972) *217 Stockholmsfamiljer (217 Stockholm Families)*. Stockholm: Tiden.

Kamerman, S.B. and Kahn, A.J. (1981) *Child care, family benefits, and working parents*. New York: Columbia University Press.

Konsumentverket (1984) 'Tids nog . . . En undersökning om svenska folkets tidsanvänding' ('Time Enough . . . A Study of the Use of Time by the Swedish People'). Report from Allmänna byrån 1984: 6–13.

Lamb, M.E. and Levine, J.A. (1983) 'The Swedish Parental Insurance Policy: An Experiment in Social Engineering', in M.E. Lamb and A. Sagi (eds) *Fatherhood and Family Policy*, pp. 39–51. Hillsdale, NJ: Lawrence Erlbaum.

Lassbo, G. (1985) 'Föräldrars fritid' ('Parents' Leisure Time'). Rapport No. 1985: 4, Institutionen för pedagogik, Göteborgs Universitet.

Liljeström, R. (1978) 'Sweden', in S.B. Kamerman and A.J. Kahn (eds) *Family Policy: Government and Families in fourteen countries*, pp. 19–48. New York: Columbia University Press.

Liljeström, R. and Dahlström, E. (1981) *Arbetarkvinnor i hem- arbets- och samhällsliv (Working Class Women at Home, at Work, and in Public Life)*. Stockholm: Tiden.

Moen, P. (1985) *Work and Parental Well-being: Social Change in Sweden*. Ithaca, NY: Cornell University.

Myrdal, A. and Myrdal, G. (1934) *Kris i befolkningsfrågan (Crisis in the Population Question)*. Stockholm: Tiden.

Official Statistics of Sweden (1975) 'Hur jämställda är vi?' ('How equal are we?', Living conditions, Report No. 1975: 20.

Official Statistics of Sweden (1981) 'On Children's Living Conditions', Living conditions. Report No. 1981: 21.

Official Statistics of Sweden (1982a) 'Women and Children: Interviews with Women about Family and Work', Forecasting information, Report No. 1982: 4.

Official Statistics of Sweden (1982b) 'Perspectives of Swedish Welfare in 1982', Living conditions, Report No. 1982: 33.

Official Statistics of Sweden (1983) 'Work and Children — Employment Patterns among Women in the Child Bearing Ages', Forecasting information, Report No. 1983: 4.

Official Statistics of Sweden (1984) 'Children — but how many? Interviews with Women about Children, Family and Work', Forecasting information, Report No. 1984: 4.

Pleck, J.H. (1983) 'Husband's Paid Work and Family Roles: Current Research Issues', in H. Lopata and J. Pleck (eds) *Research in the Interweave of Social Roles, Families and Jobs*, pp. 251–333 (Vol. 3). Greenwich, CT: JAI Press.

Riksförsäkringsverket (1984: 6) 'Föräldrapenning för till-fällig vård av barn 1982'

('Parental Insurance for Short Term Child-Care in 1982'), Statistisk rapport No. 1984: 6.

Riksförsäkringsverket (1984: 12) 'Föräldrapenning för till-fällig vård av barn 1983' ('Parental Insurance for Short Term Child-Care in 1983'), Statistisk rapport No. 1984: 12.

Riksförsäkringsverket (1984: 14) 'Särskild föräldrapenning 1983' ('Special Parental Insurance in 1983'), Statistisk rapport No. 1984: 14.

Riksförsäkringsverket (1985: 4) 'Föräldraledighet i samband med barns födelse. Barn födda 1978–1982' ('Parental Leave at the Birth of a Child. Children born 1978–1982'), Statistisk rapport 1985: 4.

Riksförsäkringsverket (1985: 8) 'Föräldraförsäkringen 1984' (The Parental Insurance in 1984), Statistisk rapport 1985: 8.

Rosengren, A. (1985) '2 barn och eget hus' ('2 children and owning a house'), in Familjenormer — familjeformer, pp. 18–21. Stockholm: Forum för Kvinnliga Forskare och Kvinnoforskning. Rapport 1985: 2.

Sandqvist, K. (1982) 'En beskrivning av FAST-familjerna och deras sociala förhällanden' ('A Description of the Families of the FAST-Project and their Living Conditions), Stockholm Institute of Education, Department of Educational Research, Report No. 2, 1982.

Sandqvist, K. (1985) 'Jämställda pappor — finns dom?' ('Equal Fathers — do they exist?), in Familhenormer — familjeformer, pp. 114–21. Stockholm: Forum för Kvinnliga Forskare och Kvinnoforskning. Rapport 1985: 2.

SCB (The Central Bureau of Statistics) (1966) Statistical Abstract of Sweden 53.

SCB (The Central Bureau of Statistics) (1976) Statistical Abstract of Sweden 63.

SCB (The Central Bureau of Statistics) (1981) Statistical Abstract of Sweden 68.

SCB (The Central Bureau of Statistics) (1985) Statistical Abstract of Sweden 72.

Schönneson, L. (1985) 'Hennes och hans äktenskap' (His and her Marriage), Projektet parrelationer i barnfamiljer, Report No. 1. Delegationen för jämställdhetsforskning.

Socialstyrelsen (1984) Amning. En bok om amning och bröst-mjölk. H-fakta (Breast-feeding. A Book about Breast-feeding and Breast Milk). Stockholm: Liber.

SOU (Swedish Official Report) (1975: 62) 'Förkortad arbetstid för småbarnsföräldrar' ('Shortened Work Hours for Parents of Young Children').

SOU (Swedish Official Report) (1978: 55) 'Att sambo och att gifta sig' ('To Cohabit and to Marry').

SOU (Swedish Official Report) (1979: 89) 'Kvinnors arbete. En rapport från jämställdhetskommittén' ('Women's Work. A Report from the Equality Committee').

SOU (Swedish Official Report) (1982: 36) 'Enklare föräldraförsäkring' ('A Simpler Parental Insurance').

SOU (Swedish Official Report) (1983: 51) 'Ensamföräldrarna och deras barn' ('The Single Parents and their Children').

Sundström, M. (1983) 'Kvinnor och deltidsarbete' ('Women and Part-time Work'), in M. Lundal (ed.) Kvinnan i ekonomin, pp. 70–81. Malmö: Liber.

Swedish Institute (1968) 'The Status of Women in Sweden', The Swedish Government's Report to the United Nations Economic and Social Council. Stockholm.

Trost, J. (1983) 'Män och Chushållsarbete' ('Men and Household Work'). Uppsala Universitet, Family Reports, 2.

Wistrand, B. (1981) Swedish Women on the Move. Stockholm: The Swedish Institute.

10
Problems in role-reversed families

Graeme Russell

Recent approaches to the study of families have been characterized by a focus on all family members, the diversity of patterns, and on family change. This contrasts with earlier approaches which emphasized mothers, two-parent families in which the father was employed and the mother was the full-time child-carer, and which assumed stability. There is more sensitivity now to the dynamic nature of family patterns and to the ways in which these are affected by economic and social change. Much attention has been given, for example, to two family types that have increased dramatically in recent years in response to these changes — dual-worker or dual-career families in which there are young children, and single-parent households. Researchers have also turned their attention to other family types that have not been as obvious in terms of increased numbers, but which have been equally or even more obvious because of their marked divergence from traditional divisions of labour or beliefs about the needs of children. One such family type is that in which couples have reversed the responsibilities for paid work and child-care, where the mother is employed full-time and the father is the primary caregiver of preschool children.

Probably the most fundamental defining characteristics of a reversed role family pattern are: mother employed full-time and father at home as the day-to-day child-carer of preschool children. How to take account of the fathers' employment status, however, is more problematic. Like many mothers, fathers who are at home as full-time caregivers sometimes have part-time jobs (during the evenings, on weekends, or working from home). Their contribution to family income, however, is minor compared to the mother's. For the purposes of this chapter, both paternal part-time employment and paternal unemployment groups will be included.

Reversed-role families have attracted a good deal of research and media attention in western countries, and they have been the subjects of films — e.g. *Mr Mom* in the US — and stage plays — e.g. *The Perfectionist* in Australia. This family type has also featured in debates about changing male/female relationships. There is a growing view that a reversed-role pattern or one in which fathers are highly participant in child-care, will facilitate more fundamental changes in male/female relationships, and could be instrumental in increasing the opportunities for women in the paid workforce (Russell, 1983, 1984). Thus some have advocated reversed- or shared-role patterns in the belief that they will enhance the common good of the community. Others point out that many couples may want to reverse roles because it best suits their family needs, and they have advocated that more attention be given to policies and practices which will expand the choices for couples to adopt such a pattern.

Overall, there has been a noticeable trend for researchers and social commentators to emphasize the potential positive aspects of reversing roles for a period of time, and the desirability of it being considered as a viable alternative. In contrast, very little attention has been given either to the potential problems associated with changing work/family responsibilities in such a dramatic way, or to the fact that for many couples, reversing roles may not be a matter of choice — they may be thrust into it by unemployment or other economic circumstances. It seems especially important therefore to examine closely the antecedents and consequences of reversing family roles, and to emphasize both the potential and actual positive aspects, as well as the potential and actual difficulties experienced. This is the approach taken in this chapter.

The chapter is divided into five sections. In the first, characteristics of 'reversed-role' families are described. Personal, family and social factors which either antecede or facilitate the adoption of this pattern are examined in the second section. The third examines problems families have reported they experience in attempting to adjust to reversed roles. This analysis focuses on personal adjustment, family relationships and relationships with significant others. The problems people experience in maintaining reversed roles is the focus of the fourth section. It addresses the question of why it is that so many families revert to traditional roles in a relatively short time. The fifth section summarizes the implications of findings for changes in family policies and practices, both to expand the options for people to reverse or share paid work and family roles, and to help families adapt to and maintain these patterns.

Unless otherwise indicated, the findings discussed here are based on thirty-seven of the shared caregiving families described in Russell (1983). This subsample consists of those families in which the mother was employed full-time and either the father was unemployed ($n=16$) or he was employed part-time ($n=21$; average number of hours employed $= 15$). The majority of these families were recruited either after they had responded to notices on university or community noticeboards or after they had been approached at playgroups or preschools. The average age of the fathers was 32 years, and of the mothers was 31 years. Twenty-five percent of fathers and 63 percent of mothers had either university degrees or college diplomas. The average occupational status ranking of mothers was higher than that of fathers (mean for mothers = 3.6, fathers = 4.3; based on a 7-point scale, where 1 = high status), with the majority of mothers being employed in either professional or semi-professional jobs (e.g. school teacher, nurse). Families had an average of 1.7 children, with the mean age of the youngest child being 2.8 years.

Reversed-role family patterns

It is difficult to estimate how many 'reversed-role' families there are, or whether their numbers are increasing. I have estimated that in Australia they constitute between 1–2 percent of families, a figure which corresponds to between 10,000 to 15,000 families. Reversed-role families have been noted by researchers in several different countries: Sweden (Lamb et al., 1982), Australia (Harper, 1980; Russell, 1983); in the US (De Frain, 1979; Field, 1978; Levine, 1976; Radin, 1981, 1982), and in Israel (Sagi, 1982). Few of these studies have provided detailed information about family life-styles, maternal employment patterns, or divisions of labour for child-care. Rather, researchers have tended to state simply that mothers were employed (without giving information about the nature of their jobs, hours of employment or work schedules), and either that fathers were the primary caretakers, or that they performed proportionally more of the child-care than the mothers did. It is not always clear, therefore, to what extent employment and child-care patterns have been reversed.

From the information that has been provided, however, it is obvious that the fathers described do take a major responsibility for day-to-day child-care. In Radin's (1982) US study, her father-prime or reversed-role group were reported to perform 57 percent of child-care tasks. In my group of reversed-role families, fathers spent an average of 33 hours per week taking sole responsibility for their children during the day when they were awake (compared to 13 hours per week for mothers and 1 hour for traditional fathers), and they performed 51 percent of child-care tasks (compared to 11 percent for traditional fathers), spending an average of 10 hours per week doing them.

Other findings from my study indicate, however, that reversing employment and child-care jobs, does not necessarily lead to fathers assuming the overall responsibility for children in the way that traditional mothers do. Many mothers retained greater responsibility for decision-making, planning, monitoring and anticipating the needs of the children, and 'took over' when they arrived home from work. On the other hand, findings also indicate that paternal unemployment does not necessarily lead to a major shift in traditional male household jobs or in notions about overall responsibility for family financial management and breadwinning. A mother being employed is frequently considered as a short-term option rather than a fundamental long-term change in family responsibilities.

Factors which either antecede or facilitate role reversal

Reversed-role families depart from traditional patterns in three ways: (i) the mother of a preschool child is employed; (ii) the father is not the breadwinner; and (iii) it is the father who provides the day-to-day child-care. The latter two in particular are quite radical departures from traditional family ideologies and beliefs about the needs of children. For this type of family pattern to either be adopted in the first place or continued for a reasonable period of time then, suggests that the underlying determinants must be very strong indeed. Few studies have considered questions of antecedents, however, and therefore it is not possible to make clear-cut statements of cause and effect. Furthermore, samples have rarely been selected in a random fashion, and have tended to be biased towards the professional middle class.

Several recent economic and social trends have probably been instrumental in the emergence of reversed-role families, particularly trends associated with increases in unemployment, the women's and the men's movements, increased employment and career opportunities for women, and changes in leave provisions for parents (notably in Sweden). These factors are clearly implicated in the explanations given by parents for reversing roles (Kimball, 1984; Radin, 1985; Russell, 1983). Some couples explain their decision to change in terms of economic necessity, either because the father has lost his job, or because the mother can earn more money. Another group say that they chose to change, mainly because of the strong desire of the mother to pursue a career, and to a lesser extent, because the father has little interest in his job or career, or wants to opt out of the workforce for a while. Other analyses (Kimball, 1984; Radin, 1985; Russell, 1983) show that a reversed-role pattern is associated with mothers having higher status, and potentially more rewarding jobs than their spouses. Egalitarian beliefs about child-care responsibilities and employment opportunities for women is a further explanation noted in the literature. This is more likely to be given by professional or highly educated couples.

Although family financial or employment situations are clearly prominent in parental explanations and therefore need to be given high priority in any discussion of possible antecedents, it is obvious that these factors cannot explain everything. Many people have the same economic and career demands, or in the case of Sweden, have the same leave options, but they do not reverse roles. Commenting on findings that having flexibility in work hours and leave provisions does not result in a marked increase in fathers' family involvement, Lamb et al. (1984) argue that it might only be fathers who are highly motivated and who have confidence in their skills, who will respond to changes in policies. Research findings lend some support to this hypothesis.

In my study, reversed-role fathers, in comparison with traditional fathers, were more likely to have attended childbirth classes and the actual birth, and to have read books on child-rearing, indicating that indeed these fathers were more highly motivated and committed. Given these experiences too, it could reasonably be expected that they would have a higher level of knowledge and skills appropriate to the job of child-carer.

Other findings show, however, that many fathers (like many mothers!) become caregivers without having a high level of child-care or domestic knowledge or skill. Beliefs about potential parenting competence therefore, might be critical for some couples. A common objection to fathers being primary caregivers is that they are not competent or are not as sensitive to children as mothers are (Russell, 1983). In a survey of traditional families (Russell, 1983), 78 percent of fathers and 66 percent of mothers agreed that there was a maternal instinct which enabled mothers to be more competent caregivers, and 51 percent of fathers and 35 percent of mothers thought that fathers did not have the ability to care for children. In contrast, while nearly 50 percent of parents in reversed-role families agreed that mothers had a head start because of biology, 88 percent thought that fathers could be competent caregivers. We cannot know, of course, whether the experience of this family pattern has changed these parents' beliefs, but it is a reasonable hypothesis that the beliefs people hold about parenting will have a powerful influence on the type of child-care arrangement they adopt (especially when they perceive the particular arrangement to have possible negative consequences for their children).

Given both that there is an absence of role models for reversed role-families, and that this pattern contradicts accepted cultural beliefs, another possibility is that it is only people who are high on self-esteem and independence who will either contemplate, adopt, or feel comfortable in going against the tide in this way. We might also expect that parents who reverse roles will be more likely to be androgynous — that is, they will endorse traditional masculine characteristics (e.g. independence, self-confidence, assertiveness), as well as traditional feminine characteristics (e.g. interpersonal sensitivity, expressiveness). Findings, however, do not give consistent support to this hypothesis. Studies by Russell (1983) and Kimball (1984) provide positive evidence, whereas those of De Frain (1979), Lamb et al. (1982), and Radin (1982) provide contrary evidence.

Arguments about relationships between personality variables, and family life-styles also present problems with regard to conclusions about cause and effect. We cannot be certain about what is causing what — whether the life-style is a consequence of personality factors, or whether the personality factors are a consequence of the life-style. Further, it may yet be that while personality factors are not critical for whether or not a reversed-role pattern is adopted, they may be critical for the process of adjustment.

Comparisons with traditional families also show that reversed-role families are more likely to have fewer and older children, with very few at all having young babies. A father caring for older children conflicts less with cultural beliefs about the desirability of breastfeeding, the importance of mother–infant bonding, and the very strong belief that babies need their mothers (cf. Lamb et al., 1982). It may be too that fathers will either only take on or continue in this life-style when child-care demands are low and therefore they either anticipate or actually experience few difficulties in adjusting (cf. Radin, 1985). The difficulties, both practical and psychological, that a reversed-role pattern generates for fathers and mothers, how they cope with these demands and with the reactions of significant others, are discussed in the next section.

Difficulties experienced

As was indicated above there are many reasons why people adopt a reversed-role pattern. Some are thrust into it, and are continually looking for an opportunity to revert to traditional roles, whereas others are very enthusiastic, displaying a sense of missionary zeal about it. The exact nature and the consequences of the difficulties experienced will obviously depend on factors such as: whether parents have chosen to reverse roles, whether they are satisfied with this family pattern (irrespective of whether they have chosen it or not), their degree of commitment and sensitivity to children, and individual personality characteristics. Unfortunately, studies have not paid adequate attention to these mediating variables and therefore it is only possible here to report general patterns of findings. Difficulties experienced by families, as reported in the literature, cover three major areas: problems of personal adjustment, changes in family relationships (parent–child and couple), and reactions of significant others.

Personal adjustment

Fathers. Few fathers are able to anticipate the difficulties they experience in staying at home and caring for children. Although many look upon their new job with enthusiasm and have expectations about achieving things while at home (e.g. renovating the house), most are forced to revise their expectations. Similar to most 'new' mothers, 58 percent of my sample of reversed-role fathers reported difficulties in adjusting to the demands of child-care and housework (the relentlessness, boredom, physical work, and lack of adult company). Seventy-four percent of mothers also reported that their partners experienced such difficulties. As would be expected too, fathers who felt they had been forced to reverse roles reported more problems than those who had chosen to.

One of the most obvious of the possible difficulties fathers might experience is feeling threatened in their identity and status as a male. Berger (1979) argues that problems for fathers will arise because of personal doubts and fears, and from men being 'exposed to new parts of themselves (e.g. becoming more expressive and vulnerable)'. Cultural stereotypes of masculinity do not include nurturant or care-giving behaviour, and a major aspect of male socialization in most western societies is the expectation that they will fulfil an in-strumental role in the paid workforce and be the breadwinner. Despite this, only five out of thirty-seven of my sample of reversed-role fathers reported any serious difficulty with their identity as a male. There are two possible explanations for this finding. First, fathers may have found it difficult to admit to these doubts during an interview. Or, it may only be those fathers who do *not* identify strongly with cultural stereotypes of masculinity who become involved in this type of family pattern in the first place.

Nevertheless, 40 percent of fathers rated the loss of status and reduced self-esteem associated with paid employment as a major disadvantage of their life-style. In contrast, 42 percent rated the freedom from career and work pressures as a major advantage. As would be expected, most of those in the first group were from families forced into the lifestyle, whereas most in the second group had chosen to reverse roles.

Despite these difficulties, fathers also report enhanced self-esteem, self-confidence or satisfaction with their parental role (Gronseth, 1978; Lamb et al., 1982; Lein, 1979; Russell, 1983; Sagi, 1982). Perhaps it can be argued that this is a consequence of fathers having taken on a job which males are not normally expected to be capable of performing, being subjected to criticism from others, and experiencing difficulties in adjusting, but after all that, considering themselves and being considered by others to have been successful.

Mothers. Difficulties experienced by mothers are similar to those noted in the maternal employment literature. Although the majority report increased satisfaction, self-esteem and independence associated with employment (Radin, 1985; Russell, 1983), most (68 percent) also report constant physical and emotional exhaustion associated with having dual roles. The other major difficulty mentioned by mothers is coping with the guilt of leaving their children (reported by 26 percent of mothers). Coping with the mother's exhaustion and emotional difficulties associated with the change was also noted as a major difficulty for fathers (26 percent).

Family relationships
Parent–child relationships. Whenever there is talk about changing family roles, one of the first questions asked is: 'What effect will it have on the children?' Findings reviewed elsewhere (Radin and Russell, 1983; Russell, 1986) generally show that reversing roles has neither a dramatic negative nor a dramatic positive effect. Rather, the most remarkable aspect of findings is how little effect the change appears to have on children. Several studies indicate, however, that reversing roles has a positive effect on father–child relationships. Both fathers and mothers rate this as one of the major advantages of fathers being at home. Nevertheless, it is not all plain sailing.

Increased tension and conflict in father–child relationships has been noted as an outcome of the frustrations and demands of being a full-time caregiver. This change is not always viewed negatively, however. Mothers in my study welcomed the better balance in parent–child relationships, and what they saw as a more realistic father–child relationship. Some fathers also looked upon it as a personal development experience, arguing that their reactions to the increased tension and conflict had provided them with new insights into themselves.

Additional difficulties have emerged from group discussions I have conducted with reversed-role fathers who have older children (most studies have been on families with young children). Fathers of teenagers report that they sometimes have conflicts because their children expect greater conformity to social norms. For one, this conflict arose because, unlike his friends' fathers, he did not help his son with his car or take him to football matches. Another father reported continuing conflicts with his teenage daughter because she did not want him to participate in her school by helping out in the canteen, or in supervising classes.

Difficulties reported by mothers mainly concern those experienced in coping with the reduced contact with their children. Thirty-two percent of mothers reported that they disliked not seeing their children as much, and they worried about missing out and losing influence over them. Consistent with this, 21 percent of mothers and 26 percent of fathers, considered that there had been a change in the nature of the mother–child relationship associated with the children being less dependent on her and not seeking her out as much for comfort and support.

Couple relationships. Difficulties in couple relationships in the first few months of making a radical change in life-styles might be expected especially if people are genuinely trying to shift responsibilities for child-care and housework. Whether this is necessarily a negative thing or not is an open question. Findings from my study indicate that those couples who confronted their conflicts, and discussed their problems openly, considered this to be a positive experience.

Although my study provides systematic data on couple relationships in reversed-role families, it also suffers from methodological limitations and therefore must be treated with caution when discussing cause and effect. It does have the strength, however, of having used two data collection methods: Spanier's (1976) Dyadic Adjustment Scale, and an in-depth interview which probed perceptions of difficulties.

Comparisons between traditional and reversed-role families on Spanier's (1976) scale revealed that the latter group had a lower total score, indicating marital relationships of poorer quality. This difference was primarily attributable to differences in responses on one subscale, *dyadic satisfaction* (this included items such as: 'having had recent quarrels', 'being irritated by one another'). There are several possible interpretations of these findings. These couples might have had poorer relationships before they changed life-styles. (Additional data suggest that reversed-role fathers who were more influential in the decision to change and chose this life-style, rated their marital relationships more highly.) Or, reversing roles does have the effect of increasing tension in relationships. Finally, it may be that because of their experiences, these parents are more sensitive to couple issues and are more open about reporting intimate aspects of their relationships.

Parents in my sample were also asked whether the change in life-style had affected their couple relationship. Fifty-three percent of fathers and 37 percent of mothers reported positive consequences in terms of increased sensitivity, understanding and equality. In contrast, 47 percent of fathers and 63 percent of mothers reported generally negative effects, including greater conflict and more dissatisfaction, and problems associated with the rushed life-style (e.g. tiredness, irritability, and spending less time together). Further, the majority of families reported that these difficulties were more acute during the first few months of changing family patterns. It was during this period when there was more uncertainty about child-care and housework responsibilities and when both parents had to cope with adjusting to the different physical and emotional demands of new jobs.

Conflicts and tensions were also found to emerge as part of the process of renegotiating family tasks and responsibilities. Mothers and fathers saw these tensions and conflicts slightly differently. One of the tensions experienced by fathers concerned the reluctance of their partner to let them make decisions about the children or housework. Some fathers resented their partners' considering them to be the secondary parent or simply 'the helper', and not allowing them to make decisions and to have the same independence to develop at home that their partner was given to develop outside the home.

These findings confirm the arguments of others (e.g. Hoffman, 1983) that some mothers may be reluctant to give up their power and status within the domestic domain. They are also consistent with findings that mothers may not be as keen to have fathers more involved in child-care as we might expect. A national survey conducted in the US has found that only 23 percent of employed and 31 percent of non-employed 'wives' would like 'more help with the children' from their husbands (Pleck, 1982). At the same time, however, the findings from reversed-role families question the suggestions by some (e.g. Bryson, 1983) that this reluctance is simply associated with the lack of power and status that women have in the public domain. Clearly there is something more involved, as the majority of women in my sample had relatively high status jobs.

Tension has also been reported to result from an apparent lack of genuine support given by mothers to their partners (Russell, 1983). Although it might be expected that mothers will be very supportive of fathers as child-carers (cf. Harper, 1980), this has not always been found to be the case. While many mothers displayed a degree of pride in the fact that their spouse was the primary child-carer, many also found it difficult to accept them in 'the domestic role', or that they could become frustrated, depressed and were not always able to keep the house 'up to standard'. Failure of spouses to acknowledge fully the problems and doubts of fathers in the caregiving role was also reported.

Findings also indicate that mothers have difficulty in accepting that their children became more attached to the father and went to him at times of stress when they needed comfort and support. Some also became irritated if their spouse's standards of child-care were not as high as theirs (e.g. many mothers considered the father to be too soft with the children). Finally, mothers often resented the status and credit that other people (and especially other women) gave their spouses because of their involvement in child-care. The comment they resented most was: 'Oh isn't he marvellous'. As these mothers pointed out, they had been the child-carer before, and no one had referred to them as being marvellous because of this.

Reactions of significant others
Berger (1979) argues that individuals in transition experience institutional constraints on their ability to change, and that they will need considerable support from significant others if they are to adapt successfully. Those who adopt a life-style which is different from the norm in three significant ways (maternal employment when having young children, father not the breadwinner and father as caregiver), are likely to encounter some type of reaction from people whom they have regular contact with, and could find that many institutions are unresponsive to their needs. Support from close friends and relatives could be crucial, as it may help couples to feel comfortable and secure in the face of more general societal disapproval.

Couples in my study reported that other people's first reactions to learning about their reversed-role pattern was generally positive — expressing surprise and interest, rather than disapproval. Fifty-three percent of fathers and 74 percent of mothers reported this reaction. Continuing positive responses and support, however, were not as evident from relatives, friends and neighbours, or from workmates. Only 35 percent of parents reported their relatives were consistently positive, 53 percent of fathers reported their male friends were negative, and 37 percent said their male workmates were negative. Overall, female friends, neighbours and workmates were seen as reacting more positively (e.g. 68 percent of mothers reported that their female workmates were positive, and 79 percent reported positive reactions from female friends and neighbours).

Although women were generally more supportive of reversed roles than men were, some fathers, and especially those who were very committed to the child-care job and had been in it for some time, frequently doubted how genuine women's support actually was. A lot is said about how men feel threatened by women changing roles, but very little is said about how women might feel threatened by men wanting to share more in child-care. Fathers who shared in child-care sometimes found themselves being described by women as just good babysitters, not being trusted by other mothers to care for their children (because of the fear of child abuse); not being accepted by women as one of the group in the neighbourhood or at school functions; and not being given genuine support during some of the tough times which recur while caring for children. Some fathers also discussed the problems of developing close supportive networks with women in the neighbourhood because of the threat many saw this as having for marital relationships. What this might mean in the longer term, however, is that fathers at home become even more socially isolated than women at home, and this lack of social support might have a major impact on whether or not families maintain this life-style over a longer period of time.

Maintaining a reversed-role family
In my study, the experience of reversing roles was found to change the views of some, and the reasons why couples continued were sometimes very different from those given for the initial change. There were two reactions which stood out as having more impact on people's explanations. For mothers, it was the satisfaction they derived from their jobs; for fathers, it was the enjoyment they derived from having improved relationships with their children. For others, however, the problems they encountered with reversing roles became more critical as time went on, forcing them to revert to traditional roles more quickly than they had originally anticipated. Three research studies have followed up reversed-role families over a longer period of time, and all point to the relative instability of this pattern.

Lamb et al. (1982), who conducted a study of Swedish families in which fathers had taken paternity leave, found difficulty in retaining a sample of families in which fathers were at home, despite their having planned to do so before the birth. Unfortunately, little data are available concerning the reasons why these families reverted to more traditional patterns so quickly.

In another study, Radin (1985), recontacted the twenty fathers from her original sample who had been primary caregivers, and found that only four were in exactly the same pattern four years later. Among the factors found to be critical for longer term stability were: residing in a community which was supportive of a non-traditional pattern; mothers having a high salary and a strong investment in their careers (and being supported in this by their families); fathers having flexibility in work hours and finding caring for children gratifying; and when the demands of child-care (in terms of numbers and characteristics of children) remained low.

I reinterviewed sixteen of my sample of thirty-seven reversed-role families two years after the initial interview. Only six were in exactly the same pattern, eight had reverted completely to a traditional pattern with the mother at home and the father employed, and two couples had separated (one of these opted for a shared custody arrangement). Neither of these separated couples felt that reversing roles had been the critical factor in their separation. Four factors were identified in this study as being more critical for reverting to traditional divisions of labour.

First, the extent to which the reversed-role pattern differed from cultural norms and expectations. Reversion was more likely when there were very young children and when the father was not employed at all. A situation in which a father is not employed and is caring for a 6-month-old, it can be argued, will generate more social disapproval than one in which a father is employed part-time and cares for a 4-year-old. The second was related to economic and employment factors. In three cases the unemployed father found a job, and in four others the reversion was associated with fathers changing to a more highly paid job. Seven out of the eight families, therefore, were better off financially after changing back.

The third factor which stood out was fathers' dissatisfaction with being unemployed and/or being at home, and more generally with their reversed-role pattern. Seven out of the eight fathers who reverted said that, all things being considered, they preferred traditional roles. Three fathers were very straightforward in their explanations for changing back; they said that they had simply had enough of staying at home, and that they had found it increasingly difficult to cope with the day-to-day demands of being a full-time child-carer in the face of implicit criticisms of male peers, and in the absence of genuine social support.

There was also some evidence of fathers reconsidering their commitments to equality. Two fathers who had originally chosen to stay at home and were amongst the most committed to equality and to the idea that men must be prepared to share child-care and housework, changed back much earlier than they had anticipated. One admitted quite openly that he had found it much more difficult than he had expected, whereas the other said the reversion was associated with the development of a lucrative business opportunity. Nevertheless, it was obvious from his responses in the initial interview that reversing roles had presented major difficulties for this father as well.

The final factor was the dissatisfaction of mothers. Seven out of the eight mothers who had reverted were very strong in their view that they preferred traditional roles. The major reason why mothers were less positive about reversed roles was that they now placed a lot more significance on the negative effects of the rushed, and physically and emotionally demanding nature of their life-style. It may be that in families where mothers experienced role overload more acutely, fathers were not highly participant in housework. Systematic data are not available on the degree to which fathers at home share in all aspects of family work, although anecdotal reports tend to suggest that mothers retain more responsibility for housework. Mothers from families who had reverted (and especially those who felt they had been forced to make the initial change), also rated their reduced contact with children as a major disadvantage of reversing roles, and spending more time with their children as an advantage of traditional roles.

Despite these difficulties, and the more negative comments about reversed roles, there did seem to be some lasting effects of the previous non-traditional life-style, however. Mothers and fathers agreed that the improved father–child relationship continued, and that fathers were more involved and more willing to take responsibility for child-care than they had been prior to having the experience of being at home. This group of fathers was also found to be more highly participant than a comparable group of traditional fathers. They were also seen by their spouses as having had a major change in attitudes towards family life; they were rated as being more sensitive to child-care issues and to the difficulties involved in staying at home.

Families who continued in a reversed-role pattern also revealed some important changes. Many reported that the fathers had become more involved and had taken over more responsibilities for the children, and especially for housework. With this, however, the nature of their problems changed. Fathers were not as concerned in the follow-up interview about their own or others' reactions to the novelty or the unusual nature of their life-style. They were more concerned with how they were coping with the mundane aspects of housework and the demands of children. They were also concerned that their contribution be given more genuine recognition by others. Fathers who stuck at the task of shared child-care often became extremely sensitive to how others reacted to them as child-carers and to their having a major responsibility and commitment to this job. Simple statements like: 'Gee, Joan must feel lucky to have you helping so much with the children' became big issues for some fathers. Would it ever be said that 'John was lucky to have Joan helping so much with the children'? This issue about fathers being given equal status and that of presuming that fathers have equal responsibility for children are central to any proposals for changes in policies and practices to help support a reversed-role pattern.

Conclusions and implications for policy and practice

The antecedents of the adoption of a reversed-role family pattern are many and varied. No simple explanation has emerged as yet, and perhaps a simple explanation is not possible given the diverse nature of this group of families. For some couples, financial factors provide the necessary and sufficient conditions for the change; for others financial factors are only the necessary preconditions — the major impetus for the change comes from strongly held beliefs about equality of opportunities for men and women; and for others, it is even more complex — the change is produced by a combination of fathers having the necessary skills and confidence, and mothers having egalitarian beliefs about parental roles, and a highly paid job with excellent career opportunities.

The finding that many families revert to a traditional family pattern perhaps is not all that surprising given recent findings about the dynamic nature of family patterns. For many, changing back was associated with the same factors that were implicated in the adoption of reversed roles — changed employment and financial conditions. Neither should reversion be all that surprising given both the extent to which this life-style is divergent from traditional family ideologies and the absence of genuine support for males in non-traditional family roles. Perhaps it is more remarkable that families adopt this pattern at all, and continue in it for the length of time that they do.

The evidence reviewed above indicates that most families encounter difficulties in reversing roles. Even those who chose to change, and were committed to equality between the sexes, found it more difficult than they expected and many reverted to traditional roles sooner than they had anticipated. Some of these difficulties are similar to those reported by parents in traditional families, e.g. coping with the constancy, the physical and emotional demands, and with the isolated nature of the full-time caregiving job, and in coping with the difficulty of balancing paid work and family commitments. Fathers at home, however, are probably even more socially isolated than mothers at home because of the absence of support systems, and reversed-role mothers no doubt experience guilt more acutely than traditional fathers do. It is also obvious that reversing roles presents additional tensions in mother/father relationships. Tension was found to be especially associated with mothers having difficulty accepting fathers 'taking over' tasks and responsibilities generally expected to be their domain. Indeed, contrary to the expectations of many that only fathers would suffer identity problems with reversing roles and would feel threatened by mothers taking over the bread-winning job, the evidence presented here indicates quite clearly that mothers experience considerable difficulty in adjusting to fathers being the primary parent.

A reversed-role family pattern is obviously one which will continue to be an option that many families will want for a period of time (even though this may be brief), that others would take if it was a more viable option, and that still others will have little or no choice about. In a recent social policy survey conducted by the author in a sample of first year university students, 80 percent said that they would like to have the option of a reversed role pattern and would like to see policies developed to make this possible. Given this situation, it seems important to address the issues raised above to help make it easier for families to reverse roles, to help them to cope during the early periods of change and to maintain the pattern as long as it suits the needs of their family.

Probably the most obvious area for change is in employment policies and career structures. Several studies (Kimball, 1984; Radin, 1985; Russell, 1983) report that these factors are instrumental both in the initial adoption of reversed-role patterns, and in their maintenance. Policies that could be considered are ones which will: expand career and employment options for women; introduce more flexibility into career structures and work hours; consider the possibility of averaging incomes over the life-cycle; and introduce parental leave schemes which give mothers or fathers the option to care for young children on a full-time basis.

While changes in employment policies may be necessary, it is also clear that they will not provide sufficient conditions for the expansion of options. A simple change to enable fathers to take paid parental leave might have little impact unless parallel policies are introduced, e.g. to encourage fathers to take the leave, or to address the possible negative attitudes of employers towards fathers who take leave. Findings noted above also indicate that economic necessity or career options for women, combined with egalitarian sex-role attitudes, were not sufficient either to guarantee a smooth change to reversed roles, or a continuation in this life-style over a longer period — even though this was what parents wanted to do. A more broadly based approach, which would facilitate fathers' adaptation to a stint at home as the caregiver, might involve an emphasis on issues such as: child-care classes for fathers (e.g. in hospitals or as community education programmes) and boys (e.g. in schools); changes in fathers' and employers' attitudes and beliefs about males' commitments to breadwinning, their employers, and to their job/careers (cf. Lamb and Levine, 1983); encourage greater recognition and acceptance by management and in personnel practices, of work/family conflicts; and encourage employers to take more account of the family responsibilities of employees, by developing alternatives to work-related skills/personal development courses for women, by offering programmes and services which might both expand men's options to participate more extensively in their families, and help employees cope with the difficulties of balancing work and family commitments.

The experiences of reversed-role mothers also indicates a need to evaluate critically approaches to increasing women's options. There are many current schemes which are aimed at increasing women's employment skills, or at broadening their options for future employment through programmes in schools. Little attempt is being made to prepare females (or males) to deal with the conflicts that they might experience between work and family responsibilities, or to explore the problems and issues associated with shared parenting. As is evident from the above review, and in articles in the popular press (e.g. Osborne, 1985; Sweet, 1984), it is not a simple matter for mothers to accept shared parenting, nor to give up the idea that they should be the primary parent.

Perhaps there is also a need for some affirmative action for males and fathers, to help encourage them to see child-care as an option, and to change their ideas about responsibilities for parenting. Such an approach would obviously help address some of the problems experienced by fathers who are forced into reversing roles through economic necessity. Critical attention could be given to the images and models of fathers and mothers portrayed in parenting books (most are still written with the assumption that it is only mothers with male children who read them), children's books, and in the media (advertisements still assume that the mother is the primary parent).

Emphasis could also be given to developing policies, services and practices which assume that mothers and fathers have equal responsibility for children, and acknowledge the fact that the father might be the primary caregiver. Most currently presume that mothers will be/are the primary parent and that the father is the primary breadwinner. This in itself represents an important barrier to the acceptance of alternative family patterns. The areas which could be given some immediate attention are: the approaches of medical professionals and groups that are concerned with childbirth education; social work, psychological and family counselling practices (e.g. more effort could be made to involve fathers in these processes); special initiatives could be taken to develop support and information groups for fathers; and some effort could be made to change the approaches of schools and other institutions which interact with or offer services to families, but which focus almost exclusively on mothers.

Finally, there is a need to evaluate critically approaches which emphasize the social barriers to women's employment options, and the development of policies to broaden these, while at the same time ignoring the possibility that many men would choose a more equal balance between paid work and family commitments if this was a realistic option. For this to become a realistic option, however, more emphasis would need to be placed on the development of parallel policies which assume parents have equal responsibility for children, and which would *support* changes in the work/family balance for *both* women and men.

References

Berger, M. (1979) 'Men's New Family Roles — Some Implications for Therapists', *Family Co-ordinator* 34: 1016–23.

Bryson, L. (1983) 'Thirty Years of Research on the Division of Labour in Australian Families', *Australian Journal of Sex, Marriage and Family* 4: 125–32.

De Frain, J. (1979) 'Androgynous Parents Tell Who They Are and What They Need', *The Family Co-ordinator* 28: 237–43.

Field, T. (1978) 'Interaction Behaviors of Primary versus Secondary Caretaker Fathers', *Developmental Psychology* 49: 183–4.

Gronseth, E. (1978) 'Work Sharing: A Norwegian Example', in R. Rapoport and R.N. Rapoport (eds) *Working Couples*. St Lucia, Queensland: University of Queensland Press.

Harper, J. (1980) *Fathers at Home*. Melbourne: Penguin.

Hoffman, L.W. (1983) 'Increased Fathering: Effects on the Mother', in M.E. Lamb and A. Sagi (eds) *Fatherhood and Family Policy*, Hillsdale, NJ: Lawrence Erlbaum Associates.

Kimball, G. (1984) 'Why do Couples Role Share?' Unpublished paper, University of California, Chico, California.

Lamb, M.E. and Levine, J.A. (1983) 'The Swedish Parental Insurance Policy: An Experiment in Social Engineering', in M.E. Lamb and A. Sagi (eds) *Fatherhood and Family Policy*, Hillsdale, NJ: Lawrence Erlbaum.

Lamb, M.E., Frodi, A.M., Hwang, C-P., Frodi, M. and Steinberg, J. (1982) 'Mother– and Father–Infant Interaction involving Play and Holding in Traditional and Non-traditional Swedish Families', *Developmental Psychology* 18: 215–21.

Lamb, M.E., Frodi, M., Hwang, C-P., and Frodi, A.M. (1983) 'Effects of Paternal Involvement on Infant Preferences for Mothers and Fathers', *Child Development* 50: 450–8.

Lamb, M.E., Pleck, J.H., Charnov, E.L. and Levine, J.A. (1984) 'A Biosocial Perspective on Paternal Behavior and Involvement', in J.B. Lancaster, J. Altmann, A. Rossi and L. Sherrod (eds) *Parenting across the Lifespan: Biosocial Perspectives*. Chicago: Aldine.

Lein, L. (1979) 'Male Participation in Home Life: Impact of Social Supports and Breadwinner Responsibility on the Allocation of Tasks', *The Family Co-ordinator* 29: 489–96.

Levine, J. (1976) *Who will raise the Children? New Options for Fathers (and Mothers)*. New York: Bantam.

Osborne, D. (1985) 'Beyond the Cult of Fatherhood: My Experience is Different from that of the Fathers I read about', *Ms* 14: 81.

Pleck, J.H. (1982) 'Husbands' and Wives' Paid Work, Family Work and Adjustment.' Wellesley College Center for Research on Women, Wellesley, Ma.

Radin, N. (1981) 'Childrearing Fathers in Intact Families: An Exploration of some Antecedents and Consequences', *Merrill-Palmer Quarterly* 27: 489–514.

Radin, N. (1982) 'Primary Caregiving and Role-sharing Fathers of Preschoolers', in M.E. Lamb (ed.) *Nontraditional Families: Parenting and Child Development*, Hillsdale, NJ: Lawrence Erlbaum.

Radin, N. (1985) 'Antecedents of Stability in High Father Involvement.' Paper presented at the Conference on Equal Parenting: Families of the future, February, University of California, Chico, California.

Radin, N. and Russell, G. (1983) 'Increased Father Participation and Child Development Outcomes', in M.E. Lamb and A. Sagi (eds) *Fatherhood and Family Policy*. Hillsdale, NJ: Lawrence Erlbaum.

Russell, G. (1983) *The Changing Role of Fathers?* St Lucia, Queensland: University of Queensland Press.

Russell, G. (1984) 'Changing Patterns of Divisions of Labor for Paid Work and Child Care.' Paper presented to the 1984 ISA–CFR International Seminar on Social Change and Family Policies, Melbourne, Australia.

Russell, G. (1986) 'Primary Caretaking and Role Sharing Fathers', in M.E. Lamb (ed.) *Fatherhood: Applied Perspectives*. New York: Wiley.

Sagi, A. (1982) 'Antecedents and Consequences of Various Degrees of Parental Involvement in Childrearing. The Israeli Project', in M.E. Lamb (ed.) *Nontraditional Families: Parenting and Child Development*. Hillsdale, NJ: Lawrence Erlbaum.

Spanier, G.B. (1976) 'Measuring Dyadic Adjustment: New Scales for Assessing the Quality of Marriage and Similar Dyads', *Journal of Marriage and Family* 38, 15–30.

Sweet, E. (1984) 'Parenting: The Electra Complex', *Ms.* 13: 148–9.

III

FATHERS AND FAMILY CRISIS

As many of the authors in this section suggest, men appear to thrive in marriage and often suffer more than their wives after separation or divorce. The following chapters describe the experiences of fathers in families undergoing problems or dissolution. By focusing upon contact between men and professionals (social workers, marital therapists and the divorce mediators) this section also provides guidelines for clinicians in a variety of settings.

Taking the example of social workers, Marsh (Chapter 11) suggests that despite the recent focus upon 'family' approaches to intervention, members of the 'helping professions' have long been hooked into a 'mother-centred' paradigm. In many cases the father is an appendage to the family who is neglected during casework.

As in social work, men tend to be somewhat removed from marriage guidance counselling (marital therapy). Blackie and Clark (Chapter 12) trace some reasons for this pattern — for example, men's reluctance to reflect upon emotional issues, particularly in public, the expectation that wives are the emotional 'experts' in families and the predominance of women in the profession of counselling. However, in three illuminating case examples Blackie and Clark show how, despite initial reluctance, men can be successfully incorporated into counselling.

Given a continuing increase in marital separation, Lund (Chapter 13) examines the experiences of men who find themselves separated not only from their wives, but also from their children. She explores the problems of establishing access and maintaining a relationship with children when the father lives apart from them. Lund shows the variations in fathering styles post-divorce and provides insights from research for clinicians who work with families after separation.

While most mothers assume custody after divorce, a small proportion of fathers do also. Men achieve custody through a diversity of pathways, which themselves may influence the way lone fatherhood is experienced. O'Brien (Chapter 14) examines one aspect of lone fathers' new life-styles — their relationships with kin and friends — and shows how interrelationships between fathers and these significant others can provide further clues about the constraints on fatherhood. The deviant status of male single parenthood can activate intense social isolation, but can also encourage high levels of dependence on kin and friends. Through an examination of these socio-kin networks, O'Brien traces the individual and social pressures which militate against a close and nurturant parental role for men.

Divorce mediation or conciliation has developed in recent years to maintain family links, particularly parenting relationships, after separation. Parkinson (Chapter 15) examines the place of fathers in this process. She uncovers why men wish to maintain contact with their children and answers the criticism raised by feminists that conciliation gives power to men after separation where previously they had little. Parkinson's chapter concludes by offering clear practical guidelines for conciliation work with all family members, including fathers.

11
Social work and fathers — an exclusive practice?

Peter Marsh

The problems and contradictions of fatherhood are issues that social workers will have to grapple with on numerous occasions. Fathers are featured in custody reports for divorce cases, thousands of children in care are looked after by foster fathers, and handicapped fathers may receive a variety of services and help. This chapter examines the way in which fatherhood has been understood within social work. It should be fruitful where research and practice should be especially relevant to our understanding of fathering in families under stress, and in particular situations of substitute fathering and step-fathering.

Fatherhood is, of course, a fast developing research topic. McKee and O'Brien (1982: 3) characterize the changes in family research over the past 15 years as a 'quiet revolution', where 'fatherhood has become a distinctive and prestigious substantive issue, and "mother-focussed" research programmes have become increasingly outmoded and criticised'. Given the clear importance of the topic within social work and the fast developing related research it would be natural to assume that there would be substantial studies by researchers within the social work discipline, and relevant extracts and summaries made from research conducted elsewhere. In fact there is surprisingly little overt emphasis on fatherhood in the social work literature. For example, the major social work abstracting journal in the UK (*Social Services Abstracts*) has almost no references to fathers or associated topics in the period 1980–5. Although, as we shall see, the picture is starting to change there has been a long-standing absence of concern with fathers which has grown relatively more noticeable as the study of fatherhood advances in the social sciences in general. To understand this state of affairs it is necessary to consider something of the history of social work itself. Such a perspective will be taken in this Chapter, using illustrations from social work practice with children in care with a particular focus on the role fathers play in the origins of care, and the importance of fatherhood to the treatment of children in care. In conclusion we shall note some of the current issues involved in the development of a father-aware practice in social work.

The missing father

Work with families in the public care system provides the sharpest example of social work's relative lack of interest in fathers, and we shall focus our attention on this area of practice research. Professional social work in child-care (in the UK) could be dated from 1948 when Children's Departments were created within local authorities (Packman, 1981). The field staff of these Departments were among the first professional social workers. They had little empirical research to guide their efforts. Training courses were rapidly established within Universities, linked with the growing social science departments (Younghusband, 1978: 80). The literature that informed the practice in the 1950s and 1960s emphasized expectations of parenting focused predominantly on mother as carer and father as worker and possibly supporter. Rapoport et al.'s skilful summary of this literature (1977: 69–75) notes that for social work, until the mid-1970s, the dominant view implied that fathers were 'peripheral' to parenting. Within this dominant framework there were voices that foresaw many of the problems that are coming into sharper focus in the 1980s. Timms (1962), for example, in a text for child-care social work notes that practice that fails to involve the father may risk reinforcing those child-care problems that are linked to the lack of involvement of father in the family itself. Regarding the provision of care Dyson (1962) notes the important potential of foster fathers. Such views were not common; the dominant theoretical paradigm remained that of a mother-centred view of child-care.

Social work was not alone in this view. Across many disciplines in the 1950s and much of the 1960s a particular framework was visible for study of the family and practice with the family. Rapoport et al. (1977: 87) summarized it as follows:

> By and large the picture . . . is one in which there was an authoritative set of formulations in the period following the Second World War that idealised a conception of the nuclear conjugal family, with relatively standardised composition, division of labour, and life-cycle timetable. This conception, with its expectations that 'normal', 'mature' men will be economic providers, 'normal', 'mature' women will be housewives and mothers – has been bolstered by clinical psychiatry (as in the work of Bowlby and Winnicott), medicine (as in the early work of Spock), sociology (as in the work of Parsons) and by professionals in law, education and social work.

There were few empirical studies of the practice of social workers in this period, but a key study of foster care by George (1970) provides a clear picture of the influence of the mother-centred views in practice. George (1970: 97) comments as follows about the differential treatment of foster mothers and foster fathers:

The contents of the reports of the child care officers as well as the number of interviews with different family members reflected the secondary position the foster father holds in social work literature . . . in one-fifth of all applications in the three departments the foster father was seen by himself once and only on one occasion he was seen twice. On the other hand the foster mother was interviewed alone in 71 per cent of the applications, in the majority of cases only once but twice in one-quarter of the cases.

George and Wilding in their study of 'motherless families' (1972), provide a supporting view of the lack of involvement of social workers with fathers. Their sample of nearly 600 lone father families highlighted the problems that these fathers face, including pressure on their time (especially because of lack of child-care support), complex feelings of depression and stress, and financial difficulties. The first two of these problems are major concerns of social work practice but in fact around 50 percent of the sample said that they had received no social work help at all; 30 percent simply not applying for help (usually citing the fact that they felt they could manage without professional help) and 20 percent being refused help. However, of the 50 percent who did receive some service around two-thirds found their contact quite satisfactory and the workers 'helpful and sympathetic' (p. 156). Nonetheless the actual service received was not ranked very highly when fathers were asked about usefulness, and George and Wilding found that social work help was relatively insignificant for lone father families.

By the mid-1970s social workers, by now organized into large Social Services Departments, had an established model of practice that gave prominence to mothers. A few dissenting voices could be found in the literature, and hints could be seen that indicated that the practice was at least starting to recognize the particular difficulties of fathers and the role of fatherhood within families. In the 1970s with the growth of fatherhood research, and the feminist critique of much family literature, it could be expected that social workers would start to embrace the new 'discovery' of fathers and question their mother-centred practice. In fact there were other major concerns that dominated the decade.

The creation of Social Services Departments from the previously separate Children's, Health, and Welfare Departments brought together for the first time social workers from child-care, mental health, and the elderly and disabled services. The creation of the new departments was not considered in detail and there was little allowance made for the scale of the exercise (Hall, 1976; Younghusband, 1978). The social workers in the three previous departments had very different traditions, there were quite different levels of qualified staff, and some of the services had been starved of resources throughout their existence. In 1974 further reorganization incorporated medical social work staff in hospitals. Coping with these multiple organizational, and administrative changes became a major concern, perhaps the major concern, for much of the 1970s. Practice developments took place in this context. Practitioners also had to respond to continuing changes in legislation, especially in the areas of juvenile crime and services for the handicapped and disabled. All in all it was not an easy time for social workers to add new social scientific concepts to their thinking. Even within the universities, where social work education was rapidly expanded, staff had to cope with multiple changes in qualification programmes and the research endeavours were correspondingly slowed.

In these circumstances it is perhaps not surprising that dominant theoretical models from an earlier era continued relatively unchallenged. As Brooke and Davis (1985: 5) have commented

> the significance and consequence of the predominance of women in the day-to-day negotiations between social workers, clients and their families have not been explicitly discussed. Most social work literature has taken for granted that this is a normal and therefore unimportant fact of professional life.

Practice in the late 1970s and the early 1980s continues to reflect this taken-for-granted role of mothers as the central feature of family life. In foster families (Rowe et al., 1984) and in work with the families of children in care (Packman et al., 1984) mothers are still the main, and sometimes the sole, focus of attention. Packman's large-scale study of child-care practice summarizes the position clearly (1984: 104–5), when she comments that social workers

> were usually able to offer an evaluation of marital relationships and of the parenting standards of the *mothers* of the children ... There was less certainty when it came to questions about the extended family, and knowledge of wider kinship networks seemed to be confined largely to those stalwart supporters – the mother's own parents. Beyond that it was shaky and faltering, as was their familiarity with the strengths and weaknesses of neighbourly relationships. Knowledge about the *fathers* of the children was also very patchy. To some extent this was inevitable. There were many one-parent families with a female head, and a father long since gone. But even where a father *was* present considerably less was known about him than about his partner, so he remained – at least in aggregated form – a rather shadowy figure. (emphasis in original)

Fatherhood, social work and care

Social work practice with families is still trailing behind the more recent research on fathers' roles, but there are signs that changes are on the way. Social work research is now developing quite fast and a wide range of research approaches (Reid and Smith, 1981) are showing results in many areas of practice (e.g. Goldberg and Connelly, 1981). In the 1980s regular *Research Highlights* have been published as a series; monographs have appeared in some quantity from the University of East Anglia, and from the Joint Unit of Social Services Research at Sheffield University, there is a new journal of *Research, Policy and Planning*, and so on. Knowledge development is on the move again. A distinctive research tradition that carefully relays and analyses clients' views is now well established (Rees and Wallace, 1982; Fisher, 1983; Shaw, 1984). Fathers and fatherhood are firmly on the agenda, although there is a long long way to go to make up for the lost decade of the 1970s. It is now time to try to gather together the few elements of past studies that focused on fathers, and look at the more recent work to sketch, very tentatively, some of the issues concerning fatherhood that are emerging.

This modest preliminary effort to piece together the bits of knowledge that we have of fathers within social work will continue to focus on the British child-care system. It is a fruitful area for fatherhood studies, and has recently been the subject of much social work research attention.

As the discussion progresses it will be clear that Packman's picture of a practice that focuses on mothers to an extent which can effectively exclude fathers is borne out by other studies. It would be easy to be very critical of social workers, even if the relative youthfulness of the profession was stressed in mitigation. It is therefore important to bear in mind that the professional denial of a role to fathers is widespread. Social work practice compared to, say, that surrounding the birth of children (e.g. Jackson, 1984; Brown, 1982) seems relatively benign.

In child-care practice social workers will face the widespread cultural assumption that mothers will take the major role in external negotiations and discussions about their children (Sharpe, 1984; Osborn et al., 1984). They also face problems in finding fathers, when around one-third of the families with children in care are headed by single mothers, and many of the two-parent families have step-fathers (Marsh et al., 1985). There are significant barriers in the way of including fathers in child-care social work.

Children in care and their families come in many shapes and sizes. Problems, routes of entry to care, legal matters, family compositions and so on are visible in a wide variety of forms. Packman's recent study (1984) has given us one useful way of simplifying this picture by suggesting that three groups of children can be identified. The groups are not mutually exclusive, and not clear-cut, but they do provide a useful framework for consideration of care. They are 'ideal types', derived from research. Firstly, there are the 'victims' who suffer at the hands of their parents and need protection. Usually this will be provided on the basis of decisions reached in court. Then there are the 'villains' who commit some form of criminal offence and who are sentenced to care by the courts. 'Villain' has an unfortunate ring to it, implying serious crime, and perhaps also implying a classification of personality type. Neither factor should be associated with the use of the term here. The majority of crimes committed by juveniles are small in scale but high in nuisance value (petty shoplifting, vandalism and the like), and the majority of juveniles cease to commit crimes as they mature into adulthood; 'villain' is a convenient shorthand and should not be taken as anything more. Finally, there are the 'volunteered' where care is requested and needed as a service and where the courts are rarely involved. It should be borne in mind that these categories may not correspond to parental or child views of events. Marsh et al. (1985: 14) for example, noted that 'the criminal element in behaviour and the use of compulsory care were important but not dominant features of the families' experiences'. That is to say that 'villains' may have been willingly volunteered and 'volunteers' may have been villainous or felt treated like villains. Nonetheless the 'ideal types' of villains, victims and volunteers will be a useful aid to our discussion and analysis especially in clarifying the types of care that particular research studies cover, and in examining the distinctive roles that fathers might play within each ideal–typical category. We shall look first at the origins of care, and then at the involvement of fathers once children are in care.

Family dynamics antecedent to care

It is now well documented that juvenile crimes and delinquency are associated with lack of parental supervision, and a low level of family rules and their enforcement concerning staying out, bed-times, manners and so on (West and Farrington, 1973, 1977; Wilson and Herbert, 1978). Some of these youngsters will enter the care system as the villains that we have noted earlier. Riley and Shaw (1985) looked in detail at families with children aged 14 and 15, when crimes are most likely to occur, and where research has been surprisingly absent in the past. They held separate interviews with teenagers and parents of a representative sample of around 750 families in England and Wales. The parent was usually the mother, but the interviews with fathers proved particularly interesting. Around two-thirds of the mothers worked outside the home, mostly part-time, and a majority were reasonably satisfied with the relationship with their teenage children. There was no link found between working mothers and teenage self-report of delinquency. On the other hand, working fathers, nearly all full-time, were much less happy with their relationship with their child. Almost half felt that they spent insufficient time with them and they usually blamed their work for this state of affairs. For both boys and girls the lack of a close relationship with father appeared to be one of the factors associated with delinquent behaviour. Lewis et al. (1982: 191) found similar connections, with low father participation in middle childhood being almost the sole parental factor related to the acquisition of a criminal conviction by age 18 to 20. Shaw and Riley (1985: 22) summarize their main report as follows.

> there are indeed a number of aspects of family life which are important in relation to teenage delinquency, and a number of areas over which parents can expect to have some influence, including teenagers' attitudes to crime, their choice of friends and the central importance of maintaining close family relationships between parents and teenagers. It is also evident that both boys and girls were more likely to be delinquent if they had delinquent friends, did not regard stealing as particularly wrong and were not very close to their fathers.

Our own study (Marsh et al., 1984, 1985; Fisher et al., 1986) based on a sample of children and families who were experiencing care, can add more detailed child and parental views to this area. We were able to see children, mothers and fathers separately, and we conducted around 330 interviews based on a sample drawn from 350 children in care. Seventy-nine fathers were seen individually and one group interview also took place discussing themes that appeared to be arising in the research (for a discussion of the research approach see Phillips and Marsh, 1984). Our study covered 'victims', 'villains' and the 'volunteered'.

The parents in our study were notably concerned about the likelihood of their children getting into trouble, and they regarded the process of child development as one which led to a natural testing of the limits and rules of social conduct, and a risky experience of contact with other, potentially delinquent, children. We characterized this as a parental view (usually echoed by their children) that children were primed, simply by virtue of being children to encounter trouble, and they were most likely to do this in the (city) streets.

The parents interviewed by Shaw and Riley appeared to underestimate the likelihood of teenagers committing delinquent acts. Those we interviewed were under no such illusion. They thought that their rights to control their children were less obvious than in their own childhood and that this made the task especially hard. Over two-thirds of mothers and fathers felt their rights had decreased as compared with those they ascribed to their parents. They thought that the task of giving discipline should ideally be shared between two parents, but there was a particular weight to a father's punishment that was difficult for a mother to replicate. Control and discipline were, in their view, most effective if they directly preceded or followed the relevant event. Immediacy of response was important. So matters of discipline could not await a father's return, even if it was thought more appropriate that the father handled it.

In practice, as has been noted earlier, many families had no father at home to provide this service. Around half of the children had a father or father figure present (other studies found similar figures, e.g. Millham et al., 1984: 191). One-third of the children lived in single-parent families headed by the mother, and when a father figure was present it was equally as likely to be a step-father as a natural father. When a new father figure arrived he sometimes selected the parts of the fathering role that he was prepared to undertake. Both fathers and mothers described to us this adoption of different parts of the father role with different children, 'the eldest one, she's not his, you see'. At times it was actually difficult to detect from mothers and children that there was a father figure in the family, because of the lack of involvement that he had with his new children.

Mothers described to us the difficulties that they had in persuading a new husband or cohabitee to take on the role of discipline giver. They recognized that it might expose him to extra problems, that it could lead to increased arguments with the new children and the risk of rejection by them. In short it was, in their eyes, a threat to the stability of the new family. Attempts to involve father figures were handled with due care in the light of this. Mothers therefore felt themselves to be burdened with a lack of societal support for discipline and control and the absence of a father figure (physically or socially) pushed them into a role they were ill equipped to carry out. Not surprisingly mothers found this situation increasingly desperate. Some responded by calling in uncles, or trying to make the eldest boy into a responsible figure whose job it was to set standards, but these were seen as temporary solutions. They offered only marginal relief.

The problems grew increasingly difficult as the child to be controlled grew older. This was particularly because of the common parental view that increasing age increased the need for occasional very firm control. Views on the extent to which firm control directly required physical punishment differed between fathers and mothers. Both were agreed that some physical chastisement was needed but there was a different degree of emphasis given to it.

Mothers discussed discipline and control in terms of the importance of children showing respect for adults. They encouraged this by discussion and by example of the sort of relationship that should exist between the child and the adult world. If firm control was needed this

approach led mothers to try other sanctions before any use of physical punishment. They did not reject such punishment, they regarded
its presence as a symbolic deterrent, to be used with some care, which
backed up the development of an appropriate relationship between
adult and child. Their inability to give such physical punishment to
older children reduced their control by significantly reducing their
credibility.

Fathers, on the other hand, tended to see a more direct link
between physical punishment and firm control. It was the view of
many fathers that physical punishment at an early stage was effective
in decreasing disobedience. They thought that a quick smack was
often a better way to demonstrate firmness than discussion or some
form of sanction. Limited physical punishment was, in their view,
part of the standard range of techniques for setting clear limits for
children; it was, if necessary, an ingredient of day-to-day control.

Social workers see families under stress, and in the shorthand we
have used here they help the 'villains', the 'victims' and the 'volunteered' when care is needed. Fatherhood clearly plays an important
role in the origins of that need for care. The 'villains' are likely to
have a poor relationship with their father. In all groups the mother
may regret the absence of a father for specific aspects of care and
control and find the resultant burden an ingredient in her need for
outside help. The differences that appear to be present in father's and
mother's views of control may also form an important backdrop to
care.

Social work research in the 1980s is therefore starting to make its
own modest contribution to the study of fatherhood especially in
examining the role of the father in families under stress. It is interesting to speculate on future themes that may develop as research in
social work brings the father more clearly into its remit.

Fathering and the origins of care appear to intertwine in complex
ways. Problematic relationships between fathers and their children
characterize many of the care families. It may be that different forms
of this problem are linked to different forms of child behaviour. We
have seen that poor relationships between children and fathers play
some role in delinquent behaviour (the 'villains' in care), and that the
physical absence of fathers plays some role in internal family stress
leading to breakdown and care (the 'volunteered' in care). In our
own research we looked at the family composition of these two
groups (Marsh et al., 1984: 7). Around 40 percent of court admissions, approximating to 'villains', were from two natural parent
families. Only around 18 percent of voluntary admissions, approximating to 'volunteers', are from such families. Are there hints here
that the physical absence of fathers is prominent in the origins of

internal family breakdown, while poor relationships with fathers within the family are implicated in families with delinquent children? Might physical absence of fathers be more associated with children's behaviour problems within the family, and the social absence of fathers within families be more associated with children's public behaviour problems? Whether or not these hints have any substance will no doubt become clearer as our knowledge develops over the coming years.

Fathering during care

We have considered some issues of fatherhood and the origins of care, but what happens to fathers, and to fathering, when care is under way? The majority of children in care should maintain links with natural or step-parents and will go home to them at some time in their childhood. Around half of all admissions are likely to be home in 3 months, and only perhaps 5 percent of all admissions need complete separation from parents because of abuse (see Millham et al., 1984). The majority of care work should try to prevent permanent family breakdown (Fisher et al., 1986), and as problems between fathers and children are likely to feature as one of the issues behind entry to care, so part of work in care will often need to try and rectify such problems. We have noticed before that achieving this is fraught with problems. Poor or non-existent relationships may have built up over years and prove intractably difficult to change. With this firmly in mind what do we currently know about the interconnection of fatherhood and treatment in care?

Three rather different situations need to be distinguished. Firstly, the provision of care when a father figure is present, or potentially present within the family. Secondly, care for families where fathers are very unlikely to be involved due to a variety of reasons such as their own firm choice or the hostility of others. Finally, care for the small minority of cases where fathers have hurt their children and protection is an important element of the work. We shall both review current practice, and see what indications there are of developments that link fathering and work in care.

Despite the fact that most children in care are going to maintain contact with their families, there is evidence that parental involvement with their children in care is lower than it should be (Fisher et al., 1986; Millham et al., 1984). There are indications that this is a rather worse problem for fathers than mothers. For example, when social workers at the end of 6 months reviewed the cases of children in care, Millham and his colleagues (1984: 234) found that

in 39% of cases access between the child and natural mother was not even raised as an issue and contact with father or the wider family received even less consideration.

At the end of one year they found (1984: 280) that social work contact with parents had notably diminished as there was 'virtually no communication with a third of mothers', and 'fathers fared even worse with 80 per cent of them uninvolved with social workers'. Clearly the level of parental involvement is not satisfactory in terms of the aims of maintaining family links and keeping families intact. The particular situation of fathers is notably bad, and a cause for some concern. Indeed Packman and her colleagues (1984: 322) found faint suggestions that removal to care may directly exacerbate difficulties in father–child relationships. This may have a link both with the finding noted earlier of social workers' relative exclusion of fathers from their immediate concerns, and the way that fathers respond to the institution of care itself. Jenkins' (1981: 328) American study of parents of children in care, for example, hints that fathers may experience greater feelings of shame than mothers. Detailed examinations of the responses of fathers to the changes in their role when their children enter care are unfortunately not available at present.

Current progress
Are there signs that the mother-focused practice developed in the 1950s and still prominent in the 1980s is starting to change? Certainly the practice models available to social workers have expanded to include ones that would emphasize father awareness. These newer models are clearly becoming more dominant in the 1980s. Family therapy, derived from developments in many disciplines, and task-centred practice derived from empirical research in social work are two prominent examples.

A small number of social workers have been active in the development of family therapy from its beginning, but it is only very recently that approaches within this tradition are being used at all widely within social work. The past few years have seen a sudden large increase in the social work texts available, all of which emphasize the roles of *all* family members (Masson and O'Byrne, 1984; Barnes, 1984; Manor, 1984; Treacher and Carpenter, 1984). A few limited social work references to the specific role of fathers, are starting to appear. Schulman (1981), for example, discusses issues in helping fathers and families cope with the changes involved in divorce, and in becoming step-families. Wylder (1982) suggests that including the divorced father in family therapy may lead to greater future family stability.

Family therapy looks set to develop much more widely in social work over the coming years and fathers will clearly feature more strongly as it does so. Family-based models of work are also developing within a social work practice model called task-centred work. This is a contract based, time-limited model of practice that has developed as a result of empirical research over the past two decades. Its origins lie in a study by Reid (1963), who has been the leading research practitioner in this field. His text and research study *The Task-centred System* (1978) provides the most general formulation of the model. In recent years the model has strongly emphasized the inclusion of all family members, and new developments in this direction have been devised and tested (Reid, 1985; Fortune, 1985). Links with family therapy are quite strong and a coherent family-based approach may be forged from the two models.

There are therefore positive signs that a more father-aware practice may be developing. Insofar as it does it will also need to take account of those situations in care where the father is not able to become involved. Developments have hardly begun here and only tentative discussions of substitute fathering featuring the use of foster fathers (Davids, 1971) and male residential staff (Brody, 1978) can be found in the literature. It will also need to cover the small minority of families in care where fathers have abused their children, and again developments appear to be rather thin. Martin (1984) for example reviewed sixty-six child abuse studies from within various disciplines published between 1976 and 1980. Twenty-two of the studies were only of mothers, two were only of fathers, and thirty-six made no differentiation between parents. None of the studies discussed the specialized treatment needs of men and women. It is clear that all the disciplines concerned with child abuse are rather slow in incorporating fatherhood into their frame of reference.

The future

Social work has not been in the forefront of developing a father-aware practice. As we have seen, much of its theoretical legacy from the 1950s and 1960s offered an approach that effectively moved fathers to the margins of social work concerns, and could effectively exclude them from social work practice. After such a lengthy hiatus in the 1970s when fatherhood research developed rapidly but social work practice marked time, there are signs of change in the 1980s. Contributions to our knowledge of fathering in families under stress are now being made by social work researchers, deficiencies in practice are being examined, and new family approaches are developing. In this chapter we have seen, for example, that delinquency may be associated with poor relationships with fathers, and that fatherhood is an important part of the analysis of the origins of care. It has also been shown that mothers in families under stress regretted the social or physical absence of fathers for specific aspects of care and control of children, and they found the resultant burden one ingredient in their need for outside help. Our body of knowledge is therefore growing, but there is a very long way to go. Studies of the substitute and supplementary father role are signally lacking, fathers in child abuse cases are not receiving enough attention, and work on handicapped fathers and elderly fathers would be particularly welcome. These will come, as there is no doubt that fatherhood is now firmly on the agenda of social work practice and research.

References

Barnes, G.G. (1984) *Working with Families*. London: Macmillan.

Brody, S. (1978) 'Daddy's Gone to Colorado: Male-Staffed Child Care for Father-Absent Boys', *Counselling Psychologist* 7(4): 33–6.

Brooke, E. and Davis, A. (eds) (1985) *Women, the Family and Social Work*. London: Tavistock.

Brown, A. (1982) 'Fathers in the Labour Ward: Medical and Lay Accounts' in L. McKee and M. O'Brien (eds) *The Father Figure*, pp. 104–19. London: Tavistock.

Davids, L. (1971) 'Foster Fatherhood: The Untaped Resource', *The Family Co-ordinator* 20(1) (Jan): 49–54.

Dyson, D.M. (1962) *No Two Alike*. London: Allen and Unwin.

Fisher, M. (ed.) (1983) *Speaking of Clients*. Joint Unit for Social Services Research, University of Sheffield.

Fisher, M., Marsh, P. and Phillips, D. (1986) *In and Out of Care – The Experiences of Children, Parents and Social Workers*. London: Batsford.

Fortune, A. (1985) *Task-Centred Practice with Families and Groups*. New York, USA: Springer.

George, V. (1970) *Foster Care*. London: Routledge and Kegan Paul.

George, V. and Wilding, P. (1972) *Motherless Families*. London: Routledge and Kegan Paul.

Hall, P. (1976) *Reforming the Welfare*. London: Heinemann.

Goldberg, E.M. and Connelly, N. (eds) (1981) *Evaluative Research in Social Care*. London: Heinemann.

Jackson, B. (1984) *Fatherhood*. London: Allen and Unwin.

Jenkins, S. (1981) 'Separation Experiences of Parents whose Children are in Foster Care' in P.A. Sinanoglu and A.N. Maluccio (eds) *Parents of Children in Placement: Perspectives and Programs*, pp. 327–35. USA, Child Welfare League of America.

Lewis, C., Newson, E. and Newson, J. (1982) 'Father Participation through Childhood and its Relationship with Career Aspirations and Delinquency', in N. Beail and J. McGuire (eds) *Fathers – Psychological Perspectives*, pp. 174–93. London: Junction Books.

Manor, O. (ed) (1984) *Family Work in Action – a Handbook for Social Workers*. London: Tavistock.

Marsh, P., Phillips, D., Sainsbury, E.E. and Fisher, M. (1984) 'In and Out of Care', Report to the ESRC.

Marsh, P., Fisher, M. and Phillips, D. (1985) 'Negotiating Child Care', *Adoption and Fostering* 9(3): 11–17.

Martin, J.A. (1984) 'Neglected Fathers: Limitations in Diagnostic and Treatment Resources for Violent Men', *Child Abuse and Neglect* 8(4): 387–92.

Masson, H.C. and O'Byrne, P. (1984) *Applying Family Therapy – A Practical Guide for Social Workers*. Oxford: Pergamon.

McKee, L. and O'Brien, M. (eds) (1982) *The Father Figure*. London: Tavistock.

Millham, S., Bullock, R., Hosie, K. and Haak, M. (1984) 'The Problems of Maintaining Links between Children in Care and their Families – A Study of the Child Care Process', Report to the DHSS April 1984, University of Bristol: School of Applied Social Studies, Dartington Social Research Unit.

Osborn, A.F., Butler, N.R. and Morris, A.C. (1984) *The Social Life of Britain's Five-Year-Olds*. London: Routledge and Kegan Paul.

Packman, J. (1981) *The Child's Generation: Child Care Policy in Britain*, 2nd edn. Oxford: Basil Blackwell.

Packman, J., Randall, J. and Jacques, N. (1984) 'Decision-Making on Admissions of Children to Local Authority Care', Report for DHSS.

Phillips, D. and Marsh, P. (1984) 'Doing Social Work Research', *Research, Policy and Planning* 2(2): 21–7.

Rapoport, R., Rapoport, R.N., Strelitz, Z. and Kew, S. (1977) *Fathers, Mothers and Others*. London: Routledge and Kegan Paul.

Rees, S. and Wallace, A. (1982) *Verdicts on Social Work*. London: Edward Arnold.

Reid, W.J. (1963) 'An Experimental Study of Methods Used in Casework Treatment', Columbia University PhD thesis.

Reid, W.J. (1978) *The Task-Centred System*. New York: Columbia University Press.

Reid, W.J. (1985) *Family Problem Solving*. New York: Columbia University Press.

Reid, W.J. and Smith, A.D. (1981) *Research in Social Work*. New York: Columbia University Press.

Riley, D. and Shaw, M. (1985) 'Parental Supervision and Juvenile Delinquency', Home Office Research Study No. 83, HMSO.

Rowe, J., Cain, H., Hundleby, M. and Keane, A. (1984) *Long-Term Foster Care*. London: Batsford.

Schulman, G.L. (1981) 'Divorce, Single Parenthood and Step-Families: Structural Implications of these Transitions', *International Journal of Family Therapy* (Summer): 87–112.

Sharpe, S. (1984) *Double Identity: The Lives of Working Mothers*. London: Penguin.

Shaw, I. (1984) 'Literature Review – Consumer Evaluations of the Personal Social Services', *British Journal of Social Work* 14: 277–84.

Shaw, M. and Riley, D. (1985) 'Families, Teenagers and Crime', *Home Office Research and Planning Unit – Research Bulletin* No. 19: 20–2.

Timms, N. (1962) *Casework in the Child Care Service*. London: Butterworth.

Treacher, A. and Carpenter, J. (1984) *Using Family Therapy*. Oxford: Blackwell.

Wilson, H. and Herbert, G. (1978) *Parents and Children in the Inner City*. London: Routledge and Kegan Paul.

West, D. and Farrington, D. (1973) *Who Becomes Delinquent?* London: Heinemann.

West, D. and Farrington, D. (1977) *The Delinquent Way of Life*. London: Heinemann.

Wylder, J. (1982) 'Including the Divorced Father in Family Therapy', *Social Work* (Nov): 479–82.

Younghusband, E. (1978) *Social Work in Britain: 1950–1978 – A Follow-up Study*, Vols 1 and 2. London: Allen and Unwin.

12

Men in marriage counselling

Senga Blackie and David Clark

In this chapter[1] we shall examine some of the roles of men and fathers as clients in marriage guidance. We shall explore the organizational and practice implications of men's involvement in an agency which concerns itself particularly with the institution called marriage and with personal relationships generally. There would appear to be a *prima facie* case for arguing that men's participation in such an agency will be problematic; we shall therefore try to show some of the ways in which the problems are resolved — or not — when men become involved in marriage counselling.

Before considering that involvement however, it is important to take note of a range of variables which show up differences between men and women in aspects of marriage and personal relationships. For despite certain rhetorics about 'companionate' marriage and 'symmetrical' families (Fletcher, 1977; Young and Wilmott, 1975) there is now a large body of unequivocal evidence to show how marriage and family life remain the sites of important *divisions* between men and women. These divisions — in attitudes, experience and rewards — will clearly play a part in shaping the activities of men within a marriage counselling service and form the necessary backdrop to more detailed enquiries.

A recent review (Macintyre, 1985), for example, in drawing on a range of epidemiological studies, posits a close relationship between health and marital status. Taking into account standardized mortality rates as well as chronic and acute illness episodes, it is clear that in general the health of those who are married is better than that of their single, widowed, divorced or separated counterparts. More importantly, these differences are greater for men than for women. The implication of such material is that 'marriage is more protective of good health for men than it is for women — or, alternatively, that being single, divorced or widowed is worse, compared to marriage, for men than it is for women' (Macintyre, 1985: 18). In health terms therefore, male partners have more to lose by the ending of a marriage — a factor which might have some bearing on the experience of those of them who go into counselling.

It would be reasonable to infer from the health evidence that the adverse effects for men of separation and divorce tell us something about their dependence within marriage. This might be seen at both the material and the emotional levels, for men not only receive a variety of domestic servicing from their wives, but are also likely to regard them as their *only* source of emotional support. Insofar as heterosexual men are capable of any sharing of feelings and emotions with another person, it is likely to be with their female partner or wife, rather than some other friend, colleague or workmate. A spate of recent books on men and masculinity (Ingham, 1985; Ford, 1985; Tolson, 1977; Hodson, 1984) portrays men as emotionally and psychologically fragile, highly defended and buttressed in this vulnerability by a number of structural and cultural artefacts which support and sustain an illusory self-image.

This paradox is extensively articulated by Eichenbaum and Orbach (1984) who argue that whilst men's *dependency* needs are more hidden within the culture, they are also more likely to be met. Dependence on mother is replaced by dependence on wife, who as Hodson (1984: 20) points out, is only referred to as 'mother' in some marriages. For women, however, there is no such reciprocal relationship, but only 'crises' of dependency. It is for this reason that Eichenbaum and Orbach seek to deconstruct the concept of psychological dependency, which is to be understood as a gendered phenomenon, shaped by both internal and external processes. Likewise its correlate: 'the ability to listen, to care, to nurture, to relate intimately, to be emotional — is not just there by nature or magic' (Eichenbaum and Orbach, 1984: 71). One of patriarchy's most powerful myths is therefore the one of male independence. The myth bolsters stereotypes of masculinity and dictates a public script for male–female relationships.

This is clearly visible in men's and women's differing *expectations* of marriage and family life. These may be seen in assumptions about the primacy of the male breadwinning role over that of wives, as revealed in Mansfield's study of newly-weds (1985); in conflicting perceptions of the apparently 'joint' decision to start a family (Simms and Smith, 1982); and in the individual or marital conflicts which may follow the arrival of a first baby (Clulow, 1982). As Richman (1982) has shown, fathers' experiences of childbirth serve to highlight some of the contradictions of their role, revealing the 'hidden side' of masculinity (Richman, 1982: 103), perhaps allowing the brief exposure of 'private' feelings and emotions prior to their recontainment in the routines of work and 'public' life. Simms and Smith point out, however, that an awareness of the new responsibilities of fatherhood is also likely to increase work commitment (1982: 145–7). Such a situation may therefore further redefine what we might term the emotional division of labour within the family, which is heavily prescribed by gender roles and which creates a variety of internal tensions for men and fathers.

For these sorts of reasons it is important to go beyond cross-sectional approaches to understanding men and fathers and to take into account changes over the life course (Cohen, 1986). The meaning and experience of personal relationships, marriage and father-hood are likely to modify in relation to the ageing process and changing employment, housing and financial circumstances. Burgoyne and Clark (1984) have shown how these may interact to produce particular influences upon married couples and to define a context in which 'marital problems' may take shape. With the exception of violent marriages (Dobash and Dobash, 1980; Pahl, 1985) we still know very little about gender differences in the process of marriage breakdown. Although Richards (1982: 125) dismisses the notion that the majority of women petitioners in divorce cases should be regarded as an indicator of their dissatisfaction in marriage, there is other research evidence to indicate that even when women regard their husbands as satisfactory breadwinners, they find them 'inept as companions and ineffectual as confidants' (Chester, 1982). This is also a view frequently advanced by those with clinical experience in women's psychotherapy (Eichenbaum and Orbach, 1984; Greenspan, 1983). Further evidence is available from recent research on marriage counselling.

Men, fathers and marital problems

The study of clients' responses to marriage counselling is still in its infancy in Britain. Three useful monographs have been produced to date (Brannen and Collard, 1982; Hunt, 1985; Timms and Blampied, 1985). Each one has something to say about the special predicaments of men, and to a lesser extent fathers, who seek counselling for help in the marriage relationship.

Very little is known at a macro level about patterns of help seeking among those who are experiencing difficulties in marriage, though the Working Party on Marriage Guidance asserted that 'the specific agencies are consulted only by a small proportion of people with marital problems' (1979: 24). However, it is important to recognize that 'consulting' about difficulties in personal life may stretch over a wide continuum, including various informal and semi-formal networks, as well as the 'professional' help of trained workers. In general though, the evidence reviewed by Brannen and Collard does suggest that women are more likely than men to seek any outlet for self-disclosure (1982: 31); this was borne out by the same authors' own study of marriage counselling clients in which eighteen out of twenty-two men interviewed had a 'negative attitude' to self-disclosure, in contrast to only seven out of twenty-six women. Hunt likewise reports that women 'are more likely than men to make the first contact with Marriage Guidance and they are also more likely to come to the first interview' (1985: 77). Women are also more inclined to continue with counselling than men, even if their partner drops out after the first interview. This in turn was supported by Timms and Blampied's study of fifty marriage counselling clients, in which 'twice as many women as men made the first suggestion' of seeing a counsellor (1985: 21).

The evidence also suggests that even when prepared to consult a counselling agency, many men are unwilling to immerse themselves in the counselling process. Men are not short on reasons for a general antipathy towards sharing personal problems with a counsellor. Brannen and Collard list a repertoire of stock expressions emphasizing stoicism and self-reliance: 'keep a stiff upper lip'; 'soldier on'; 'sort out your own problems'; 'if I can't solve a problem then I don't see that anybody else can do anything for me' (1982: 33). Indeed for many of these men such values appeared to constitute 'an unchanging central and even fervent part of their identities' (1982: 34). Disclosure of personal difficulties, particularly of a sexual kind, might thus create a major threat to established self-images.

Timms and Blampied imply that men are likely to have specific views on counselling techniques and approaches and to place a high premium on the professional status and expertise of the counsellor (1985: 13), though both male and female clients appear to be largely uninformed about differences between statutory and voluntary agencies. Brannen and Collard speculate on a deeper explanation for differences between men and women in their expectations of counselling. 'The meaning of counselling for men and women may . . . be structured in accordance with the types of social relationships and ideologies in which they are situated' (1982: 201). Accordingly, men are more likely to expect *directive* counselling and advice-giving, reflecting their orientation to public arenas characterized by the achievement of measurable goals (1982: 201).

It has been a feature of most of the voluntary marriage counselling services that they have opted for a general orientation which is broadly client-centred and non-directive. Although the main agencies, the Marriage Guidance Councils of England, Wales, Northern Ireland and Scotland, still hold to a name which implies purposive advice from acknowledged 'experts', over the last two decades their work has owed most to humanistic psychology, and Rogerian-based and psychodynamic methods. This shift from 'guidance' to 'counselling' is not without its problems — especially in relation to clients' expectations of the service. The research evidence suggests that male clients' expectations are more likely to be disappointed than their female counterparts. Hunt is admittedly reluctant to propose that most men require a different approach to that currently on offer, but does suggest that a more 'task-centred' framework might be more effective in certain cases (1985: 79). Such an approach would involve clearer 'contracting' between clients and counsellor, as well as greater specification and articulation of the 'presenting' problem, along with a programme for action, review and evaluation. Taken a stage further, this might involve a *consultation* model for working with couples, such as that proposed by Haldane et al. (1986).

At the moment, however, the evidence in relation to any model is inconclusive. We therefore propose to examine in detail three case studies of men who were counselled within a client-centred framework under the auspices of the Scottish Marriage Guidance Council. For many of the reasons we have already identified, it will be seen that their experience of counselling was to a large extent unusual. However, insofar as they are each examples of men who came into counselling and stayed, they are worthy of detailed consideration.

Three case studies

Each of the men described here[2] had been seen by one of us (SB) as a client, prior to the present project. Accordingly, when we were asked to write about the subject of men in marriage counselling, it was decided to contact them again in order to further explore their experience of counselling. A fourth man was also approached, but declined to take part. Gordon, Neil and Alan, however, readily agreed to be interviewed by their former counsellor and it is from these recorded conversations that the verbatim quotations here are taken.

We chose these three men for various reasons. Each of them came from a different background. They differed in age and occupation and each was at a different stage in a heterosexual relationship. The number and ages of their children varied greatly, but all of them had referred to parent–child relations when presenting their reasons for coming to the agency.

Gordon

Gordon was a 27-year-old teacher, from a working class background. He had been married for five years to a schoolteacher and they had a 2-year-old daughter. Gordon came to the agency alone. He had been referred by a friend in his local church. His marriage was on the point of breaking up and he was afraid of losing contact with his daughter. His expectation of the counsellor, he recalls, was of 'someone in their forties or fifties . . . wearing a hat . . . who would tell me what to do'.

At the initial session he and the counsellor made a 'contract'. The counsellor explained to Gordon that she could not tell him what to do, but offered him the time and 'space' to talk through some of his difficulties. She told him that the aim of counselling is to facilitate change and that by listening attentively to him, trying to understand and 'check out' that understanding with him, she hoped to clarify his position and some of the feelings he had about it. She would try to communicate with him in an open and honest manner, in an attempt to help him respond in a similar way.

Gordon responded positively and decided to come for counselling and to try to get his wife to come as well. His wife never came, but Gordon took up the challenge of entering with a woman into a helping relationship which was quite unlike any other personal or professional relationship he had experienced before.

In one sense the counselling relationship is very one-sided insofar as it is only the *client's* life which is being explored; but it is in confronting the immediacy of the interaction between counsellor and client that the total involvement of both participants can lead to the building of a relationship. A relationship within which clients can begin to feel safe enough to explore thoughts, feelings and attitudes as well as to challenge their behaviour and their part in those relationship difficulties which are being experienced.

Gordon's contract with the counsellor lasted for 4 months and during that time he looked at his life from his early days, the people who were important for him, the path he had followed and the changes which had happened to him.

He described his family of origin. His father was 'rough, tough and macho . . . making money was his ambition in life . . . and I loved him'. His father was away from home regularly: 'I used to cry when he went away, I was frightened he wouldn't come back. He always did though, and he would bring me presents and cuddle me.' His mother was 'emotionally unstable . . . she was always taking pills . . . always ill . . . an embarrassment to me and my friends'. He had two sisters, one older and one younger. Both of them had problems in later life; there were illegitimate children and suicide attempts. There was also an older brother who was 'different'. He would tell Gordon that he didn't have to be the same as his father, because as Gordon put it: 'there was a sense in which I was being groomed in his image'. His brother left home quite young and now has little to do with the family.

Up until his late teens Gordon never questioned how his family lived nor his place within it, but gradually he began to change. He wanted something else. He had a girlfriend who was just like his mother, 'she was a doormat ... and I was using her like one'. His friends were all the same as his father and he wanted to be different. The woman he subsequently married was also different. She was from a well-educated middle class background and was training to be a teacher. She introduced him to a new circle of friends and eventually the drugs scene. Some of these changes caused Gordon great unhappiness; he was moving away from the family environment but still felt emotionally tied to his father. He had gone into business with his father's money, but things were going badly. There were tremendous social pressures between one set of friends and the other; and his girl friend, although boasted about by his father, never got on with him and was critical of the way he and the rest of the family lived.

He recalls his first experience with drugs.

> I was introduced to 'hash' one night by one of my girlfriend's academic friends, and I thoroughly enjoyed the experience. It gave me peace of mind. Took away all the worries I had about my father and friends and the business. For the first time in my life I didn't have to be a 'tough guy' — it was OK to show my sensitive bits ... it was also great because the next morning I didn't have a hangover.

It was during this unsettled period that Gordon married. He realized that he and his wife were very different in background, education and ability, but hoped that they could make a go of it — it couldn't be worse than his parents' marriage — and the sexual side of their relationship was very good. However the marriage never really worked out; his problems grew and he found himself resorting more and more frequently to drugs. These became the main feature of his life. He lost his business, his marriage, his friends. He found himself without a job, and involved with the criminal or near criminal element of society: 'I knew I was going down the tubes ... I had nothing and no one.' He decided one night, when he was sitting on his own in a caravan, far away from home that he would have to try to put an end to his drug taking. He went back to the family home, 'feeling like a 14-year-old ... dependent and depressed'.

During the next few months he had what proved to be two very important encounters with men. The first was a chance meeting with an old schoolfriend, whom he met whilst out walking. He talked at length with the friend, who left him saying he believed that Gordon had the ability to resolve his problems if he really wanted. As a result he went home, sold his typewriter to raise cash, and went away to a religious retreat. It was whilst there that he talked to a priest who 'listened to me and didn't judge or criticize'. Both of these encounters served to give Gordon the strength to begin his struggle against the drug habit and to look forward to a more fulfilling lifestyle.

A marriage reconciliation, followed by the decision to have a child, also gave Gordon something to work towards, although he said:

> I was filled with doubts and fears ... could I be a father? I didn't want to be the same kind of father as the one I had ... but could I be different? I also hoped that having a child would change my wife's attitude towards me ... she might become more warm and caring ... she didn't.

In common with many men, Gordon's expectation of counselling was to be told what to do, but when he realized that was not to be the case, that he would be listened to in a similar way to that in which the priest had listened to him when he was in trouble, he decided to stay. A major difference was that his counsellor was a woman and Gordon's relationships with women had not been very satisfying for him.

At the beginning of counselling, Gordon wondered what the counsellor got out of it, 'Why the interest? ... What's the reason? ... Money? ... Lip service? ... Sex?'. He knew that it was not the first and soon realized it was not the second either, but hoped that it might be the third and that if the counsellor fancied him it might lead somewhere. When this issue was confronted and he realized that even if the counsellor did find him attractive, nothing would come of it, he relaxed more and thought: 'she must be genuinely interested in me as a person'.

During his 4 months counselling he began to get to know himself better and some of his feelings, especially the anger and fear, were acknowledged. He recognized the tremendous influence of his father upon his life. Above all he began to realize in himself a sense of failure, of hating himself and being trapped. When challenged in counselling he was able to see where these feelings were coming from and how he could better cope with them. As this emotional package was unfolded, he began to feel a confidence in himself, a realization that his 'trap now had a door'.

By overcoming some of his fears and prejudices about women and learning to talk to one about some of his innermost thoughts and feelings he also found that he was more willing and able to talk and listen to his wife. Although she never came for counselling, he reported that their relationship was improving. He remained unsure that they would stay married to each other but if they were to split up, he felt more able to cope with the consequences.

Neil

Neil, separated and aged 29, had a variety of jobs before going for teacher training as a mature student. He came from a lower middle class, fanatically religious family background.

Neil's involvement in counselling came about as a result of a developing relationship with Hazel, a married woman. Hazel was concerned about the effects upon her two sons of difficulties in her marriage. Through his college associates, Neil discovered that Hazel could have an appointment at Marriage Guidance to talk over some of her fears. She went for counselling and the effect on her was so positive that Neil wondered if he could also benefit.

> I realised that intellectualising everything didn't work . . . I couldn't trust myself to handle Hazel's feelings. I also thought there might be something in it for me, although I didn't know what. I trusted the counsellor even before I met her . . . and came looking for credibility and approval.

Through what was for Neil a very painful process, he began to talk about his childhood.

> My father would beat me if I did anything wrong . . . and I was always doing things wrong. I used to feel very ashamed of myself and angry, I tried to be good but it never worked. I think that I was really scared a lot of the time that if I didn't do the 'right' thing then I wouldn't be 'saved' . . . and I would be left behind, alone, when the world came to an end.

He grew up in the south of England and had two sisters, one older and one younger than himself. As children, he and his younger sister would indulge in some sexual exploration. She sometimes told their father what had occurred and Neil would be beaten for it. His mistrust of females thus became tied in to his sexual needs, a link which he was able to make in counselling when talking of his relationship with Hazel.

When Neil was 14 years old his mother gave birth to another daughter. Only a few months later his mother died of breast cancer. In counselling he remembered his father weeping at the funeral.

> I was so angry with him . . . I had not been allowed to show my feelings as a child and I couldn't cry for my mother . . . but he did. I coped with it by shutting all my feelings away and getting on with keeping the house as neat and tidy as my mother had.

Two years later Neil's father remarried and the whole family removed to the other end of the country. Neil found life in this new family intolerable, particularly the sexual noises which came from the father's bedroom, and he left home. He spent the next five years making contact with his mother's original family, moving from job to job and looking in vain for some sense of security.

He eventually moved back to be near his father and married a girl from the church when he was 24 years old. They lived initially with her parents, a situation which he eventually found impossible. 'I became a dependent again and I resented that. They treated me as if I couldn't look after myself. I was very angry at the lack of mutual respect.' The marriage relationship was also poor and came to an end when he met and became involved sexually with Hazel.

Neil had a fairly open attitude to counselling. He had read about it and had an idea of what to expect from the counsellor. So he went along to see her knowing that he would not be given advice, that he could talk about himself and his relationships, but not knowing quite what he wanted to talk about.

> It sometimes felt like being on the edge of a whirlpool, going round and round the edges for thirty to forty minutes before plunging down into the middle of it. It didn't seem like a very efficient process.

His first 'contract' with the counsellor lasted for five sessions and was to speak about his original family. 'Looking back I think I wanted to avoid the feelings' but the counsellor challenged these and asked him to share something of them with her. When he did this he 'felt quite euphoric after expressing some of the anger and pain I felt at the loss of my mother'. The five sessions were enough for him at that time; Hazel was also coming to the end of her contract, they had decided to live together and he was 'on a high'.

Sixteen months later Neil and Hazel returned to the same counsellor for a series of six joint counselling sessions during which they realized that the intensity of their relationship was suffocating for both of them and leading to some angry, potentially violent exchanges. There were sexual difficulties to be explored as well as Neil's problem of fitting into a ready-made family. The sessions were used to recognize and ventilate these issues providing some support as the couple struggled with them.

The follow-up interview with Neil for the purpose of this chapter served to highlight for each of them the need for some separation, some space in which they might seek individually to explore further their relationship. To this end, the counsellor saw each of them separately for a further six sessions, during which time they were able to regain a sense of their own identity. They each worked towards clarifying their own wants and needs within their relationship, as well as what they were willing to give to it. They both stopped counselling together, neither of them quite sure what would happen next.

Alan

Alan's case is different from the others in that he came for the initial counselling session with his wife, Fiona. He was aged 45 years and she was 2 years older. They had been married 22 years and had 5 children, ranging in age from 18 to 7 years. Alan was an engineer, working in management and Fiona was a housewife. Marriage Guidance was Alan's 'last resort' before filing for divorce. Arguments about teenage children played a major part in the couple's difficulties and served to highlight their different attitudes and ways of dealing with conflict. It seemed that Alan believed his son's extreme antisocial behaviour was a normal part of growing up whereas Fiona found it frightening. By contrast she was able to accept more easily than Alan her daughter's boyfriends and rebelliousness. Neither was coping well with the separation of these two children from the family unit and during any fight about it she would become extremely emotional, sometimes hysterical, whilst he took refuge in his ability to rationalize the situation. Unfortunately their difficulties were exacerbated by what had become a regular pattern of over-indulgence in alcohol, leading to physical violence by both of them against one another.

Alan had made the appointment, expecting some 'expert' to come along and lecture to a group of couples on what they were doing wrong in their marriages and how to go about putting it right again. He was therefore rather taken aback to find a young woman in a small room, who did not tell them what to do, but instead asked questions and listened to the answers. Furthermore, she 'seemed interested enough to want to see us again and confident enough in her ability to help . . . although I was very unsure as to how that would happen'. By the end of the first session he says he could 'see a gleam of light . . . the counsellor had helped me to separate the problems . . . and most importantly at that stage, she had recognized that the marriage elements were quite good'.

Alan and Fiona worked with the counsellor for a period of 5 months. There were thirteen sessions, and their difficulties with commitment to the first few seemed to reflect the difficulty they were having in committing themselves to the marriage relationship. This difficulty was therefore examined in detail and resulted in years' worth of resentments, large and small, being brought out into the open and talked about frankly. At their initial contract-making session, discussion of a possible financial contribution to the agency uncovered the extent of their financial difficulties and some of the counselling time was therefore spent in looking at how they had come to be in that position; how they coped with it now and how they might be able to manage it better in the future. This resulted in a complete changeover of responsibility for the financial management within the marriage and a progressively healthier bank balance.

Parents and their marriages were also discussed and the influences of those partnerships on their own marriage helped them to focus on behaviours which they could change within their own relationship. Soon after counselling began they went to an alcohol advice centre; Fiona went to a woman's group there a few times, and eventually they both managed to stop drinking. The possibility of divorce receded further and further into the background as they began to see themselves as individuals and communicate with each other about the good as well as the bad things in their marriage. They joined forces with regard to their teenage children's behaviour and spoke with one voice on the standards of behaviour they expected and could tolerate. They also separated themselves from all of their children enough to go out together and discover that they enjoyed each other's company.

Fiona's mother's terminal illness and impending death brought the joint counselling to an end, both feeling that progress had been made and could be built upon. Alan, however, approached the counsellor asking for a new contract within which he could work on some personal issues and also where he might find support during this time of death and loss. There followed 6 months of counselling during which time he became more able to let go of certain aspects of his 'rational' approach to life. He confronted his angers and his fears, his grief at the loss of his own parents and his need for his father in times of trouble. He began to find ways of satisfying that need by communicating more openly, with his teenage son in particular as well as his other children and his wife. He worked on interdependence and began to value his family for their differences as well as their similarities.

Alan had been born into a stable, close-knit mining community.

My father wasn't a well-educated man, so he always encouraged me to stick in at school. He was determined that I wouldn't go down the pit . . . He was a family man, I remember him taking my sister and myself out for walks when she was in the pram, there weren't many men who did that in those days . . . He was also a very controlled man, I had a very controlled upbringing — everything in its place and a place for everything. My mother's father was a great influence on me as well, he was retired and lived with us for most of the time, he was a strong male character. I was brought up to take on the 'male' role in life . . . as son, brother, husband and father. I feel as if I have taken on the 'unwritten responsibilities' of these roles and that I needed to hang on to them . . . they were uncompromising, special, privileged positions and I expected others to see them in that way. Of course they didn't and that led to conflict.

The responsibilities that Alan spoke of were to do with what he learned about the 'male' role from his father — reinforced by his mother. And his conflict in that role centred on his inability to be the same kind of husband and father as his own father had been. That inability was due to the fact that he was a different person, living in a different environment, in a different age and with a different set of family relationships. Through counselling, Alan began to realize some of these differences and began to accept and value himself for being different. He also began to realize that his values in life were not so poorly matched with his father's values. He had spent the first 12 years of his marriage pursuing a career, being successful in it, but at a growing cost to his family life. He had become physically ill, his job had suffered, his marriage had suffered and after 10 years of steady deterioration threatened to break up altogether.

The counselling process helped put him back in touch with the most important things in life for him, which were his wife and his family and seemed to give him a security in his 'role' as father and husband. Although Alan expected to be lectured to on marital problems when he first came to the agency, he quickly entered into a different kind of experience; a counselling relationship with a woman counsellor.

Conclusion

These three brief case studies reveal some of the problems and contradictions which may confront those men who enter as clients into marriage counselling. In common with other material on male clients, they show how men find difficulties in forming a counselling relationship which is based on openness and the exploration of feelings, emotions and thoughts. The evidence suggests that men are not only more reluctant than women to seek some form of external help with marriage and relationship problems, but having done so are more likely to expect purposive advice from a recognized 'expert'.

Such expectations should be taken seriously and cannot be dismissed as 'presenting' issues which mask the underlying difficulties. They are one of the reasons why counselling with men in particular should involve a clear 'contract' between client and counsellor in which a framework, time scale and system of review are clarified and agreed. The case studies also reveal, however, that when encouraged in appropriate ways, some men do welcome opportunities to talk together with their partners, or individually, to a counsellor about aspects of personal life. For Gordon this meant a close examination of his relationship with his own father; for Neil the focus was upon his relationship with Hazel and her children. In Alan's case counselling provided an opportunity for him to explore with his wife the ways in which their marriage had developed over more than two decades and to place their current difficulties as parents in the context of that changing relationship. Counselling men poses specific problems, not least for women counsellors, who as we have seen may also have to contend with the sexual interests or projections of their clients. In a culture which provides few opportunities for men to explore their emotional lives, however, the counselling agencies have an important role to play in encouraging men to look beyond the available stereotypes of masculinity and fatherhood.

Notes

1. The views expressed in this chapter are those of the authors and do not necessarily represent the policies of the Scottish Marriage Guidance Council.
2. Names and other details have been changed to preserve anonymity.

References

Brannen, J. and Collard, J. (1982) *Marriages in Trouble*. London: Tavistock.

Burgoyne, J. and Clark, D. (1984) *Making a Go of It: a Study of Stepfamilies in Sheffield*. London: Routledge and Kegan Paul.

Chester, R. (1982) *Intimate Relations*, BBC *Horizon* Documentary quoted in Philip Hodson, *Men* (1984). London: BBC.

Clulow, C. (1982) *To Have and to Hold*. Aberdeen: Aberdeen University Press.

Cohen, Gaynor (ed.) (1986) *Social Change and the Life Course*. London: Tavistock.

Dobash, R.P. and Dobash, R.E. (1980) *Violence Against Wives*. Shepton Mallet: Open Books.

Eichenbaum, L. and Orbach, S. (1984) *What Do Women Want?* New York: Berkley.

Fletcher, R. (1977) *The Family and Marriage in Britain*, revised edn. Harmondsworth: Penguin.

Ford, A. (1985) *Men*. London: Weidenfeld and Nicolson.

Greenspan, M. (1983). *A New Approach to Women and Therapy*. New York: McGraw Hill.

Haldane, D., McCluskey, U. and Clark, D. (1986) 'Does Marriage Matter? A Perspective and Model for Action', *Journal of Social Work Practice* (May): 31–45.

Hodson, P. (1984). *Men*. London: BBC.

Hunt, P. (1985) *Clients' Responses to Marriage Counselling*. Rugby: National Marriage Guidance Council.

Ingham, M. (1985) *Men*. London: Century.

Macintyre, S. (1985) 'Marriage is Good for Your Health; or is it?' *Lecture given to the Royal Philosophical Society of Glasgow*, 11 December.

Mansfield, P. (1985) 'Young People and Marriage', occasional paper. Edinburgh: Scottish Marriage Guidance Council.

Pahl, J. (ed.) (1985) *Private Violence and Public Policy*. London: Routledge and Kegan Paul.

Richards, M. (1982) 'The Changing Role of Men', in S. Saunders (ed.) *Change in Marriage*. Rugby: National Marriage Guidance Council.

Richman, J. (1982) 'Men's Experience of Pregnancy and Childbirth', in L. McKee and M. O'Brien (eds) *The Father Figure*. London: Tavistock.

Simms, M. and Smith, C. (1982) 'Young Fathers: Attitudes to Marriage and Family Life', in L. McKee and M. O'Brien (eds) *The Father Figure*. London: Tavistock.

Timms, N. and Blampied, A. (1985) *Intervention in Marriage*. Sheffield University, Joint Unit for Social Services Research.

Tolson, A. (1977) *The Limits of Masculinity*. London: Tavistock.
Working Party on Marriage Guidance (1979). *Marriage Matters*. London: HMSO.
Young, M. and Willmott, P.L. (1975) *The Symmetrical Family*. Harmondsworth,
    Penguin.

13
The non-custodial father: common challenges in parenting after divorce

Mary Lund

A non-custodial divorced father faces many challenges in establishing a new relationship with his children after his marriage ends. During marriage, a father may fulfil his parenting role indirectly by supporting the mother's caretaking and by being the breadwinner. A father who divorces will probably become one of the 90 percent of men who do not get custody (Richards and Dyson, 1982; Weitzman and Dixon, 1979). In the aftermath of marital separation he may find emotional and practical obstacles to continuing a relationship with his children from a distance which require him to make more of a direct commitment to parenting than he did before the separation. As many as 50 percent of divorced fathers in the US and the UK do not overcome the challenges and have less than yearly contact with their children (Fulton, 1979; Gingerbread and Families Need Fathers, 1982). However, many fathers do master the struggle and are rewarded by good relationships that benefit both the children and fathers.

During the twentieth century there have been marked shifts in the law in the US and the UK regarding fathers' involvement with children after divorce that have paralleled trends in theory about fathers' importance in child development (Lowe, 1982; Thompson, 1983). English legal tradition originally asserted a preference for father custody after divorce, since children were property of the marriage and men were deemed best fit to look after children's moral development. The twentieth century saw women gaining legal rights and the courts considering the welfare of the children above the property rights of fathers. Women, as the parent judged to be more nurturant, were routinely granted custody of children during their 'tender years'. Courts did not recognize fathers as primary caretakers.

The problem of conflict between parents leading to marital breakdown and presumably continuing after divorce, further diminished the legal role of the non-custodial father. In *Beyond the Best Interests of the Child* (1973), Goldstein et al. argued from the point of view of psychoanalytic theory that the child's bond with one 'psychological parent' should not be disrupted, even if that means stopping contact with the other parent. In reaction to legal rulings that primarily favoured mothers after divorce, fathers' rights groups began forming in the US and UK to lobby for the importance to children of father involvement (Francke et al., 1980; Trombetta and Lebbos, 1979). Recent research on divorced families gives qualified support to fathers remaining involved with children. Early research on divorce and children showed the disadvantages of growing up in a 'single parent family' compared to 'intact families' and implied fathers had no role at all after divorce (Ferri, 1976; Levitan, 1979). Later studies in the US examined the complex variables in children's adjustment after marital separation, including parental conflict and father involvement (Hess and Camara, 1979; Hetherington, 1979; Wallerstein and Kelly, 1980). The conclusion from the largest and most methodologically sophisticated study (Hetherington, 1979) was that continued father involvement was associated with better functioning for children unless the father was 'emotionally immature' or there was intense, child-focused conflict between parents. Taken together, these American studies suggest that in the majority of families a strong father–child relationship after divorce can help ameliorate some of the ill effects of divorce for children.

Although the impact of parental conflict on children has received much attention, probably because of heated legal disputes over custody and access, there has been much less notice taken of an equally problematic outcome of divorce for children: the virtual loss of one parent. Little is known about the large percentage of fathers who slip from their children's lives. Even now with the courts shifting to encouraging father contact, many fathers do not visit children. The answer as to why children lose fathers may lie in the challenges that non-custodial fathers face, at a time in their lives when they feel least emotionally equipped to face them.

This chapter focuses on the ways divorced fathers cope with common problems in developing a new role in children's lives when they become non-custodial parents. Wallerstein and Kelly (1980) found that there was little association between the closeness in father–child relationships before and after the separation. About 25 percent of the fathers in their clinical study of sixty separating families grew more distant from their children in the space of 5 years, but another 25 percent actually grew closer. Whether or not a divorced man remains an involved father may depend on how he responds to new demands as the family changes, perhaps even more than how close he had been to his children during the marriage. Research material from a British study of divorce presented here highlights the struggle of divorced fathers to learn new ways of contributing to their children's upbringing while also dealing with the complex emotions of divorce: grief, guilt, and anger.

Divorced fathers in the Cambridge study

This chapter reports on data from thirty families from the south-east of England who volunteered to participate in a research project primarily designed to study divorced family relationships and children's adjustment. In all families, parents had been separated for at least 2 years at the time they were interviewed. Fathers fell into the following social classes (Registrar General's classification of occupations, 1970: HMSO): I Professional — six; II Managerial — eight; III Non-Manual, Highly Skilled — two; IV Manual Highly Skilled — nine; V Partially Skilled — nine; VI Unskilled — two. One child in each family, averaging 8 years old, was assessed to determine social, emotional and academic adjustment. Since mothers had care and control in twenty-seven of these families, 90 percent of the men were non-custodial fathers.

The design of the research called for interviews with both natural parents, when access was occurring, to determine the characteristics of the family. These characteristics could then be related to the assessment of how children were behaving at school and at home and how they performed on intellectual tests. Three-hour interviews were conducted with each custodial parent and 23 non-custodial parents (all those who had access, plus two who did not have access). Parents were also asked to complete a questionnaire about their interaction with each other and about the behaviour of the child focused on in the study. Children's teachers were asked to complete measures of the child's behaviour in the classroom (Rutter Behaviour Checklist, Coopersmith Inferred Self Esteem Inventory). Children were also given tests of both intellectual achievement and ability (Columbia Mental Maturity Scale, NFER Basic Mathematics Test, Neale Analysis of Reading Ability).

Based on ratings by the researchers of parental co-operation and non-custodial parent involvement from interviews with parents, families were divided into three groups. In ten *Harmonious Co-Parent* families, parents had a neutral or affectionate relationship with each other and co-operated on the issues they had in common concerning the children. In eleven *Conflicted Co-Parent* families, both parents remained involved with children, but parents were hostile and unco-operative, quite often in legal dispute over visitation or maintenance. In nine *Single Parent* families, one parent had ceased contact with the children and custodial parents varied in how co-operative they were willing to be. (There was one father-custody family in each of the three groups.)

Results showed that the 8-year-old children assessed in the study were best adjusted in the *Harmonious Co-Parent* families and least adjusted in the *Single Parent* families, according to teacher reports. A finer grained analysis showed that a friendly and co-operative relationship between parents and a visiting schedule that gave non-custodial parents extended periods of time with children were associated with children's adjustment (see Lund and Riley, 1986, for details of method and results).

The material presented in this chapter includes statistics and quotations from the study of thirty families. Some quotations are also presented from eleven non-custodial fathers who participated in a pilot project for the study. Although the original intent of the study was to explore the connection between post-divorce parenting and children's adjustment, the material presented here highlights father's experience of developing a new role in their families.

Common challenges to the non-custodial father

Similar themes emerged in the interviews with divorced fathers as they talked about the problems they faced in becoming non-custodial parents. Non-custodial fathers must cope with the practical issues of setting up access visits, establishing a new type of parenting relationship with their ex-wives, and contributing to children's upbringing from a distance and on a part-time basis. What was especially poignant was fathers' disclosure of the feelings that accompany facing these challenges.

Separation — setting up access visits

The first task of a non-custodial father is to work through his grief and anger about the separation so that he is able to start access visits. Since all but three men in the study became non-custodial fathers, the time of separation was experienced as an intense loss of the daily routine of the family. An electrical technician, 'Peter', whose wife wanted the separation, described his feelings.

> I was very happy when I was married ... everything I wished for was handed to me on a plate. I never had any hardships or anything, and then all of a sudden, sort of the whole world falls out ... all of a sudden everything stopped; it just went wrong. The house routine carries on much the same as when I was there ... I'm the kindly uncle that takes them out, on a weekend.

For the thirty families in the study, the time immediately after the separation appeared to be crucial in setting up successful access visits. In the twenty-one families comprising the *Harmonious Co-Parent* and *Conflicted Co-Parent* groups, regular visitation began within 3 months after separation. In the nine *Single Parent Families* there were sporadic attempts at visitation immediately after separation and gradually diminishing contact thereafter until it was less than yearly.

Five fathers who had stopped contact with children were interviewed. Their interview responses suggested that fathers' unresolved feelings about the separation can interfere with access. Two men, a salesman and an auto mechanic, found visiting too painful. They maintained that visits were harmful to children and that a clear break was preferable. An army sergeant was so angry at his ex-wife, he wanted no contact. A university lecturer's guilt for initiating the break-up emotionally paralysed him so he did not try visiting. A man who owned his own business was legally restrained from seeing his children because of his erratic behaviour. These men were emotionally ill-equipped to deal with the complex feelings of separation and did not get past the grief, guilt, or resentment that can interfere with visiting children.

Mothers and fathers reported that immediately after the separation everyone in the family was upset when fathers visited and then had to leave the children. Almost all parents in the study reported that early on, children were likely to cry when leaving either parent. If visiting continued that upset usually diminished as children adjusted to the pattern of the visits and became secure in the knowledge that they would see each parent again. However, some fathers said they stopped visiting or visited less frequently because children cried when they left them. These men were uncomfortable with the expression of feelings in general. The extreme position, voiced by two fathers, was the 'clean break' philosophy, that it was better for children not to see their father after divorce so they could get over him.

Peter, the father described earlier, articulated the link between his own grief and staying away from his children.

> I find it . . . it's very easy to perhaps cut yourself off and not think about it. That way the pain goes. It's, uh, you know, if you saw them every weekend it might be a bit too upsetting, so to speak.

For fathers who initiated the break-up there was also the problem of guilt interfering with setting up a relationship with their children. Nigel, a graduate research student, said:

> She also needs the children very much . . . that's really the reason I have not taken my own needs into account. This is some expression I suppose not of guilt, but of concern, for my actions or the consequences of my actions. I feel she needs the kids, so I said O.K., you have care and control, they can live with you if that's what you want.

Nigel had maintained contact with his children, but not as much as he would have liked, because he was concerned about his ex-wife's feelings.

Many men expressed helplessness in overcoming a custodial mother's opposition to their visits. Guilt about the separation could compound the problem. A university lecturer described his dilemma:

> I wanted the separation from my wife, but not from my family. That was the most painful thing. The family was almost sacred to me ...
>
> The pain was not only that I lost my children, but that the divorce caused them to gang up against me. Their allegiance always had been with their mother. Maybe I did things wrong ... I buried my head in the sand and she gathered her little ones around her to tell them I was wicked.
>
> There was no way I know of to maintain a proper relationship with the children, because of the propaganda. The only hope was that maybe I could, when they grew up.

Continued anger about the break-up also interfered with setting up contact with children. A retired army sergeant, who had not wanted the separation, described his interaction with a judge over his refusal to visit the children:

> They tried to get access arrangements started out in the courts, and the judge didn't like it when I said I'm not having anything to do with it, access. I'll never claim it, never accept it. And of course he looked quite annoyed at that. It's nothing to do with you. The kids are entitled to see you, sort of things, you know. His personal viewpoint. At this time I said this matter finishes today when I walk out of this court. I'm not going to another hearing later on to discuss it. I said the matter is finished. That's exactly how I felt.

Non-custodial fathers, who eventually had regular, comfortable visits, persevered in the beginning despite the grief, guilt and anger. Marked reduction in contact with their children was part of their loss. Of the twenty-one families in the Cambridge study, in which access was occurring, ten non-custodial parents saw their children on a fortnightly basis, and seven saw them on a monthly basis. Only four non-custodial fathers saw their children weekly or more often. When asked what they thought about the frequency of contact with their children, fourteen of the twenty-one non-custodial parents said the frequency was about right for children. However, all non-custodial parents thought the contact was too little for themselves; they would like to be able to see their children more.

Establishing a parenting relationship with ex-wives

A challenge non-custodial fathers face from separation onward is reaching agreements with custodial mothers about the children. Rarely is a separation truly mutual or amicable. No parent in the Cambridge study, even those who ended up with a harmonious relationship 2 years later, described their parting as easy. Especially when conflict remained high between parents, co-parenting required clear agreements about the way parents would interact around issues concerning the children. These agreements served as a wall between parents which allowed only an opening through which the children could pass.

The most important issue in co-parenting was access. Clear agreements about when fathers would see children and how plans could be changed facilitated an easy relationship with their ex-wives. Parents felt that these agreements were necessary, not only for their own well-being, but also for the children. A mother whose ex-husband, an unemployed cab driver, visited sporadically explained her upset:

> It hurts, I suppose, because he will not commit himself to visiting on a regular basis, which I felt was absolutely essential. All he will say is he doesn't want to be prevented from seeing them if he wants to. It upsets all of us if he just turns up on the doorstep.

Most parents kept to a minimum their contact with each other. Over half talked on the phone once a month or less. Only in the *Harmonious Co-Parent Group* did the majority say that they spoke weekly with their ex-wives. In this group, fathers felt they could flexibly schedule visits around parents' and children's immediate needs. A teacher who had an amicable relationship with his ex-wife described the way they set up visits:

> The principle is supposed to be that children ask. That's the way Joana and I like to think this is happening. If they want to come, they are welcome any time, and at the same time, if they want to do something or I want to do something in London; but it's based on every other weekend. Maybe it's being disorganized, but it's always felt important from Joana's and my point of view that it should be flexible; so I think the first time that the children said they didn't want to come because they had a party, I felt a bit stunned, and possibly the other way around, but now it doesn't really matter — it's pretty open. The children will ring me, or I will attempt to ring and talk to them. It's not an issue.

Fathers in the *Harmonious Co-Parent Group* felt more involved in their children's lives. The majority of the ten men in this group reported frequent discussions with their ex-wives about their children's health, schooling and behaviour. These fathers preferred to get information from their ex-wives, rather than directly from teachers or doctors. They seldom discussed money with their ex-wives. All but one paid regular child maintenance and most thought mothers should spend it as they saw fit. Four of them bought children some clothing or other necessities, in addition to paying maintenance. All of them discussed with their ex-wives what to get children for birthdays or Christmas, and half had bought gifts jointly with ex-wives on some occasion.

Fathers in the *Conflicted Co-Parent* group were much less likely to discuss issues concerning children with their ex-wives. Instead, over half of these fathers got their information directly from children or others. One father, a farmer, explained:

> Our daughter is a bit deaf, and often the mother might have something to say about that, but even if she tells me something I'm liable to ring up the doctor, rather than take what she's told me as true. You know I don't really believe anything she tells me. I just don't trust her now . . . It's probably me. I'm unwilling to talk to her. It's me really, who is breaking any discussion. I find it difficult to talk with her because otherwise it reawakens feelings I've sort of suppressed.

The one issue conflicted co-parents did discuss frequently was money. Half of the mothers were dissatisfied with the amount of child maintenance being paid. Seven couples had initiated legal action after the divorce in dispute over maintenance or visitation.

Curiously, some of the mothers in the *Single Parent* group reported that fathers who were not seeing their children kept up contact with their ex-wives. Two of the eight paid child maintenance, and six occasionally wrote to children or sent them gifts. Three of the mothers wrote to or occasionally phoned fathers to tell them about children. The co-operative mothers in this group believed that fathers' lack of involvement was circumstantial (one father was in a mental hospital) and wanted to keep lines of communication open so access might occur in the future. On the other hand, four of the mothers had court orders for no access because their ex-husbands had been so aggressive.

Fathers' approaches to conflict had an impact on the parenting relationship after divorce, which in turn related to children's adjustment. Mothers filled out a questionnaire about their ex-husbands' and their own behaviour. In the *Harmonious Co-Parent* group, fathers were judged to be the best problem solvers and children best adjusted at school. In the *Single Parent* group, fathers were judged to be the most aggressive in their interaction with mothers and the least likely to use problem solving and children least adjusted at school. These results suggest divorce mediation may benefit children by assisting the non-custodial divorced father to be able to face problems with his ex-wife without becoming hostile and to take responsibility for airing views and coming up with solutions.

Parenting on a part-time and long distance basis
Once a divorced father has made it clear he is going to stay involved with children through access visits and formed a working relationship

with his ex-wife about parenting issues, he then faces the ongoing challenge of being directly involved with his children. Most men want to establish a 'real' relationship with children, so they are not just seen as kindly, treat-bestowing uncles. The emotional task for the non-custodial father in part-time parenting is mustering the motivation and energy to take on a 'single parent' role for time spent with children and to find other ways of being involved from a distance. The motivation required of visiting parents can be great. The first problem they may face is distance from children, since many divorced couples find it emotionally easier not to live in the same area. In the Cambridge study, the men who were visiting children regularly lived an average of 42 miles from them.

The problem of distance is compounded by problems of housing. Seven of the twenty-seven divorced fathers in the Cambridge study did not have space for children to stay overnight, even though they had been separated from their ex-wives for over 2 years. These men shared housing with other men or lived in bedsits. They had to rely on bringing them to friends' and family's homes for visits.

A polytechnic lecturer who drove from London to the north of England to see his son told of the frustration he experienced with the practical problems of visiting:

> I travel on Friday, sleep in the car so I don't have to pay for bed and breakfast, and then fetch him in the morning.
> Saturdays are fine inasmuch as it's nice to see him. We go off to do things together, swim, eat. But then, Sundays are awkward because everything is closed. We have no place we can go and just be together.
> That's one of the reasons I don't do it so often now. When he was younger I went once a month, now it's only once every six weeks or so.
> So it's unsatisfactory as far as I'm concerned. I don't enjoy it. I feel relieved when I leave. I do it because it's important to him. He's distressed if I don't go. Although when I can have him come stay with me for longer periods, it's great, fabulous.
> It does make one feel a mixture of sad and angry, but where does that anger reside? Can't put it anywhere. I can't put it into my son, my ex-wife. It becomes an impotent rage you have to control in that situation.

The fathers interviewed in the Cambridge study voiced a strong preference for longer visits with children in fathers' homes. A father who works as a teacher explained how he would strive to make children feel at home with him:

> I suppose it's partly on principle. What I'm trying to do when they come is just to be carrying on what I would normally be doing, more or less. I've always been against this idea that it should be one long series of treats . . . certainly the times I enjoy the most is to act as if they were really living here. So a typical thing would be that they will arrive in the evening and spend some time getting a meal together and hop and dance around, or

bring games that they can play, and hear the news. Sometimes I feel a bit guilty because I keep them up late, wanting to talk to them. They have to ask to go to bed.

Fathers felt that having children stay with them in their own homes helped them relax with each other and helped children know what fathers' lives were like.

Virtually all the fathers who had access (seventeen out of nineteen) in the Cambridge study had children with them overnight on a routine basis. They also averaged a week spent with children sometime during the year, usually summer. About half of the fathers with access also telephoned children between visits to stay in touch.

Fathers in the study reported that they could easily show affection to children. Almost all said they still cuddled their 8-year-olds. Despite the lack of everyday contact, fathers and children who remained in contact enjoyed warm relationships.

Despite the reports of affection between fathers and children, non-custodial divorced fathers almost always felt that their ties to children had become more fragile. The way the fragile nature of the father–child relationship showed was that children seldom misbehaved on visits and fathers seldom disciplined or got angry with them. Fathers expressed a fear that children would not 'want to come back' if they were harsh.

The families in the Cambridge study reported that children were far less likely to be naughty or show anger to fathers. Therefore, fathers seldom needed to discipline children. A mother tells of her upset about the difference in children's behaviour in their fathers' home and hers:

He thinks they are totally at home there. I don't think he is doing anything wrong, but ... they never say no to him for anything and would never argue with him ... I said later was it because she was frightened of him getting upset, or of hurting him, or getting him angry. I think she said she's not scared of him getting angry. He won't ever get angry with them because maybe he's scared of getting angry — of frightening them so they won't want to go, and they won't argue with him in case he doesn't have them. It's interesting — I realize it was not a perfectly relaxed situation when they are with him. They probably need to spend more time so that they loosen up — he's never said anything, he's always said that they have been absolutely fantastic, great. There's only ever been a couple of times they got a bit rowdy, and that was the worst thing he ever said about them, which probably meant that they started running up and down the stairs.

Fathers' tendencies to become less effective in disciplining children after marital separation has been shown in other research (Hethcrington et al., 1976). In the Cambridge study, children were more likely to show anger to mothers than fathers, if the parents had a conflicted relationship. If parents had a co-operative relationship children were more likely to behave similarly with both parents. A lorry driver explained how his co-operative ex-wife helped resolve an incident with his daughter:

> It was Brigit that I had to smack. She rushed up into her bedroom and slammed the door and started throwing things about, and I smacked her. She said that she wouldn't come over here any more, she was quite adamant about the fact that she wasn't going to see me again. I said, well, fair enough, it's up to you to decide, and she went home. I discussed it on the phone with the wife and my mother was quite worried about her — and we all got on the phone, the wife, Brigit, my mother and me — and had a little chat, and the next time I saw her she was perfectly all right. (What did you say? I'm curious to know what turned it around?) I don't know, it was just the fact that we talked about it, blended it into the conversation with other things as well. She was determined she wasn't going to say sorry, and so was I. She was only a little girl of 10.

Remaining a 'real' parent who can discipline, after marital separation involves the risk of anger from children. Many fathers did not take that risk because they felt their time together was too precious or that the children would not want to see them. Strong backing from custodial parents about visits contributed to non-custodial parents taking on more of the disciplinarian roles.

The benefits of non-custodial father involvement for children

Although divorce certainly meant a change in father–child relationships for the families in this study, the findings suggested that they still had an influence in their children's lives. There were a variety of ways in which fathers maintained a nurturing relationship with children despite lack of day-to-day contact. The researchers rated non-custodial parents on the extent to which they shared any social, recreational or educational activities with children. These activities, plus the extent of fathers' primary responsibility for children during access visits formed the basis of the 'Non-Custodial Parent Involvement' rating used in the research (see Lund and Riley, 1986).

Non-custodial parent involvement ratings were correlated with higher scores on a test of abstract reasoning for children (r (30) = 0.46, p <0.01). There were also correlations between the length of access visits and children's positive self-esteem measures in school (r (30) = 0.30, p <0.05), and their mathematics (r (30) = 0.37, p <0.05). These results are typical of the patterns also found for the association between father involvement and children in intact families (Blanchard and Biller, 1971). Higher involvement of fathers, married or divorced, is associated with children's achievement in visuo-spatial and mathematical skills and, to some extent, with their self-esteem.

Father's involvement with children took place in the context of his relationship with his ex-wife. In this study, as in others (Hetherington, 1980; Wallerstein and Kelly, 1980) continuing conflict between parents correlated with children's behaviour problems at school (*r* (30) = 0.40, *p* <0.01). The courts in the US and the UK currently favour continued access even when there is conflict between parents. Only when there is clear danger to children because a father may be violent with the mother or them, will fathers be restrained from seeing them, as happened in four families in this study. Fathers (and also mothers) are being encouraged in conciliation courts in the US and the UK to refrain from exposing their children to continued conflict in order to keep children in touch with both parents.

Fathering from a distance has become an increasingly common experience for children. Between 30 and 50 percent of children will grow up in divorced families in the US and UK (Richards and Dyson, 1982). Still, non-custodial fathering is a role which is unclear and unexpected for most men. For most men interviewed in this study, the loss of everyday contact with children was a source of continuing heartache. 'Peter,' quoted earlier, said:

> I've done more things these last years than I've done for a long time . . . but they're not things I wanted to do. What I wanted to be was a sort of fairly loving father who came home every night and played with the children. That was about it, my ambition in my life. Just to grow old like that.

The message coming from research findings cited in this chapter is that keeping fathers involved with children is probably important for children's well-being. Non-custodial fathers do matter to children. That message may help more of them meet the challenges of becoming this new kind of father.

References

Blanchard, R.W. and Biller, H.B. (1971) 'Father Availability and Academic Performance Among Third Grade Boys', *Developmental Psychology* 4(3): 301–5.

Ferri, E. (1976) *Growing Up in a One Parent Family*. Windsor: NFER Publishing.

Francke, L.B., Sherman, D., Simone, P.E., Abramson, P., Zabarsky, M., Huck, J. and Whitman, L. (1980) 'The Children of Divorce', *Newsweek*, 11 February, 1980.

Fulton, J.A. (1979) 'Children's Post-Divorce Adjustment', *Journal of Social Issues* 35(40): 126–39.

Gingerbread and Families Need Fathers (1982) *Divided Children: A Survey of Access to Children After Divorce*. London: Gingerbread.

Goldstein, J., Freud, A. and Solnit, A.J. (1973) *Beyond the Best Interests of the Child*. New York: Free Press.

Hess, R.D. and Camara, K.A. (1979) 'Post-Divorce Family Relationships as Mediating Factors in the Consequence of Divorce for Children', *Journal of Social Issues* 35(4): 79–96.

Hetherington, E.M. (1979) 'Divorce: A Child's Perspective', *American Psychologist* 34(10): 851–8.

Hetherington, E.M. (1980) 'Children and Divorce', in R. Henderson (ed.) *Parent–Child Interaction: Theory, Research and Practice.* New York: Academic Press.

Hetherington, E.M., Cox, M. and Cox, R. (1976) 'Divorced Fathers', *Family Coordinator*, 25: 417–28.

Levitan, T.E. (1979) 'Children of Divorce', *Journal of Social Issues*, 35(4): 1–25.

Lowe, N.V. (1982) 'The Legal Status of Fathers: Past and Present', in L. McKee and M. O'Brien (eds) *The Father Figure*, pp. 26–41. London: Tavistock.

Lund, M.E. and Riley, J. (1986) 'Children's Adjustment After Parents Separate: The Importance of Post-Separation Family Characteristics', submitted for publication.

Richards, M.P.M. and Dyson, M. (1982) *Separation, Divorce and the Development of Children: A Review.* London: Department of Health and Social Security.

Thompson, R.A. (1983) 'The Father's Case in Child Custody Disputes: The Contributions of Psychological Research', in M.E. Lamb and A. Sagi (eds) *Fatherhood and Family Policy*, pp. 53–100. Hillsdale, NJ: Lawrence Erlbaum.

Trombetta, D. and Lebbos, B.W. (1979) 'Co-Parenting: The Best Custody Solution', *The Los Angeles Daily Journal Report* 79(12): 11–23.

Wallerstein, J. and Kelly, J. (1980) *Surviving the Breakup.* London: Grant McIntyre.

Weitzman, L.J. and Dixon, R.R. (1979) 'Child Custody Awards: Legal Standards and Empirical Patterns for Child Custody, Support, and Visitation After Divorce', *University of California Davis Law Review* 12: 472–521.

14
Patterns of kinship and friendship among lone fathers

Margaret O'Brien

When marriages end, only a minority of families are reorganized in such a way that the mother becomes the non-custodial parent and the father the parent with major responsibility for care of the children. Becoming a lone father with full-time care for the children is therefore a highly unusual and unanticipated life event.[1] Until the 1970s lone fathers remained relatively unresearched by social scientists. However, by the mid 1980s over twenty major projects had been conducted into this family form (see O'Brien, 1984; Santrock and Warshak, 1986 for reviews). A welcome development has been the growth of studies exploring specific aspects of father–child relationships in lone father households. However, detailed work into the adult dimension of lone fathers' post-divorce adaptation is lacking. The purpose of the present chapter is to redress this imbalance by focusing on two such aspects – lone fathers' relationships with kin and friends.

The manner in which a lone father relates to significant others can give important clues about how he negotiates his change in status. In turn, the ways in which individuals interact with him can illuminate the dimensions involved in the social management of lone fatherhood. Given that family researchers have shown that divorce alone can completely change social relationships (e.g. Miller, 1970; Duffy, 1982), it is important to uncover what effect the further ingredient of becoming a *male* single parent adds to this state. As Hart (1976: 159) has commented:

> Losing a marriage partner means more than just the experience of material deprivation and social stigma. It also means a complete transformation in the nature and extent of relationships linking the individual to others in his social universe.

Many popular and academic authors have assumed that lone fathers' kin and social relationships are somewhat advantaged compared with both other single or married men and especially women in equivalent circumstances (Marsden, 1969; Sanctuary and Whitehead, 1972). Their scarcity is thought to attract 'support', particularly from female kin and other women. Marsden (1969: 241) has argued:

> The 'motherless' child, that is the child who has no mother figure, is a very rare phenomenon in our society — a father without a wife can usually call on female kin to bring up his children, or he can advertise with community approval for a woman housekeeper.

Sociological research on kinship and friendship suggests a different outcome (e.g. Blau, 1961; Rosow, 1970; Allan, 1979). This predicts that the scarcity of male single parenthood has an undermining influence on lone fathers' contact and intimacy with friends and kin. From her research on friendships amongst the elderly, Blau argues that the *prevalence* of any status change is a key factor in determining the extent of its deviance. A change which places individuals in rare and unusual positions was found to have a negative influence on relationship maintenance and formation. From these findings one would expect male single parents, when contrasted with peers of similar age, gender and class, to experience widely different, possibly impoverished, socio-kin relationships.

The small amount of empirical data on kinship and friendship amongst lone fathers has produced fragmentary and often contradictory results. For instance, American studies have highlighted lone fathers' social integration and connectedness to support systems (e.g. Orthner et al., 1976; Hanson, 1981), whilst British work has pointed to the relative isolation of many lone fathers (George and Wilding, 1972; Hunt, 1973).

It is noticeable that the early American researchers often portrayed a rather rosy and proselytizing view of their respondents. Bartz and Witcher (1978: 35), for example, suggested that 'fathers with custody are now modelling — for the sake of their children and society — the adaptive role behaviours necessary for the family to preserve its socialization function in a changing culture'. In Britain the idea of lone father as a social pioneer was notably absent. Instead, with the exception of Hipgrave's (1978) research, UK investigators regarded male single parenthood as a social problem — an aspect of 'family disorganization' or 'incompleteness' (George and Wilding, 1972: 178–9). This variation in intellectual orientation, together with the differences in the samples used in both countries (UK samples included more blue-collar workers and unemployed respondents), might well explain the disparity in research findings on lone fathers' relationships with kin and friends.

In addition the work carried out in both countries has been marred by methodological weaknesses. Investigators have concentrated on the frequency of contact between lone fathers and significant others, leaving the context and subjective perceptions of these relationships insufficiently examined.

Kin relationships among lone fathers

In the present study, where lone fathers were compared with a pair-matched control group of married fathers,[2] the data suggested a complex pattern of kin association for male single parents. Before these data are presented the methodology will be briefly described.

Quantitative and qualitative indicators of kin association were employed. In a tape-recorded, semi-structured interview informants were asked how often they typically had contact with important family members. Also information on respondents' feelings towards kin was ascertained. Each was asked whether he perceived his kin as an important source of support in his life (at the time of the interview) and secondly, if he felt kin members usually gave the support he expected of them. The definition of 'support' was left open, so that respondents were able to talk about any particular aspect they wished (a similar format was used when the area of friendship was explored).

The results suggested that for lone fathers, frequency of kin contact measures (except with in-laws) were positively correlated with subjective measures of kin importance. The more contact a lone father had with his sister for instance, the more likely he was to perceive her as a provider of support and vice versa.[3] There was no such linear correlation for the married respondents. Thus, a married man might have felt his father was an important source of support without seeing him very much.[4] The difference in results here is related to the meanings individual respondents attribute to the notion of support, and to the social context in which it does, or does not, take place. One context in which mutual support might occur is when kin co-reside. While rare, this arrangement illuminates the different connotations support has for married and lone fathers, and will be considered in more detail below.

Contrary to expectations, the *overall* frequency of contact between lone fathers and their *parents* was not very different to that of men in nuclear family households.[5] Of those whose parents were still alive, about one-third in both groups saw their mothers and fathers at least monthly, with the rest having less frequent contact. However, a closer inspection reveals distinctive within-group patterns. Of the forty-six lone fathers who had a living mother, nineteen (42 percent) did not see her any more frequently than at 6-monthly intervals including five who had no contact with her at all. The comparable proportion of married informants in such a position was 29 percent. Whilst at the other extreme lone fathers were more common in a subgroup who saw their mothers or fathers *daily*.[6]

FIGURE 1
Married and lone fathers' contact with siblings

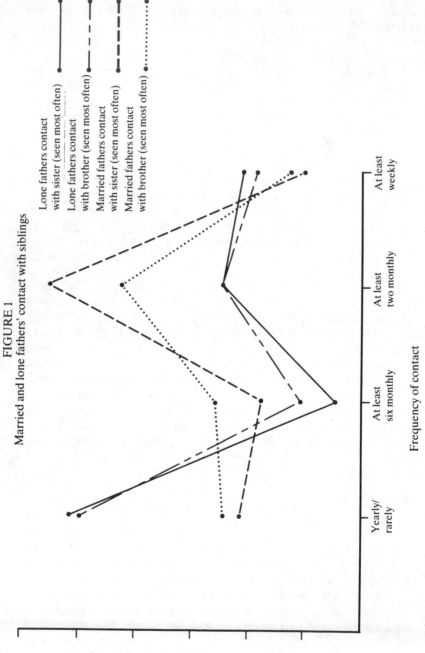

Lone fathers contact
with sister (seen most often)
Lone fathers contact
with brother (seen most often)
Married fathers contact
with sister (seen most often)
Married fathers contact
with brother (seen most often)

Frequency of contact

Proportion of respondents (in percent)

At least
weekly

At least
two monthly

At least
six monthly

Yearly/
rarely

This bimodal patterning of lone fathers' contact with their kin (to have either high or low contact) becomes emphasized when *sibling* relationships are examined. As indicated in Figure 1, there are sub-groups of lone fathers who have very high or very low levels of association with their brothers and sisters. This configuration of results is particularly exaggerated for lone father–sister rela-tionships. Lone fathers either see their sisters weekly (20 *v*. 8 percent of married men) or rarely, if at all (51 *v*. 21 percent of married men): a finding which may help us understand the apparent contradictions between the empirical studies cited above. It seems that lone fathers are more likely than married men to become isolated from or inte-grated into kin networks and, as will be seen later, other social networks. The experience and status of lone fatherhood brings with it either marginality or social inclusion.

Co-residence with kin

Three of the lone fathers lived with kin (Mr Cab, Mr Hack, Mr Shad). These men and their children resided respectively in the home of a brother who was single, a male cousin who was a retired bachelor, and in Mr Hack's case with his family of origin. Mr Hack, a stock-jobber's dealer, returned to his mother's home 2½ years after the marriage break-up, under the condition that he could have his finan-cial share of the property and after ensuring that he and his sons had sufficient physical space in the house. Mr Hack's mother was di-vorced and lived in a ten-roomed house with two of her younger sons; at the time of interview all six kin members cohabited. One of the reasons why Mr Hack had not returned home sooner was because his family had always disapproved of his wife — 'They'd have only said I told you so'. Mr Hack was doggedly insistent on sharing the house-work with his mother and on remaining responsible for the care of his children.

For Mr Cab and Mr Shad the co-residential arrangement was perceived as more temporary and inconvenient. Both had lost their homes due to dramatic events around the time of marital separation — Mr Cab had kidnapped the children, taking them abroad, whereas Mr Shad lost his money and home fighting for child custody.

In the married sample, there were two instances of residence with kin (Mr Sales, Mr Stuart). However, the basis of their relationships were different: the parents of these married men had moved into their children's home. For the Sales, the arrangement came about because of parental ill-health, whereas Mr Stuart had asked his mother to come and stay after her retirement. Thus, the direction of dependency between generations was in reverse for the married and lone fathers. Furthermore, no married respondent resided with a sibling or other extended family member, and the only married man who saw his sister daily worked with her.

The nature of support provided by co-resident and highly involved kin incorporated physical contact, material aid, child-care assistance and adult companionship. Married respondents did not appear to need or expect such support. Indeed some anticipated that at their stage of life they should be in a position to supply material and emotional sustenance for their own parents. As one such married father put it 'we support them rather than them supporting us'. Lone fatherhood, it appears, interrupts the 'ideal' male life course.

As mentioned above, not all lone fathers experienced a high level of association with their kin. Indeed some respondents felt they had no family support at all. In the next part of the chapter the contexts and factors related to both high and low engagement with kin will be considered in more detail.

Transgenerational influences
The way in which a man became a single parent after the breakdown of his marriage appeared to have important connections with the nature of his kin relationships. As described elsewhere (O'Brien, 1982), respondents in the present study moved from married fatherhood to lone fatherhood through three main pathways. There was a *hostile seeking* route where men fought for custody of the children often against the wishes of their ex-wives ($n = 20$); a second route was one of *passive acceptance* where respondents had single parenthood thrust upon them by their spouses' desertion ($n = 19$); a final pathway was where respondents reached a mutually agreed compromise over child-custody with their ex-wives — the *conciliatory negotiation* route ($n = 20$).[7] At the time of interview hostile seekers expressed a higher level of engagement with kin than men in the other two groups.

Seventy percent of hostile seekers who had kin networks described these relatives as a very important source of support. This strong attachment to kin was expressed by fewer passive acceptors (44 percent) and only 11 percent of the conciliatory negotiators. The three lone fathers who resided with extended family and the three lone fathers who worked with kin had become single parents through the hostile seeking route (only one of these men had worked with his family before marital separation). At the time of interview, then, hostile seekers' everyday lives were often bound up with those of their extended family members.

One of the reasons for this heightened interconnectedness was the wish of some of these lone fathers to involve and implicate the extended family in the marital drama. For instance, Mr Last (a draughtsman) enlisted his mother's assistance in his legal fight for child-custody.

> My mother had a part-time job but she gave that up and went to court with me and told the magistrate that she was quite willing to look after them. So they're in my custody but she's allowed access. The same at school — only me or my mum can pick them up. I signed a paper at school indicating that the mother (his ex-wife) is to have absolutely no access to them at all.

This respondent's mother, prompted by her son, was taking sides, allying with him against her daughter-in-law. In part she colluded with Mr Last's negative representation of his wife, possibly maintaining the hostile and acrimonious barriers between the couple. Mr Last remarked that the 'whole experience' had brought him closer to his family:

> If you would have asked me before she left whether ours was a close family I would have said no, not close. But I think it's got closer this year.

In contrast to this strong positive identification with natal kin, hostile seekers' relationships with their *in-laws* were much less harmonious. Not surprisingly, lone fathers had significantly less association with parents-in-law compared to the married men,[8] but this tendency was especially marked for hostile seekers and passive acceptors. With the hostile seekers overt distancing between the two sets of family of origin seemed to predominate. Often both sets of kin adopted the 'appropriate' husband or wife and so partially mirrored the battle going on within the marital unit itself. As Mr Last's mother declared about his ex-wife's family:

> If you go down to their house, just down into town, you'll see his mother-in-law, his father-in-law, her and her boyfriend and their baby all living together. It's disgusting.

For hostile seekers in particular, the nature of the marital break-up and child-custody allocation reflected and even intensified interactional patterns for dealing with conflict already present in respondents' wider kin networks.

Social class, kin relationships and lone fatherhood

The majority of British community and occupational studies have pointed to the prominent role of kin in working-class patterns of support and sociability (Bott, 1957; Dennis et al., 1956), particularly the 'power of the mum' in the geographically stable communities of Ship Street in Liverpool (Kerr, 1958) and in London's Bethnal Green (Young and Willmott, 1962). In the present study respondents were not attached to one specific neighbourhood or community, and in fact lived in a variety of places throughout the London area. It was therefore not possible to relate directly type of neighbourhood to kin association. If, however, the occupational index of social class is used, some interesting relationships can be identified.

Firstly, there was a tendency, not found in the married sample, for working-class lone fathers to attach more importance to kin support when contrasted to their middle-class counterparts. Thus, 42 percent of working-class lone fathers felt that kin support was very important in comparison to 31 percent of the middle-class group. These feelings of kin association found expression also when frequency of contact measures between kin members were examined. Lone fathers who had high (i.e. weekly) rates of contact with their *mothers* and *fathers* were significantly more likely to be working class.[9]

These social class differences in frequency of contact with parents were not found within the sample of married men. A different pattern appeared to be in operation here: working-class married men had more frequent associations with their *mothers-in-law* and with their *brothers*.[10] The former finding perhaps affirms the primacy of the mother–daughter relationship for wives over the mother–son relationship for husbands, that has been found in many working-class married households (Young and Willmott, 1962; Komarovsky, 1967).

In working-class families when a wife departs, leaving her husband with the children, the power of the husband's mother is often reasserted.[11] This particular chain of events occurred for Mr Eye, an unemployed shop assistant who felt his mother provided some 'feminine' influence for his daughter.[12]

> If you've got a boy you've got the same interests, for example, like football, cricket, wrestling, boxing, camping, walking, hiking, etc. but when it comes to things that are strictly female sort of things like dress-making she loses out. I feel inadequate but I'm lucky because she can get it with granny. It's passing the buck which is inadequate but it's the best thing that's available.

Another working-class respondent, Mr Pent, argued very strongly that *mothers* were the only people lone fathers could rely on: 'the only real person I can rely on, and you'll find that with a lot of people, is their mother'. Thus the prominent place of mothers in some men's lives before marriage may have been reactivated when they became single fathers. Conversely, the working-class man's link with his mother-in-law, most usually sustained by his wife, is clearly severed when this transition occurs.

These data indicate that the ways in which men become single parents, their current levels of kin association and their overall occupational statuses are intimately connected. Further research is needed to tease out the relative importance of each variable.

Lone fathers who had low involvement with kin
As suggested earlier some lone fathers had little physical contact with, or support from, their kin. A number of the reasons for this were common to both lone and married fathers, such as geographical distance, death or family tensions and dissatisfaction. However, some explanations were given only by male single parents and seemed to derive from their ambiguous status. Mr Allan, for instance, had noticed his father's confusion and disappointment when he became a single parent. This uneasiness, he remembered, had started earlier. A year before this informant's marriage had ended he had moved from journalism to full-time study, a step which his father had thought was unwise. Then after the break-up Mr Allan was at home even more with the children. This upset his father considerably: 'He's disappointed that I haven't followed the pattern.' The 'pattern' for a man from Mr Allan's conventional middle-class background was certainly not to move from the successful world of journalism into the more deviant world of child-care and housework.

Other lone fathers also mentioned how becoming lone parents had diminished their standing in their families and resurrected quiescent rivalry between siblings. One such respondent, Mr Pattern, an unemployed printworker, felt that he was no longer a 'proper man' in the eyes of his family, having been left by his wife (for another man) and, moreover, having been left with the children. The family gradually moved away from Mr Pattern, being unsure of how to react towards him in the delicate circumstances: 'when you have an accident, whenever anything happens there's a great tendency (for relatives) to pretend it never happened'.

The general upheaval and upset associated with the marital separation was another reason why some lone fathers turned away from kin rather than towards them. Some respondents felt ashamed and attempted to conceal the changes that were going on in their lives, while others wanted to protect their parents from the 'sordid mess'. One lone father rejected his parents totally for a short time after the separation, because he felt that they had ill-prepared him for adult life and relationships. Thus, as well as family moving away from their kinsman at a time of crisis, a kinsman may retreat from his family, especially if he blames them in some way for the events he has experienced.

While geographical distance influenced levels of kin contact for both married and lone informants, this often had a specific and special significance for lone fathers. They were usually more tied to the home and its immediate locality than were the married respondents.[13] Moreover, geographical relocation may create psychological distancing between generations of families so that when a personal crisis does happen it may be less likely that kin can give, or will offer appropriate support. One example of this process was provided by Mr Wood (a shopfitter) who had moved, 12 years previously, a relatively short distance from the East End to an outer London borough. Although he hated the lack of 'community spirit' in his new area, he had found it hard to 'fit in' whenever he returned home. Over the years these visits had ceased. Consequently, when Mr Wood's wife left him and the children, his family did not turn to him and neither did he ask them for assistance. He commented: 'They're all too busy.' In the 2 years since separation he had employed a variety of au-pairs to help with the housework and child-care: functions which might have been carried out by his mother or sister had he not moved away. The mother–son link had been severed and it was difficult to pick it up again.

Friendship and lone fatherhood
Relationships with friends and social life experiences provide a further window through which the contradictory elements of male single parenthood can be viewed. As with kin relationships, lone fathers are more likely than married men to lead a life of either social isolation or frenetic socializing.

Friendship and social life: lone and married fathers compared
One of the interesting findings from the present study was the prominence and salience of friends and social activity in the lives of most of the lone fathers interviewed. Lone fathers were twice as likely as married men to feel that friends were particularly important to them.[14] Table 14.1 shows a tendency for lone fathers to socialize more than married men. However, it also points to a subgroup who rarely, if at all, participated in social activities outside the home (a

TABLE 14.1
Frequency of social activity by fathers' parental status (in percent)

	Married fathers (n = 37)	Lone fathers (n = 59)[a]
At least once a week	24	29
At least once every fortnight	24	31
About once every month	14	17
Once every couple of months	35	7
Rarely goes out	3	17

Chi-square = 15.0, [df = 4], $p = 0.004$.
[a] Owing to rounding up/down in this table and Table 14.2 some column percentages may total 101 or 99.

larger proportion than that found in the married sample). Three lone fathers considered themselves to be 'friendless', whereas all married men reported having at least one friend apart from their wives.

> People, friends are my hobby now. I have more time for all things and to do the things I want to do.
> (Mr David, a teacher)

> Friends are critical ... I have a kind of sorority which is enormously important to me. These are mutual friends of my ex-wife and myself who are very close to me and who are my means of coping with a full-time job, children and everything, which is a *family*.
> (Mr Roberts, a University lecturer. Emphasis added)

Friends of lone fathers who had comforted and helped around the time of marital separation were often singled out as particularly salient:

> I have one or two very good friends ... one, who coincidentally is a psychiatrist, was very good when we broke up. I used to stay with him at weekends. Another good friend had been through a similar thing.
> (Mr Side, Senior Personnel Manager)

In fact, friends were mentioned most frequently as the first port of call when the marriage was breaking down. Just under 30 percent of the sample described turning to friends at this time.[15] As Allan (1979: 141) has commented: a 'crisis is the crux of real friendship, the assumption being that at such times only the few — the real and true friends — will remain loyal'. Friends proved especially important for those who had been single parents for longer periods.[16] This finding points to the possibility that having close friendships can sustain and enable men to maintain their single parenthood state over time. Moreover satisfaction with friends was associated with a measure of personal well-being (the General Health Questionnaire, GHQ) — a correlation not found for satisfaction with kin.[17]

Since married men, in form if not in substance, had a friend at home — their wives — they may have attached less significance to the concept of friend as confidant, a concept implicit in many lone fathers' accounts of friendship. (Also for married men friendship satisfaction was not significantly related to the GHQ score.) As Mr Median (a researcher) put it:

> I'm not the sort of person who has a close friend, an intimate in that way ... you know, Carol and I are like that and that's sufficient ... I've got one or two friends I can go out with and drink, or have lunch with and get into conversations about current events as they affect us immediately but I don't feel a need and don't really want to have a kind of gossipy close relationship. No, I don't work on that level I don't think.

Moreover, for some the ideology of being a 'family man' appeared to preclude an active social life or a high profile involvement with friends outside the home.

> When you have family you don't have your own social life or friends. Anyway we are staying in, saving up to buy a house. (Mr Marl, park-keeper)

> When you have a family that is growing up they need time. They expect time and as a result one doesn't have a social life in the sense of what one had when one was younger or what one might have. It just doesn't translate in that sense. One tends to devote oneself to the family, the children.' (Mr Money, accountant)

However, friends and socializing were not absent from the lives of the married men of the present study. A closer consideration of, firstly, the issue of gender in respondents' friendships and, secondly, the nature of a social life for lone and married fathers will further illuminate the differential meanings given to these domains.

Gender aspects of friendship

As indicated in Table 14.2, at the time of interview married men were significantly more likely than lone fathers to have either male friends (57 percent) or friendships with other couples (38 percent),[18] while lone fathers either mixed with both women and men (53 percent), or reported having mainly female friends (12 percent). Many married men felt that cross-sex friendships were taboo.

TABLE 14.2
Sex and marital status of friends by fathers' parental status (in percent)

	Married fathers ($n = 37$)	Lone fathers ($n = 59$)
Mainly male friends	57	24
Equally male and female friends (non-couples)	5	53
Couples (male and female)	38	7
Mainly female friends	0	12
No friends	0	5

Chi-square = 41.1, [df = 4], $p = 0.000$.

The relationships lone fathers described with their women friends were in the majority of cases non-sexual — only a minority ($n = 9$) were depicted as girlfriends. Usually the platonic aspect of the relationship was emphasized. Many of the women had young children and the presence of children appeared to be a common interest. Women friends were typically relatively recently acquired, with few knowing the respondent before he had separated from his wife. Such women had been met in the neighbourhood, whilst collecting the children from school, at the local park or at one-parent family group meetings. Old venues acquired different significances, whilst other venues were experienced for the first time.

> Yes, I have a great number of friends. I just recently found out that three-quarters of them are all in Gingerbread (a one-parent family organisation), that is my main life-line really . . . they're more women than men. But it's only platonic. (Mr Ring, school caretaker)

It seemed that caring for children single-handedly could buy some men entry into 'women's territory'. Lone fathers may have become in the eyes of other women, 'honorary women' or 'honorary mothers' for according to respondents it was women, rather than men, who took an interest in their single-parent responsibilities.

> Women are openly curious as to how you manage, whether or not the house is clean and how often you cook. (Mr Wish, Director of Housing, Social Services)

> I think that a lot of women I meet in the streets, shops etc were always very touched by the fact that I was carrying a girl around on my back while shopping. However, I don't yet know if I got such strong reactions from men or whether they just ignore it. (Mr Canada, teacher)

The finding that only 24 percent of lone fathers had mainly male friends in comparison to 57 percent of married respondents, is suggestive of a shift from 'male' to 'female' concerns amongst lone fathers. Being part of a male friendship group was, for some, difficult to combine with looking after children on a full-time basis.

> Your friends drop away and all my friends were workmates, especially being in the print. They rarely live in your neighbourhood . . . Pub friends don't tend to be a lot of good . . . they only want to know you for a drink or a game of darts, so when you stop going down the pub they drop you out. When you see them down the road they say 'Good morning', 'Hello', no more than that, you know. (Mr Pattern, ex-print worker)

Nevertheless, a group of lone fathers, as indicated in Table 14.2, *did* have mainly male friends. This number included men who managed to maintain the male friendships they had before divorce, men who were very wary of women (because of their marital experiences) and respondents who had become close to other lone or divorced fathers. For example Mr Plat met 'Gus' at a Gingerbread group meeting, where they got on well. Very soon after this meeting, Mr Plat let out his spare room to Gus, who had access to his own children on alternate weekends. During these weekends both sets of 'families' would eat and go out together. On weekdays each man would take turns in cooking the meals and Gus kept 'an eye on the kids' when Mr

Plat was doing his nightly check-over of the housing estate for which he was a caretaker. It seemed that both men gave each other much support and comfort. Similarity in marital status and concern over children had helped to draw these two men together and override the possibly divisive dimension of gender.[19]

Lone men also tended to have fewer friends who were couples. Much has been written about married couples' 'fear of contamination' once a friend's marriage comes to an end (e.g. Miller, 1970) and also about the divorced woman as 'fair-game' (Goode, 1956). Less has been said, however, about couples' perceptions of the divorced man and the lone father. It seems that they have to cope with two, often conflicting aspects of the lone fathers' situation, since he is viewed as both a *lone parent* and a *single man*. The couple might therefore be aware of the lone father's responsibilities and wish to give him support and assistance; but they would also recognize that without a wife, he is deprived of female intimacy. Thus the lone father is often regarded as a sexual risk or simply an odd man out:

> If you're a family man, you're reliable, come to work on time. You're not going to fiddle with the girls or boys for that matter. (Mr Roberts, University lecturer)

> It's my observation that when you're on your own with a family you get the worst . . . whereas before when you were married and as a couple you had no difficulty . . . now you're a little bit of a risk . . . you're the odd man out all the time. (Mr Baker, assistant headmaster)

No lone fathers in this study described incidents where they had actually pursued other men's wives (which is not to say this activity never occurred), although one respondent described the opposite sequence of events — namely, other men's wives showing some sexual interest in him.

> After it got around I was amazed at the number of women who offered to sleep with me, it was quite staggering. I don't know if they thought they were doing me a favour or if they wanted a bit of variety from their husbands. That was quite surprising. (Mr Side, senior personnel manager)

It seems that the divorced man, like the divorced woman, is also perceived by some as 'fair game'.

The social life of lone fathers

Lone fathers are formally 'bachelors' or 'single men'. For the majority of the men in this study the state was an involuntary one. Only 19 percent of respondents had actively wanted to separate; the remainder were left by their wives. The consequent feelings of rejection experienced in the context of their marginal status appeared to encourage a social withdrawal amongst a subgroup of respondents. As seen in Table 14.1, 17 percent of lone fathers ($n = 10$) rarely went out of the house socially. These men described a lack-lustre life centred around the home, the children and the television, attributing such labels to themselves as 'a lone wolf' and 'a hardened eunuch'. These tended to be older men and those who had been separated for longer periods of time.[20] However, psychological factors such as mistrust of the outside world, particularly women, emerged in interviews as important qualitative data to consider.

By contrast, many of the highly socially active lone fathers appeared to be re-entering a second phase of 'single-hood' with all its associated attributes: relative independence, a variety of sexual partners and so on. Recently separated lone fathers described feelings of nervousness, fear and excitement about the prospect of being single again.

> There are tons of things I want to go and do and see ... but basically relationships with other women are a completely new experience for me. I can remember the cattle-market period of my youth going to dances, chatting-up the birds. I had a period when I'd had enough of that ... it'll be difficult to bring them (women) back here ... they'd (the children) all be sitting looking and everything. (Mr Allan, ex-journalist)

Mr Allan had only been separated for 3 months and his excitement about embarking on a 'new' social life was tempered both by family responsibilities and lack of confidence in dealing with the opposite sex after 10 years of marriage (he was 35 years old at the time of interview). Mr Allan wondered especially if other women would be put off him because he had been left by his wife.

A special social outlet for lone fathers, as distinct from married men, was the range of one-parent family organizations such as Gingerbread. Seventy percent of respondents had visited a single-parent family group (mainly Gingerbread) since their marriage had ended, but only half of this number were regular attenders at the time of interview. Frequent attenders tended to be men who were recently separated and those who still felt upset about the end of their marriage.

Certainly one reason for lone fathers to become involved in one-parent family groups was to increase their opportunities for meeting women and so widen the possibilities of developing new couple relationships. Nearly 40 percent of those who had some contact with these groups cited their most useful function as providing companionship and a social life. Since only single parents participated in such gatherings lone fathers no longer had the insignia of peculiarity or misfit. However, even in such special environments several men experienced moments of difference precisely because of their unique status as *male* single parents. Complaints were voiced about female domination, 'being left out' and being surrounded by 'men-haters'. In some cases therefore marginality was re-experienced by lone fathers in one-parent family groups, resulting in further social withdrawal and isolation.

In general, for lone fathers the more active their socializing the greater the sense of social life fulfilment they voiced — although there were exceptions.[21] Being able to get out of the home environment on a regular basis meant an escape from daily housework and the demands of children. It also provided an opportunity to befriend other adults. Often lone fathers who were satisfied with their social life compared it favourably to the 'rut' they had been in during marriage, even if they had not wanted their marriage to end:

> The difference between myself perhaps and a married person is that I'm not restricted in any way in deciding what to do with my time. (Mr Kingston, senior computer analyst)

Such men pointed out that they were sometimes the envy of their mates and that they had more control over their daily living than they had ever previously experienced. Notwithstanding these remarks more lone fathers than married men were very dissatisfied and disillusioned with their social lives (48 v. 22 percent), including Mr Baker who socialized a great deal.

> Well I'm discontented because it's really an emotional thing. I mean I've got a very wonderful varied cultured life you know, for example last year looking up in my diary I attended two hundred happenings of a cultural nature. But it's a very lonely existence really . . . you get the worst part of every deal. If you've never been married you don't know what you're missing but if you've been married . . .

It seemed that no degree of frenetic socializing could compensate for Mr Baker's acute sense of loss and loneliness. An important factor to note here, however, was that Mr Baker did not have a girlfriend and mostly went out on his own. 'Socializing alone' is perhaps a contradiction in terms and indeed researchers have commented on how difficult it is to manage public encounters as a single person in a milieu of 'withs' (Davis and Strong, 1977). This prescription to be part of a couple militates against a satisfactory social life for a single parent. Lone fathers whose social nexus included a girlfriend or a platonic woman friend reported a more contented social life which fits in with this suggestion. As does the finding that married men's satisfaction with their social lives was related not to a general activity level, but instead to their regularity of socializing with wives.

Thus, the context of an activity as well as its enactment must be taken into account in order to understand fully the special social life of lone fathers, and indeed of married men.

Conclusion

The overall picture that comes from this study is that being a male single parent does indeed transform relationships with kin and friends. When compared to men in nuclear family households, lone fathers appear embedded in a different set of socio-kin relationships. The attributes of the status — being a man, having experienced marital separation and caring for young children without a live-in partner — create a complex of contradictory images which provoke contradictory responses in others. The lone father is a unique sort of family man whose position invokes both support and disdain, admiration and suspicion.

As far as relationships with kin are concerned, in contrast to the married sample, lone fathers showed a polarized pattern. There were subgroups of lone fathers who had very high, possibly overinvolved associations with kin and there were others who experienced very low, disengaged levels of association. There was no evidence for heightened female kin support, although sisters often occupied special places: taking the samples as a whole, lone fathers' contact with female kin was no more frequent than that reported by married fathers. However, since the study excluded fathers who had not maintained overriding responsibility for the care of their children, the amount of such aid may have been underestimated. This possibility should be investigated in future research, as should the relative influences of social class, and the manner in which men became custodial parents; variables found to be crucial in structuring post divorce kin relations.

The salience of friendship and a social life was another point of difference between lone and married fathers. Becoming a lone father necessitated constructing a different identity. Part of this process involved extending outwards, embracing new individuals and places. One interesting finding was the significance of other women in the lives of lone fathers, not just as sexual partners but more importantly as platonic friends, with a common concern — children. It was suggested that lone fathers, as a consequence of their shift in parental status, may have been perceived by these women as 'honorary mothers' or even 'honorary women'. However, since they were at one and the same time also male and single, lone fathers' public personae contained contradictory elements and strains in social interaction often resulted. There was indeed a subgroup of respondents who were social isolates rarely moving outside the home. These tended to be older men and those who had been single parents for longer periods of time.

This comparison of socio-kin relationships among two types of fathers has highlighted the constraints on men who occupy rare parental roles. It has been shown that such states can provoke the extreme outcomes of social marginality or absorption. However, the study also suggests that a move into the private domain of home and child-care can open up for men the possibility of closer relationships of a different kind with women.

Acknowledgements

I would like to thank Jane Ward and Sylvia Hudson for their help in the preparation of the manuscript. I would also like to thank Charlie Lewis for his useful comments on earlier drafts.

Notes

1. Lone fathers headed 1.5 percent of Great Britain families with dependent children in the 1979–81 period (Popay et al., 1983). The corresponding proportion for the United States was 1.6 percent (Glick, 1979). Divorced and separated fathers constitute approximately 60 percent of the American total. A commensurate breakdown is not available for the UK period cited above although earlier data from Finer (1974) suggest a similar proportion.

2. Fifty-nine London-based men who had main care of their dependent children after marital separation were interviewed once. One of the children was in the age range 5–11 years. The sample was stratified by social class of father and sex of child. Men had been apart from their wives for an average of 3.1 years. Married fathers were pair-matched to two-thirds of the lone fathers in terms of the latters' occupation and age, family size and sex of target child ($n = 37$) (O'Brien, 1984).

3. Respondents' perceptions of kin support were categorized on a 5-point scale from 'very important' to 'not at all important'. Frequency of kin contact measures were positively correlated with perception of kin support: mother, Kendall's tau = 0.52, $p = 0.00$; father, Kendall's tau = 0.59, $p = 0.00$; sister, Kendall's tau = 0.43, $p = 0.00$; brother, Kendall's tau = 0.36, $p = 0.0002$.

4. However, the results pertaining to married men and their contact with mothers-in-law and brothers also gave indications of following the lone father pattern (Kendall's tau = 0.20, $p = 0.06$ and Kendall's tau = 0.26, $p = 0.06$ respectively).

5. Forty-six lone fathers had a mother who was still alive; 33 percent, 26 percent, 20 percent and 22 percent usually saw her at least monthly, 2-monthly, 6-monthly, yearly/very rarely. The respective proportions for married fathers ($n = 31$) were 29 percent, 42 percent, 3 percent, 26 percent.

Thirty-nine lone fathers had a father who was still alive; 31 percent, 28 percent, 18 percent, and 23 percent usually saw him at least monthly, 2-monthly, 6-monthly, yearly/very rarely. The respective proportions for married fathers ($n = 25$) were 32 percent, 36 percent, 8 percent, 24 percent.

6. Thirteen percent of lone fathers had daily contact with their mothers and fathers compared with 9.6 percent and 8 percent respectively for married men.

7. These groups did not significantly differ in terms of their age, length of marriage, length of marital separation, age and sex of children. However, they did

significantly differ as regards their own and their ex-partners' social class and current family size. Conciliatory negotiators and their ex-partners were found in the higher status social class categories whilst passive acceptors and their ex-partners were located in the lowest status social class categories (the hostile seeker respondents were intermediate between these two groups). Family size (the number of children resident with father) followed a similar pattern with conciliatory negotiators having a smaller family size and passive acceptors having a large number of co-resident children (O'Brien, 1984).

8. Four percent of lone fathers had seen either parent-in-law in the last month. In contrast, 41 percent of married men had been in contact with their mothers-in-law and 33 percent had been in contact with their fathers-in-law in the last month.

9. Chi-square = 11.0, [df = 4], $p = 0.08$; chi-square = 12.9, [df = 4], $p = 0.04$ respectively. The 'middle-class' category included those in social classes I and II (Registrar General Classification of Occupations, 1970) and the 'working-class' category incorporated the remainder.

10. Chi-square = 13.9, [df = 4], $p = 0.03$; chi-square = 10.7, [df = 4], $p = 0.05$ respectively.

11. In the present study, however, cases of complete grandmotherly takeover were excluded specifically in order to study men who had major responsibility for their children.

12. Mr Eye had a boy and a girl. There was no significant relationship between sex of children and frequency of grandmother contact.

13. It was of interest that slightly more lone than married fathers had lived in their present home for 10 years or over (17 percent, v. 8 percent respectively). Hunt (1973) has also commented on male single parents' relative residential stability.

14. Fifty-eight percent of lone fathers felt that friends were very important to them at the time of interview, in contrast to 30 percent of married fathers (chi-square = 12.0, [df = 1], $p = 0.01$).

15. Twenty-four percent of lone fathers turned to professional agencies (such as medical or counselling agencies), 22 percent to kin. Seven percent reported turning to no one whilst the remaining respondents utilized other strategies such as self-improvement activities.

16. Respondents' perceptions of friendship importance were categorized on a 5-point scale from 'very important' to 'not at all important': Kendall's tau = 0.16, $p = 0.07$.

17. More symptomatic scores on the GHQ (Goldberg, 1972) were positively associated with dissatisfaction with friends (Kendall's tau = 0.38, $p = 0.0005$). The latter variable was categorized on a 5-point scale from high to low satisfaction.

18. There was a significant tendency for working-class married men's friends to be exclusively male. Middle-class married respondents were more likely to mention being friends to the female in a couple (chi-square = 6.8, [df = 1], $p = 0.03$). There were no class differences for lone respondents.

19. Brown and Stones (1979) have written about their experiences in setting up lone fathers' support groups for lone fathers who need to meet men in a similar situation to themselves.

20. There was a significant tendency for older respondents to socialize less often than their younger counterparts (Kendall's tau = 0.17, $p = 0.04$): 71 percent of the short-term separated (up to 1½ years) went out at least once every fortnight in contrast to 55 percent of the medium-term separated (between 1½–3½ years) and 50 percent of the longer-term separated (over 3½ years).

21. Activity of socializing was categorized as in Table 14.1 and satisfaction with

social life was categorized on a 5-point scale from 'very satisfied' to 'not at all satisfied'. Kendall's tau = 0.53, *p* = 0.000.

References

Allan, G.A. (1979) *A Sociology of Friendship and Kinship*. London: George Allen and Unwin.

Bartz, K. and Witcher, W. (1978) 'When Father Gets Custody', *Children Today* 7 (5): 2–35.

Blau, Z. (1961) 'Structural Constraints on Friendship in Old Age', *American Sociological Review* 26: 429–39.

Bott, E. (1957) *Family and Social Network*. London: Tavistock.

Brown, A. and Stones, C. (1979) 'A Group for Lone Fathers', *Social Work Today* 10 (47): 10–13.

Classification of Occupations (1970). London: HMSO.

Davis, A. and Strong, P. (1977) 'Working Without a Net: The Batchelor as a Social Problem', *Sociological Review* 25: 109–29.

Dennis, N., Henriques, F. and Slaughter, C. (1956) *Coal is Our Life: An Analysis of a Yorkshire Mining Community*. London: Tavistock.

Duffy, M. (1982) 'Divorce and the Dynamics of the Family Kinship System', *Journal of Divorce*: 3–18.

Finer, M. (1974) 'Report of the Committee on One-Parent Families', Cmnd. 5629. London: HMSO.

George, V. and Wilding, P. (1972) *Motherless Families*. London: Routledge and Kegan Paul.

Glick, P. (1979) 'Children of Divorced Parents in Demographic Perspective', *Journal of Social Issues* 35(4): 170–82.

Goldberg, D. (1972) *The Detection of Psychiatric Illness by Questionnaire*. Windsor: OUP.

Goode, W. (1956) *Women in Divorce*. New York: The Free Press.

Hanson, S. (1981). 'Single Custodial Fathers', paper presented at National Council on Family Relations Annual Meeting, Wisconsin.

Hart, N. (1976) *When Marriage Ends: A Study in Status Passage*. London: Tavistock.

Hipgrave, T. (1978) 'When the Mother is Gone: Profile Studies of 16 Lone Fathers with Pre-School Children', unpublished MA theses: University of Nottingham Child Development Research Unit.

Hunt, A. (1973) *Families and their Needs, with Particular Reference to One Parent Families*. London: HMSO.

Komarovsky, M. (1967) *Blue Collar Marriage*. New York: Vintage Books.

Kerr, M. (1958) *The People of Ship Street*. London: Routledge and Kegan Paul.

Marsden, D. (1969) *Mothers Alone: Poverty and the Fatherless Family*. London: Allen Lane, Penguin.

Miller, A. (1970) 'Reactions of Friends to Divorce', in P. Bohannan (ed.) *Divorce and After*. New York: Doubleday.

O'Brien, M. (1982) 'Becoming a Lone Father: Differential Patterns and Experiences', in L. McKee and M. O'Brien (eds) *The Father Figure*. London: Tavistock.

O'Brien, M. (1984) 'Fathers Without Wives: A Comparative Psychological Study of Married and Separated Fathers and their Families', PhD dissertation. LSE: University of London.

Orthner, D., Brown, T. and Ferguson, D. (1976) 'Single Parent Fatherhood: An Emergent Family Lifestyle', *The Family Co-ordinator*, 25: 429–37.

Popay, J., Rimmer, L. and Rossiter, C. (1983) 'One Parent Families: Parents, Children and Public Policy', occasional paper No. 12. London: Study Commission on the Family.

Rapoport, R.N., Fogarty, M.P. and Rapoport, R. (eds) (1982) *Families in Britain*. London: Routledge and Kegan Paul.

Rosow, I. (1970) 'Old People: Their Friends and Neighbours', *American Behavioural Scientist* 14(1): 59–69.

Sanctuary, G. and Whitehead, C. (1972) *Divorce and After*. London: Gollancz.

Santrock, J.W. and Warshak, R.A. (1986) 'Development, Relationships, and Legal/ Clinical Considerations in Father-Custody Families', in M.E. Lamb (ed.) *The Father's Role: Applied Perspectives*. New York: Wiley.

Young, M. and Willmott, P. (1962) *Family and Kinship in East London*. Harmondsworth: Penguin.

15
Fathers and conciliation services

Lisa Parkinson

Divorce and family break-up
On current trends one in three marriages in England and Wales is likely to end in divorce within thirty-five years of marriage (Haskey, 1982) but marriage remains a very popular institution in spite of this high divorce rate. Over one-third of new marriages in 1984 involved a remarriage for one or both partners. But the hope of finding lasting happiness with a new partner may not be realized, as second marriages are even more likely than first marriages to end in divorce (*Social Trends* 14, 1984). Separation and divorce do not only affect adults. They have major consequences for children (Wallerstein and Kelly, 1980; Mitchell, 1985), two-thirds of whom are under 11 when their parents divorce while a quarter are under 5. For many families, separation and divorce bring severe disruption in every aspect of their lives, often involving several changes of home and acute financial problems (Southwell, 1985). Women struggling to bring up children on a low income carry a heavy burden of responsibility, often with very little support, and men who live alone after the break-up generally find their loneliness extremely difficult to cope with.

Research studies in Australia, Britain and the United States show that divorce is very painful for men as well as for women (Weiss, 1975; Burns, 1980; Kitson, 1982; Ambrose et al., 1983; Jordan, 1985), but men seem to have greater difficulty than women in expressing their deepest feelings, particularly their fears and hurts, and may therefore find it harder than women to come to terms emotionally with their divorce (Goldsmith, 1980; Kressel, 1985). There are few signposts to guide men towards the new role of divorced father and those that do exist may carry contradictory messages, suggesting that access visits to children are important in theory but unimportant in practice. One or two visits per month are often considered sufficient but it is very hard for children and fathers to sustain a relationship with such limited contact. If the visits become strained and artificial, or if the parents move some distance apart, the contact may become tenuous and finally cease altogether. Research on access to children is scarce but suggests that at least 25 to 30 percent of fathers lose touch with their children soon after the separation (Maidment, 1976; Eekelaar and Clive, 1977; Mitchell, 1985).

Changing attitudes to parental roles
The present high rates of divorce undermine traditional beliefs in the sanctity and permanence of marriage. They also challenge our assumptions about gender roles both within marriage and after divorce. The growth of the women's movement has encouraged women to look beyond a narrow domestic role as housewife and mother, while the greater acceptance of men's nurturing qualities makes it more natural for fathers to be seen taking care of their children instead of merely providing for them. Parents who enjoy a collaborative approach to child-rearing may find this works very well if they agree how parental tasks and responsibilities should be shared. But uncertainty about their respective roles may increase tension between couples who fail to explore their expectations of marriage and each other. They may become increasingly disillusioned, especially if one partner ignores the other's complaints or distress. Communication in these troubled marriages is often problematic and as the gap widens between each partner's perceptions and concerns, the two sides of the marital coin — the husband's and the wife's — may present a totally different picture, depending on whose side is being looked at. Bernard (1973) suggested that each marriage contains two marriages — his and hers — which often involve marked differences or contradictions. This seems even more true in divorce, where the unresolved conflicts of the marriage may turn into bitterly fought contests over what constitutes 'the best interests of the child'. Although some fathers convince themselves that the children will suffer less if they withdraw from their lives altogether, many others struggle to remain actively involved and may desperately need encouragement and support.

Men and the legal process of divorce
The present law of divorce in England and Wales is still fundamentally adversarial. Unlike other European countries such as France, Sweden and West Germany, English law does not permit joint petitions and joint custody orders are the exception rather than the rule. Only 12 percent of custody orders in 1984 granted legal custody of the children to both parents jointly (Parkinson, 1986) and the courts' practice of rubber-stamping unilateral applications from one parent (Eekelaar, 1984; Maidment, 1984) gives a strategic advantage to the petitioner while the respondent parent may feel humiliated and redundant. Seven out of ten petitions are filed by wives (*Social Trends* 14, 1984) and although many husbands refuse to accept that

their marriage has broken down irretrievably, hardly any of them untimately defend the divorce because of the difficulty of obtaining legal aid for a defence that is unlikely to succeed, while private litigants may be deterred by prohibitive legal costs. Arrangements for the children can easily become a new battleground in which bitterly divided parents inflict fresh wounds on each other. Some fathers, finding a lack of what they consider just and fair treatment, resort to desperate actions such as snatching the children, assaulting their former partner and behaving in ways that harm their children and themselves. The longer the battle continues, the more intractable it generally becomes.

Only about 10 percent of divorces involve contested custody and access proceedings but a research survey of recently divorced couples in south-west England and Wales (Davis et al., 1982) found that 29 percent of parents reported disagreeing with each other about arrangements for the children. Many fathers feel unfairly deprived of parental responsibilities which could still be shared to some extent, and their experience of the legal process of divorce may leave them bitter and disillusioned. Some refuse to pay maintenance (support payments) as a form of retaliation, and court orders for defined access and maintenance may prove unenforceable in practice, since the intense emotional conflicts associated with marriage breakdown and divorce need more than purely legal solutions.

Some countries, including Australia, New Zealand, Sweden and West Germany have abandoned all fault-based grounds for divorce, whereas English divorce law perpetuates the outdated concept of the matrimonial offence, even though the Divorce Reform Act 1969 made irretrievable breakdown of marriage the sole ground for divorce. A no-fault divorce can be obtained in England after 2 years' separation where the respondent consents to the divorce or after 5 years without consent, but many petitioners are unwilling to wait as long as this. Those who want a quick divorce use fault-based evidence to conform to the law's requirements, and the proportion of petitions based on the respondent's 'unreasonable behaviour' actually increased from 28 percent of divorces in England and Wales in 1974 to 41 percent in 1984 (*Judicial Statistics*, 1976, 1985). Nine out of ten of these 'behaviour' petitions are filed by wives. All at once, a husband may be faced with the prospect of losing his wife, his home, his children and possibly a substantial part of his income, for what is allegedly all his own fault. He has to decide within a matter of days whether to let the divorce go through undefended and whether to accept the proposed arrangements for the children. These are major decisions which couples may be unable to discuss with each other unless they are helped to do so. Many of them separate after an argument or crisis, without any agreed plan for the future, and they may then find that the only means of communication is via solicitors. Solicitors are often more conciliatory in their approach to divorce than is commonly supposed (Davis et al., 1982; Kressel, 1985), but negotiations conducted between solicitors may not ease the feelings of anger and devastation which often accompany divorce nor help parents to talk directly with each other when their solicitors withdraw. Solicitors have a primary duty towards their own client and even if they seek a negotiated settlement, separate legal advice to each party tends to polarize their positions and attitudes. Professional advisers may also take a very directive role, possibly instructing the divorcing couple not to communicate with each other. Without this direct contact, each partner may harbour unchecked suspicions and fantasies about the other and become less and less able to liaise with each other concerning the children. The legal divorce may take place in a way which leaves the couple emotionally still tied to each other, yet unable to take joint decisions (Bohannan, 1970. Parkinson, 1985).

Conciliation services

Divorcing couples who want to remain on reasonably good terms may look for a private forum where they can discuss their decisions and practical arrangements informally, without abdicating control of their affairs to the court. Specialist conciliation and mediation services (the terms tend to be used interchangeably in Britain) have sprung up in many parts of the country since 1978 to provide this alternative forum. Their objective is to help couples at any stage of separation or divorce to reach agreed decisions, especially where their children are concerned. The need for conciliation was identified over 10 years ago by the Finer Committee on One-Parent Families (Report, 1974) who criticized the adversarial system in divorce, recommending that conciliation (which the Committee distinguished from reconciliation) should be used as far as possible as a means of settling disputes and avoiding litigation. The Finer Committee proposed that conciliation services should be provided under the aegis of a new, unified family court which would replace the dual jurisdictions of the divorce courts and the magistrates' domestic courts. Twelve years later, we still have the same uncoordinated system, despite continuing pressure for family courts and divorce law reform. However, the call for conciliation met an enthusiastic response from small groups of lawyers, court welfare officers and social workers who worked together to establish locally based conciliation services in the court itself or in the community. Many areas in England and Wales and some parts of Scotland now have some kind of conciliation scheme, linked by broadly similar objectives but with wide variations in their structure, staffing and working methods (Parkinson, 1986).

The extensive experience of conciliation and mediation in Canada and the United States has influenced developments in Britain, although in this country conciliation is provided almost entirely by statutory and voluntary agencies and so far we do not have individual mediators setting up in private practice, as they do in North America. Although English divorce law seems archaic compared with some other European countries, this country seems ahead of most of Europe in developing a network of conciliation schemes. The net still has many gaps and lacks the funding to assure its future, but it is continuing to grow. West Germany and the Netherlands have a few divorce counselling bureaux which also undertake conciliation, while in France the key figure in the legal process of divorce is a specialist judge who combines his inquisitorial role with a form of judicial conciliation.

Court-connected conciliation in England and Wales
Many divorce courts and some domestic courts in England and Wales have taken initiatives in the last 10 years to introduce conciliation procedures in contested cases, instead of listing them for a full hearing in court. The Committee on Matrimonial Causes Procedure (Booth Committee) set up by the Lord Chancellor in 1982 has recommended (Report, 1985) that conciliation should become an integral part of court procedure in contested cases and that courts should be empowered to adjourn contested cases to allow conciliation to take place. Some courts such as the Principal Divorce Registry in London use a system of in-court conciliation in which parents are invited to talk with a welfare officer acting as a conciliator, to see whether agreement can be reached on the spot. The time that can be allocated to each case is often very short and from the parents' point of view the system may seem geared to obtaining quick settlements without allowing them sufficient time to explore their differences and re-establish direct contact. Davis and Bader's (1985) follow-up research at Bristol and Newport County Courts questioned how far conciliation in the context of a court hearing actually benefits fathers, mothers or children. Just over half the parents who were interviewed said they had been upset, angry or disappointed with the outcome of their conciliation appointment, compared with 35 percent who had felt pleased or relieved. This form of court-controlled conciliation does not necessarily produce lasting agreement or resolve hurt and angry feelings, though it helps some couples to sort out their difficulties at a relatively early stage. The researchers found that even a brief attempt at conciliation at the court encouraged some parents to get

together afterwards and renegotiate their arrangements on their own, without returning to court.

Unequal power in conciliation
There is concern particularly among feminists that some women are disadvantaged in conciliation because they may be less assertive, articulate or informed than their husbands (Bottomley and Olley, 1983). Feminists believe that men will exploit an informal process of negotiation by bullying or browbeating tactics and that women will lose the protection afforded them by the due process of law. Preliminary evidence from British researchers does not so far substantiate these concerns (Davis and Roberts, 1984).

One of the major differences between divorce mediators in North America and conciliators in Britain is that the latter deal predominantly with child-related issues and rarely become involved in negotiations over finance and property. Couples are encouraged to reach agreement in principle over the payment of maintenance (child support) and the occupation of the matrimonial home but in most cases conciliation takes place in conjunction with legal advice to each party from their solicitors, who continue to deal with issues of finance and property. Restricting conciliation to child-related issues has both advantages and disadvantages (Milne, 1983). Custody and access disputes are often inextricably linked with issues over property and maintenance. On the other hand, the focus on child-related issues concentrates attention on the children and may reduce the risk of them being used as bargaining counters.

Conciliators are not completely neutral in that there is generally a presumption in favour of access taking place and this creates a potential alliance between the conciliator and the parent seeking access — usually, though not invariably, the father. Many British conciliators favour some form of co-mediation where resources permit because working in a pair or team helps them keep track of the unequal positions and discordant needs of each partner and their children, while exploring possible solutions. A recent American study (Waldron et al., 1984) found some evidence that a male–female mediator pair was more effective than two female co-mediators. A male–female pair may be able to balance inequalities of bargaining power and address underlying issues of gender roles without either parent feeling misunderstood or disadvantaged during a process which often exposes very raw angry feelings. However, the use of two workers cannot guarantee perfect balance and mediators' effectiveness probably depends more on their skills and personal qualities than on their gender per se.

Research to compare the outcomes of conciliation in the longer term with those reported by a control group of litigated cases suggests that conciliation is associated with more co-operative attitudes between parents, more regular access to children and greater compliance with the terms of negotiated agreements, including financial settlements (Pearson and Thoennes, 1984). However, many questions still need to be explored. The number of variables involved in conciliation make evaluation very difficult and simple comparisons between court-connected and independent schemes may not be valid because they may be catering for different sections of the divorcing population at different stages of the legal process.

Independent conciliation services
Court-based services can be used as a mandatory filter for all contested cases after proceedings have been started, whereas independent services have to attract customers and conciliation can take place only if both parties agree to participate. Even if they both attend, they are not necessarily inclined to co-operate with each other. The parent who fears losing in court may hope for a 'better deal' in conciliation or see it as the only possibility of breaking a prolonged deadlock. Concern about children is often very strong, though some parents are so overwhelmed by their own crisis that they find it hard to separate their children's needs from their own. Most independent services in Britain offer a free or almost-free service financed by grants, donations and payments from the legal aid scheme.

These services complement court-related schemes by being available at an early stage, before as well as after legal proceedings are commenced, and in being directly accessible to the public, taking referrals from solicitors as well as from the parties themselves. Self-referrals are usually initiated by one party rather than by both together, by individuals who often feel a desperate need to regain some control of their lives. They may turn to a conciliation service and respond in varying degrees to its focus on decisions for the family as a whole, rather than on individual reactions and adjustment in the longer term.

Why do men seek conciliation?
Referrals to marriage counselling services are initiated predominantly by women (Heisler, 1984), but Yates (1984) found that self-referrals to conciliation services were made slightly more often by men than by women. Most couples in her survey had been married for 5 years or more and a considerable number had been married over 15 years. Fathers of school-age children are likely to be strongly attached to them and may want an equal say in decisions about them

as well as about the divorce itself. Conciliators try to help parents focus on the present and future without getting caught up in recriminations about the past, and men may find this approach more acceptable and relevant to their needs than other legal and welfare services because it is non-stigmatizing, impartial and quickly accessible in crisis situations. The issues they bring to conciliation usually fall into one or more of the following categories.

Access to children. Problems over access to children are by far the most common reason for referral to conciliation services. Many fathers, including unmarried ones, want access to their children or more access than they are currently getting but mothers may be reluctant to let the father take sole charge of the children even for short periods. Sometimes a father comes to realize that the children need time to adjust to being with him on his own before they are ready to accept his new partner. In other cases, a mother may be helped to accept that the children need to see their father even though she finds the contact very painful. Planning access arrangements in detail and negotiating over particular obstacles can help parents anticipate difficulties and discuss possibilities that neither had previously considered. Trial arrangements can be tested out before any binding agreement is reached, and if one or both parents cannot manage regular face-to-face contact when the children move between them, additional sources of help may be suggested, involving a mutually trusted relative or possibly an access centre.

Joint legal custody. Fathers who are anxious to go on playing a central role in their children's lives may feel very threatened by the prospect of sole custody, care and control of the children being 'awarded' to the mother. Fights over custody are often about its symbolic meaning rather than over practical arrangements (Patrician, 1984) and many parents need help to maintain their co-parenting relationship while disengaging as spouses. One case comes to mind in which the husband had made a suicide attempt because he felt he was losing everything he cared about most deeply. His wife wanted a divorce but did not want to deprive the children of their father. She reassured him during conciliation about the importance of his continuing role as father and they agreed that although the children would live with her, they would share joint legal custody. This seemed to make the pain of the divorce more bearable for the father, without undermining the mother's position.

Care and control of children. Fathers who want to obtain or retain care and control of their children may fear that the court will be biased against them unless they can prove that the mother is unfit to have care and control. This can lead them to make exaggerated allegations in affidavits to the court, but parents who denigrate each other are likely to add greatly to their children's distress, as well as suffering themselves. Parents who are treating their children as possessions or pawns may need to consider the alternatives in a less destructive way. There may be no ideal solution that is fully acceptable to them both, but with help and support some become more able to look at difficult questions from various angles, recognizing that their children need two psychological parents, whichever parent has day-to-day care.

Private negotiations. Co-operative couples who agree in principle about their divorce may nonetheless want to talk through their decisions together, using conciliators as a neutral sounding-board. These couples often fear — with justification — that an adversarially structured legal process may whip up hostility between them. They may also feel that conciliators with a mental health or social work background are more appropriately trained than lawyers to help them work out detailed arrangements for their children. Conciliators need to explain that they are not substitutes for solicitors and that both parties should seek legal advice before finalizing their arrangements. Provisional agreements can be drafted by solicitors in the form of applications to the court for consent orders and it is encouraging that solicitors seem much more inclined to support agreements reached in conciliation than to advise their clients against them.

Conciliation as a means of achieving reconciliation. Individuals who are desperate to prevent a divorce sometimes contact a conciliation service in the hope of achieving a reconciliation. Conciliation is not directed towards achieving a reconciliation and the outcomes vary: some couples separate and expect to divorce with consent 2 years later, some agree to an undefended divorce with conciliation on other issues and some decide to remain together. Couples who reconcile are usually referred to a marriage guidance counsellor for further help.

Two illustrations of conciliation in practice
The following brief examples based on two cases referred to an independent conciliation service may help illustrate how the process works in practice. Names and other identifying details in these cases have been changed.

Case example 1. Conciliation in an access dispute
Barry and Pauline D were referred for conciliation by their solicitors and both accepted the offer of a joint appointment to discuss their difficulties over access arrangements. They had separated very recently and Pauline was about to file a divorce petition based on Barry's 'unreasonable behaviour'. Their only child, Mandy, was 10 years old and physically handicapped. She attended a special school and needed a lot of care. Pauline was refusing to let Barry have access to Mandy on the grounds that he upset her and did not know how to look after her properly. Barry argued that he had always helped to look after her and that it was altogether wrong to cut her off from him and also from his parents, whom she loved greatly. Both he and Pauline were feeling extremely hurt and upset about the breakdown of their marriage and their own distress inevitably coloured their perceptions of Mandy's needs. Pauline said she did not want Mandy to lose contact with Barry but she was understandably very protective of her and needed to regain some trust in Barry as a reliable and caring father. Detailed arrangements were discussed and both parents agreed to try them out over a period of several weeks. As they worked reasonably well in practice, Pauline became less fearful about letting Mandy go out with Barry and more willing to share parental responsibility with him. When their divorce took place a few months later all applications were made with consent and both parents attended the court appointment to discuss the proposed arrangements for Mandy with a judge in chambers. They were encouraged to contact the conciliator again if further problems arose but both said they felt more able to sort out arrangements for Mandy as the tensions between them were more manageable.

Case example 2. Conciliation in a custody dispute
Ann T had left her husband, Donald, to live with another man who had left his wife and children. This man subsequently returned to his family but Ann felt that her 15-year marriage to Donald had broken down totally and that reconciliation was out of the question. Donald had started divorce proceedings on the basis of her adultery, which she admitted, but they were unable to agree about the custody, care and control of their two children, Mark aged 14 and Tania aged 12. Consequently they were also in dispute about the occupation of the matrimonial home and financial matters. Mark and Tania had become very involved in the conflict between their parents and found it intolerable to be caught in the middle, with the result that Mark sided with his father while Tania defended her mother and attacked both Mark and her father.
    Ann and Donald eventually decided that Mark and Tania should

continue to live with their father with frequent access to their mother and that they would spend alternate weekends and a major part of each school holiday with Ann. Mark and Tania began to settle down once they could see that their parents were prepared to co-operate and that they did not have to choose between them. Both solicitors were helpful in advising on financial and property matters and negotiating an agreement to preserve the joint interest in the matrimonial home. Contested court proceedings over custody, care and control were avoided and both parents felt that the agreement to share joint custody, with care and control to Donald, represented far more than a mere compromise. All four members of the family understood it to signify that Ann and Donald were still parents, despite the ending of the marriage, and once they stopped using the children to carry messages and demands between them the stress on the whole family was greatly reduced.

Main strategies of intervention in conciliation
The main strategies of intervention used in these two cases may be summarized as follows:

1. Simultaneously engaging both partners to work on a mutually agreed agenda. This even-handed approach contrasts with the partisan role of solicitors and with the therapeutic alliance which is often formed between a professional worker and one partner from a troubled or broken relationship. Wiseman and Fiske (1980) found that the process of involving both partners in decision-making was associated with better psychological adjustment to the divorce compared with cases where only one partner was seen. This is particularly significant for respondent husbands since they are often excluded from the decsion-making process. Valuing their opinions, perceptions and objectives helps restore their self-esteem and may open the way to joint problem-solving instead of the fight-or-flight reactions which are so common in an adversarial divorce.

2. Providing space and structure. Couples who are unable to talk to each other at all or who cannot engage in any constructive discussion may need neutral ground and the firm structure which conciliation can provide. The greater the conflict, the more structure may be needed, at least initially. Structure can be provided in a number of ways, including the use of time-boundaries for each phase of each session, rules to help contain conflict (such as prohibiting interruptions), and careful phrasing of questions (such as asking 'how?' rather than 'why?' type questions).

3. Redefining roles in the family. Spousal and parental roles are often intertwined and it is very difficult to sever some strands in the bonds which tie couples to each other without cutting other strands at

the same time. Focusing on the father's role after separation may clarify what parents expect or can accept from each other. Paradoxically, this can help mothers just as much as fathers, since mothers need some relief from the psychological and economic stresses of being a full-time single parent. Sometimes one parent and the children move swiftly into a new family structure with a stepparent and possibly stepchildren and the strains of this rapid transition can be enormous for all concerned. Rivalry between the natural father and the stepfather is common, with each feeling threatened by the other's existence. Stepfamilies often struggle to become the same as 'ordinary families' by blocking out the past, instead of trying to come to terms with it (Visher and Visher, 1979). Mediators who work from a basis of systems theory have commented that this helps them conceptualize the multiple changes which divorcing and divorced families need to negotiate if they are to avoid overwhelming conflict or loss of attachment (Ahrons, 1980; Robinson and Parkinson, 1985).

4. A pragmatic, task-centred approach. Brannen and Collard (1982) found significant gender differences between men and women in their expectations and experience of marital counselling. Men seemed to prefer a problem-solving approach which focused on explicit goals, whereas women were primarily looking for a supportive, listening relationship. Hunt's study (1985) of marriage guidance clients likewise suggested that the methods used by marriage guidance counsellors may match the needs of female clients more closely than those of their male clients. The working methods used by conciliators are still evolving in Britain and there is considerable variation but attention is often given to apparently minor and concrete details, if they are emotionally significant to both parties. Some issues become highly charged emotional conductors and parents may be helped to manage powerful currents of feeling if they learn to deal with the conductor rather than with the actual current. Conciliators may therefore draw from a range of practical strategies, such as setting a specific task to be accomplished before the next session or negotiating a quid pro quo agreement on a concrete issue. In the second case referred to, both parents found it helpful to work out who should telephone whom at a specific time on certain days of the week. This helped them avoid endless wrangles and recriminations in which the children had been pressed to take sides with one parent against the other.

Conclusion
Conciliation draws knowledge and expertise from more than one professional discipline and is rapidly becoming a discipline in its own right (Haynes, 1981; Folberg and Taylor, 1984). Practitioners seem

to agree that specialist training is needed to develop practical skills in conflict management and to distinguish the role of conciliator from that of legal adviser, social worker or therapist (Parkinson, 1986). It is particularly important to clarify the confidentiality of conciliation in relation to solicitors, other agencies and the court. The National Family Conciliation Council (NFCC), a voluntary association of independent services, has drawn up a Code of Practice for conciliators, in consultation with the Law Society's Family Law Committee and the Solicitors' Family Law Association, which defines the main principles and objectives of conciliation and sets out some basic ground-rules (NFCC, 1985).

Deutsch (1973) has emphasized that disputes can be settled through win–win outcomes and not only through win–lose outcomes. Conciliation should be measured by the durability of agreements and parents' increased ability to co-operate and negotiate with each other rather than by the number of recorded settlements which may prove unworkable in practice. Children's needs inevitably change over time and arrangements may need to be varied. Parents who can look to each other for some understanding and support are less vulnerable to the stresses they encounter as their children grow up and as different problems arise. Although conciliation cannot be appropriate or effective in all cases, it offers an informal process of conflict management which can be more finely tuned to the needs of individual fathers, mothers and children than formal institutions are likely to be.

References

Ahrons, C. (1980) 'Re-defining the Divorced Family: A Conceptual Framework', *Social Work* (Nov): 437–41.

Ambrose, P., Harper, J. and Pemberton, R. (1983) *Surviving Divorce — Men Beyond Marriage*. Brighton: Wheatsheaf Books.

Bernard, J. (1973) *The Future of Marriage*. Harmondsworth: Penguin Books.

Bohannan, P. (1970) *Divorce and After*. New York: Doubleday.

Booth Committee (Committee on Matrimonial Causes Procedure) (1985) Report. London: HMSO.

Bottomley, A. and Olley, S. (1983) 'Conciliation in the USA', *Legal Action Group Bulletin* (Jan): 9–11.

Brannen, J. and Collard, J. (1982) *Marriages in Trouble — The Process of Seeking Help*. London: Tavistock.

Burns, A. (1980) *Breaking Up: Separation and Divorce in Australia*. Melbourne: Nelson.

Davis, G. and Bader, K. (1985) 'In-Court Mediation: The Consumer View', *Family Law* 15 (1 and 2): 42–9, 82–6.

Davis, G. and Roberts, M. (1984) 'Conciliation: The Consumer View', unpublished paper given at a conference in Bromley, Kent, 6 July.

Davis, G., MacLeod, A. and Murch, M. (1982) 'Divorce and the Resolution of Conflict', *Law Society's Gazette* (13 Jan): 40–1.

Deutsch, M. (1973) *The Resolution of Conflict*. New Haven: Yale University Press.

Eekelaar, J. and Clive, E. with K. Clarke and S. Raikes (1977) *Custody After Divorce*. Oxford: Centre for Socio-Legal Studies.

Eekelaar, J. (1984) *Family Law and Social Policy*, 2nd edn. London: Weidenfeld and Nicolson.

Finer Committee on One-Parent Families (1974) Report, Cmnd. 5629. London: HMSO.

Folberg, J. and Taylor, A. (1984) *Mediation — A Comprehensive Guide to Solving Conflicts without Litigation*. San Francisco: Jossey-Bass.

Goldsmith, J. (1980) 'Relationships between Former Spouses: Descriptive Findings', *Journal of Divorce* 4(2): 1–20.

Haskey, J. (1982) 'The Proportion of Marriages Ending in Divorce', *Population Trends* 27. London: HMSO.

Haynes, J. (1981) *Divorce Mediation*. New York: Springer.

Heisler, J. (1984) *The National Marriage Guidance Client 1982*. Rugby: National Marriage Guidance Council.

Hunt, P. (1985) *Clients' Responses to Marriage Counselling*. Rugby: National Marriage Guidance Council.

Jordan, P. (1985) *The Effects of Marital Separation on Men*. Sydney: Family Court of Australia, Research Report No. 6.

Judicial Statistics (1976) and (1985). London: HMSO.

Kitson, G.C. (1982) 'Attachment to the Spouse in Divorce: A Scale and its Application', *Journal of Marriage and the Family* 44: 379–93.

Kressel, K. (1985) *The Process of Divorce*. New York: Basic Books.

Maidment, S. (1976) 'A Study in Child Custody', *Family Law* 6(7): 195–202; and 6(8): 236–41.

Maidment, S. (1984) *Child Custody and Divorce — The Law in Social Context*. Beckenham: Croom Helm.

Milne, A. (1983) 'Divorce Mediation: The State of the Art', *Mediation Quarterly* 1: 15–31.

Mitchell, A. (1985) *Children in the Middle*. London: Tavistock.

National Family Conciliation Council (1985) 'Extended Code of Practice for Family Conciliation Services', *Family Law* 15: 274–6.

Parkinson, L. (1985) 'Divorce Counselling', in W. Dryden (ed.) *Marital Therapy in Britain*, Vol. 2, pp. 207–37. London: Harper and Row.

Parkinson, L. (1986) *Conciliation in Separation and Divorce — Finding Common Ground*. Beckenham: Croom Helm.

Patrician, M. (1984) 'Child Custody Terms: Potential Contributors to Custody Dissatisfaction', *Mediation Quarterly* 3: 41–57.

Pearson, J. and Thoennes, N. (1984) 'Mediating and Litigating Custody Disputes: A Longitudinal Evaluation', *Family Law Quarterly* 17(4): 497–524 and 535–9.

Robinson, M. and Parkinson, L. (1985) 'A Family Systems Approach to Conciliation', *Journal of Family Therapy* 7(4): 357–77.

Social Trends 14 (1984). Central Statistical Office, London: HMSO.

Southwell, M. (1985) 'Children, Divorce and the Disposal of the Matrimonial Home', *Family Law*, 15, 184–6.

Visher, E.B. and Visher, J.S. (1979) *Stepfamilies: A Guide to Working with Stepfamilies and Stepchildren*. New York: Brunner Mazel.

Waldron, J.A., Roth, C.P., Fair, P.H., Mann, E.M. and McDermott, J.F. (1984) 'A Therapeutic Mediation Model for Child Custody Dispute Resolution', *Mediation Quarterly* 3: 5–20.

Wallerstein, J. and Kelly, J. (1980) *Surviving the Breakup — How Children and Parents Cope with Divorce*. London: Grant McIntyre.

Weiss, R. (1975) *Marital Separation*. New York: Basic Books.

Wiseman, J.M. and Fiske, J.A. (1980) 'A Lawyer–Therapist Team as Mediator in a Marital Crisis', *Social Work* (Nov): 442–5.

Yates, C. (1984). 'National Family Conciliation Council Research Project', unpublished report. University of Essex, Law Department.

Notes on contributors

Kathryn Backett is currently Research Fellow in the Research Unit in Health and Behavioural Change, University of Edinburgh, and is working on a project examining the development of lay health beliefs in families. She was previously Research Fellow in the Department of Sociology, University of Edinburgh, where she carried out a project examining fertility and family planning practices in a working-class community (publication forthcoming).

Senga Blackie is Researcher at the Scottish Marriage Guidance Council.

Julia Brannen is a sociologist at the Thomas Coram Research Unit, University of London Institute of Education. She is currently carrying out research on dual-earner households. She has also conducted research on marital and family relationships, mental health and help-seeking behaviour and is co-author (with J. Collard) of *Marriages in Trouble: the Process of Seeking Help* (1982). She is a convener of the Resources within Households Study Group.

David Clark has researched and published widely on issues relating to marriage and family life. He has a special interest in the sociology of divorce and remarriage and is co-author, with J. Burgoyne, of *Making a Go of It* — a study of stepfamilies in Sheffield. He is currently Director of the Scottish Marriage Guidance Council.

Sarah Cunningham-Burley is a sociologist, currently working at the MRC Medical Sociology Unit, Glasgow. Her research interests focus on the family and health, and on qualitative methods. She has conducted empirical research projects on 'Becoming a Grandparent', and 'The Cultural Context of Childhood Illnesses'. She has published papers on a variety of aspects of grandparenthood, and is joint editor (with Neil McKeganey) of *Enter the Sociologist* (1987).

Jarmila Horna is Associate Professor of Sociology in the Department of Sociology at the University of Calgary, Canada. Her primary areas of research and teaching are cross-cultural studies of the family, multi-dimensional perspectives of family leisure, and patterns of leisure choices and participation. She edited a Special Issue of *The Journal of Comparative Family Studies* and published numerous book chapters, papers in conference proceedings and journal articles mostly in *Loisir et Société, Family Perspectives, World Leisure and Recreation* and *Canadian Slavonic Papers.*

Michael E. Lamb is Professor of Psychology, Psychiatry and Pediatrics at the University of Utah, Salt Lake City. His research on fathers and children is among the best-known research in this field. Some of his latest books include *Fatherhood and Family Policy*, with Abraham Sagi (1983) and *Infant–Mother Attachment* (1985), *The Father's Role: Applied Perspectives* (1986) and *Adolescent Fatherhood* (1986).

James A. Levine is Director of the Fatherhood Project at Banks Street College, New York City. He is author of *Who Will Raise the Children?*, *Day-Care and the Public School* and *Child Care and Equal Opportunity for Women.*

Charlie Lewis is a Lecturer in Developmental Psychology at the University of Reading. His main research has examined men's involvement in parenthood and parent–infant interaction. In 1986 his study *Becoming a Father* was published by the Open University Press.

Mary Lund is Assistant Professor in the Department of Psychology, UCLA, California. She has written articles on divorce and children caught in the middle for various scholarly journals.

Eugen Lupri is Professor of Sociology at the University of Calgary, Canada. His major research interests are in the sociology of the family, gender relations and theory. He has contributed numerous chapters to books and monographs and published articles in many scholarly journals. His most recent book is *The Changing Position of Women in Family and Society: A Cross-Cultural Comparison* (1983). A monograph, *Reflections on Marriage and the Family in Canada: A Study in the Dynamics of Family and Work Roles*, is nearing completion.

Peter Marsh is Lecturer in Social Work Studies at the University of Sheffield. His research, practice and publications are primarily in the field of children and families. Recent work includes *In and Out of Care* (1986), a study of client and social worker views of the statutory child-care system.

Peter Moss is a Senior Research Officer at the Thomas Coram Research Unit, University of London Institute of Education. He is currently carrying out research on dual-earner households and on women who have a first child when under 20. He has also conducted research on children with mental handicaps and their families, residential care for children and the transition to parenthood. He is co-author of *All Our Children*, *Nurseries Now* and *Work and the Family*. From 1987, he will be Co-ordinator of the European Childcare Network.

Margaret O'Brien is a Senior Lecturer in Psychology at the Department of Sociology, North East London Polytechnic. She co-edited *The Father Figure* (1982) with Lorna McKee. Her current research interests include the position of male clients in therapeutic settings.

Lisa Parkinson is currently Training Coordinator at the National Family Conciliation Council. She has a special interest in joint custody and the position of fathers during and after divorce. She is the author of *Conciliation and Divorce — Finding Common Ground* (1986), two chapters in W. Dryden's *Marital Therapy in Britain*, Vol. 2 (1985) and has contributed to many scholarly journals.

Joseph H. Pleck is Program Director, Male Role Program, Center for Research on Women, Wellesley College, Wellesley, Massachusetts. His work focuses on male roles, sex roles, and sex-role attitudes, and on family roles, work and family issues and work schedules. His recent books include *The Future of Fatherhood*, *Working Wives, Working Husbands*, *Research in the Interweave of Social Roles* (with Helena Lopata), and *The Myth of Masculinity*.

Martin Richards is at the Child Care and Development Group, Cambridge.

Graeme Russell is Associate Professor of Psychology at Macquarie University, Australia. He is the author of *The Changing Role of Fathers* and *A Practical Guide for Fathers*.

Karin Sandqvist is currently Research Fellow in the Department of Educational Research, Institute of Education, University of Stockholm. She is the author (with B.-E. Andersson) of *Family Support and Development: A Presentation of a Swedish Longitudinal Research Project of Families with Small Children* (1982), *En beskrivning av FAST-familjerna och deras sociala forhallanden* (A description of the FAST project and their living conditions) (1982) and 'Jamstallda pappor — finns dom' (Equal fathers — do they exist), in *Familjenormer — familjeformer* (1985).

Index